Direction and Destiny
in the Birth Chart

CPA Seminar Series

Direction and Destiny in the Birth Chart

Howard Sasportas

Centre for Psychological Astrology Press
London

First published April 1998 by The Centre for Psychological Astrology Press, BCM Box 1815, London WC1 3XX, GB, Tel/Fax 0181-749-2330.

This paperback edition published 2002.

DIRECTION AND DESTINY IN THE BIRTH CHART

ISBN 1 900869 22 5

British Library Cataloguing-in-Publication Data. A catalogue record for this book is available from the British Library.

Printed in Great Britain by Antony Rowe Ltd, Chippenham, Wiltshire, SN14 6LH.

Table of Contents

Preface

Astrological literature, like the products of any other creative profession, is variable. Some works are painstaking and original but difficult to comprehend; some repeat, reargue, or regurgitate ideas belonging to others; and a very few reflect true inspiration, insight, and originality combined with grace of expression. Astrological teachers, like those working in any other sphere of knowledge, are also variable. Some are competent but uninspiring; some are profound but inarticulate; and a very few combine the qualities of wit, inspiration, profundity, articulateness, soundness, and human warmth. Howard Sasportas was one of these very few, as both a writer and a teacher.

When Howard died in 1992, the astrological community recognised that it had lost one of its best-loved and most original thinkers. The two books which he wrote – *The Twelve Houses* and *The Gods of Change* – have become astrological classics which will undoubtedly remain in print for many decades, standing as definitive works on their subjects. The work which he produced jointly with others – *The Sun-Sign Career Guide* which he wrote with Robert Walker, and the four volumes which he and I compiled from seminars we gave for the Centre for Psychological Astrology in London and Zürich (*The Development of the Personality, Dynamics of the Unconscious, The Luminaries* and *The Inner Planets*), have helped to make his astrological work more accessible to both the astrological student and the general public. His worldwide lectures made him a well-loved figure in the international astrological community, and attendance at any of these lectures was always a joy and a gift.

But those who knew his work best were those who regularly attended his seminars for the CPA in London. At these seminars the students could enjoy his unique and unforgettable combination of intuitive insight, humour, warmth, inspired interpretation, and profound grasp of human nature. Howard was deeply mystical, and expressed his spiritual beliefs freely and regularly in his seminars. But he never lost sight of basic human psychology, nor of the need for the astrologer to grasp fundamental human motivations and conflicts in everyday life. He was always kind and compassionate when responding to questions and offering interpretations. He perpetually emphasised the importance of a spiritual overview. Yet he could pack

---

a powerful punch and did not shrink from direct confrontation when necessary. It is this rare blend of spirituality and down-to-earth, trenchant observations of human psychological dynamics which makes his work so unusual and memorable.

Since his death students have repeatedly requested transcripts of Howard's CPA seminars. It seems appropriate now, perhaps more as a celebration of his birth than a memorial to his death, to publish three of the best of the seminars in book form. Howard would have been fifty years old on 12 April, 1998. The publication of this volume has been timed to coincide with that date; it is an honouring of his entry into life, and a distillation of what he was able to contribute to astrology in the time he was given. These three seminars all deal with the themes of direction and destiny in the birth chart, a subject with which he, as an Aries with a Capricorn Ascendant, was deeply concerned. In personal consultation work he had the gift of inspiring his clients and highlighting potentials for the future which gave them renewed hope and new directions to pursue in life. These seminars convey the same optimism and boundless vision of human possibilities. Howard's astrology was always on the side of the individual, and on the side of that which supports and enhances life and freedom of choice.

Because he is not here to edit his own work, I have altered as little as possible in these seminars. Some grammatical changes have been necessary because the speaking style of any teacher is inevitably different from his or her writing style, and no one, however articulate, speaks to a group in a day-long seminar in complete, grammatically correct sentence structures. As an American living in England, Howard's teaching style was "mid-Atlantic" – an unusual blend combining the best of the speaking and thinking qualities of both countries. But apart from the kind of editorial "tidying up" which makes a spoken seminar flow coherently as a book, the seminars are offered here as they were given, complete with jokes both tasteful and otherwise, allusions to friends, casual references to his own birth chart, and spontaneous dialogue with members of the seminar group. He referred constantly to the work of other astrologers and psychologists, and was always generous in giving credit to their writing; the references have been footnoted whenever possible so the reader can avail himself or herself of these sources.

These seminars were given during 1990 and 1991, but the interpretations and perspectives offered do not date, and are as relevant to the astrologer in the next millennium as they were to the astrologer in the 1990s. We cannot know how Howard's astrology might have developed, had he been able to continue his work. I have no doubt that he would have continued to grow in stature and depth, offering innovative perspectives which incorporated any new astrological and psychological insights that came his way. Howard's work never stood still, as befits a cardinal sign; he was perpetually seeking new ways of looking at things, astrologically, psychologically, and spiritually. We can only mourn what we have lost, yet at the same time celebrate what we have – a legacy which can help us all to become not only better astrologers but also better human beings.

Liz Greene
Zürich, January 1998

Part One: Vocation

This seminar was given on 7 July, 1991 at Regents College, London as part of the Spring Term of the seminar programme of the Centre for Psychological Astrology.

Vocation as a calling

Let me give you the definition of the word "vocation" which I found when I looked it up in the *Concise Oxford Dictionary*. There are actually two definitions, and the first one is quite important. It says: "A divine call to, or sense of fitness for, a career or occupation." They actually use the word "divine". They give examples such as: "He felt no vocation for the ministry." "She has never had the sense of vocation." "He has little vocation for literature." Then they give as the second meaning – the more common one, I think – an employment, trade, or profession. So you could say, "Some vocations are overcrowded," or "That vocation won't earn him much money."

The word "vocation" stems from the Latin noun *vocatio*, which means "a call" or "a summons". In the 9th grade at school I won an award for being the best Latin student. I don't remember any Latin at all now. The same thing happened when I did the Faculty Diploma exam – I did well on the astronomy section, which I learned by rote for the exam, and then I forgot all of it the next day. But at least I can throw *vocatio* at you. It comes from the verb *vocare*, which means "to call". A lot of what I have to say today plays on this idea of a calling. The dictionary did pick it up. A vocation can be understood as a calling from God to do something, or, as I would probably say, a calling from your deeper core Self. What I am trying to get at is that I think a real vocation has to do with the outer expression of something inside you. It has to do with your inner life.

I would describe vocation as a summons from your deeper Self, a call from somewhere inside to express yourself through some sort of service or work. I think you all understand what I mean by a summons from the Self. The way I understand it as well is that it is related to the Sanskrit or Hindu term *dharma*. This is not the same as *karma*, although karma comes into vocational issues a lot. Dharma has to do

_____

with your life pattern, and with being who you are. It is the dharma of a fly to buzz, the dharma of a lion to roar, the dharma of an artistic person to create. Sometimes you get flies trying to roar, or lions buzzing, but the idea is that each of us should try to discover our pattern – that thing in us which will unfold into what we are meant to become – and cooperate with its realisation. St. Augustine said, "There is an I inside me which is more myself than myself."

I know I am labouring this point. But understood in this way, the whole issue of vocation is not really about making money. It is not about winning approval, or gaining recognition, or gaining status, or showing your Mummy and Daddy what a big, important boy or girl you can be. It is more than just trying to be useful or keeping yourself occupied. What is it they say about workaholics? The workaholic attempts to find meaning through work. But the individual with vocation, on the other hand, finds meaningful work. There's a difference. Workaholics try to give structure and meaning to their lives through work, often because they have to keep busy in order to avoid facing a terrible depression or other things which they would have to face if they stopped working. So they try to find meaning to their life through work. But the individual with a vocation is looking for meaningful work.

Inner and outer

To repeat, for those of you who arrived late: If vocation is understood as a summons or calling from your inner Self, and if it is part of your dharma or life purpose to find your vocation, then we are talking about vocation as a correlation between your inner Self and what you do in your external life. One of the ways I understand the 6th house and the sign of Virgo is that they reflect the process of getting the outer forms of your life to be as true a representation as possible of what you are inside. It is a meeting of outer and inner – trying to get the outer structures to be a mirror of what you are inside. This means trying to get the work you are doing to be a true reflection of your essence, your being, your myth, the gods and goddesses that are most prominent in your inner world. It is even about trying to get the way you dress, or what your home looks like, to be a true reflection of who you are.

When you interpret Virgo and the 6th house, you are dealing with the definition of the individual as a unique person with this particular trait and not that particular trait, with this particular way of looking at things and not that particular way. We distinguish ourselves by what we are not, as much as by what we are, and we really fine-tune our individuality by the time we get to Virgo and the 6th house.

I also think that this requires continual adjustment. Richard Idemon called the 6th house "the house of repair and maintenance". This conveys the idea that you have to keep adjusting the outer forms of your life as you change or contact new things inside yourself. If you go through some sort of breakthrough or shift, or a part of you which you have not been in touch with starts to appear, then in a 6th house way you may have to adjust the work you are doing to fit that, if possible. You may want to adjust the colours you wear, the way your home looks, to create a more accurate reflection of what you are becoming inside. This is the true meaning of inner and outer. Anything that has an outside has an inside. As Marilyn Ferguson wrote in *The Aquarian Conspiracy*, "Our true vocation is to be ourselves."[1] This means being who you are, no more and no less. There is a Hassidic story about a Jewish rabbi called Rabbi Suscher. He said, "When I get to heaven they will not ask me, 'Why were you not Moses?' Instead, they will ask me, 'Why were you not Rabbi Suscher? Why did you not become that which only you could become?'"

It's also described in other ways. There is a quote by the existential thinker Paul Tilly, and it goes something like this: "Man's being is not only given to him, but demanded of him. Man is asked to make of himself what he is supposed to become, to fulfil his destiny." This is actually quite a meaty quote. It is saying that we are given a being, we are given an essence, we are given an inner nature; and although at the deepest level my beingness is the same as your beingness, each of us as an individual also reflects some individual aspect of the divine, some face of the greater cosmos which – when put together – will make a whole. It is something about becoming what you are meant to become to fulfil your destiny. This means that there is a little bit of responsibility here, a little bit of will to actualise, to become conscious and make certain choices to grow into what you are

---

[1] Marilyn Ferguson, The Aquarian Conspiracy: Personal and Social Transformation in the 1980's, J. P. Tarcher, 1987.

---

meant to become. You can't just sit there and expect it to happen. The deeper Self has an active component in it as well.

I am trying to distinguish between a job or career and a vocation, which is a calling from your deeper Self. It is very true that some people have to have certain jobs or careers in order to earn money, or to have some security in their lives. And it may not be what they feel is their true vocation. I have a lot of questions about the whole issue of vocation, some of which are unanswerable, and we will be getting into these later in the morning. I am pretty clear in my mind about how I want to run the day. After I throw out some unanswerable questions, which we won't discuss because they are unanswerable, I want to look at the traditional significators for vocation – the hard-core, traditional astrological significators given in textbooks. This really amounts to the earthy houses – the 2nd, 6th, and 10th. Then I want to open it up and talk about how, in fact, the whole chart gives clues to your vocation, not just the 2nd, 6th, and 10th houses.

The whole chart is a clue to vocation, just as the whole chart is a clue to your physical appearance. Some people say the Ascendant and the chart ruler, or the MC and its ruler, determine how you look. I think you physically embody everything in your chart, just as I think defining your true vocation embodies everything in your chart. To find a true calling you need to use as much of your chart as possible, not just what is in the 10th, or the aptitudes suggested by the 6th, or what might earn you money in the 2nd. To find your true vocation, you have to find the gods that you answer to, the deities within which are the most primary to you, the myths which are closest to you as suggested by the chart. And you have to find some way to live out those myths in order to be who you are. This will become clearer as we go through the day.

The Sun-sign

Let's consider the Sun-sign. I am going to get very basic here. I feel that, in order to be fulfilled, in order to feel whole, in order to feel good about yourself, you really need to be expressing and manifesting and shining the constructive qualities of your Sun-sign. If someone comes to me for a reading, and I cannot hear or see their Sun-sign in them, I'm not happy. If someone comes who is an Aquarian, and they are very subjective and very emotional and don't seem to have any objectivity or perspective, I'm not happy, because the Sun-sign is probably the closest thing to the inner Self in the chart. If you are not living that, you are not being who you are. The philosopher Kierkegaard said, "The most common form of despair is not being who you are." An even deeper form of despair is trying to be someone other than who you are. I am just using the Sun-sign as an example – it isn't the only thing we need to look at – but I know that we need to develop our Sun-signs.

I don't believe you are born expressing your Sun-sign immediately. Your Sun-sign is given to you, but also demanded of you. I don't go along with the kind of Sun-sign astrology which says, "If you are an Aries you are dynamic and forceful," or, "If you are a Gemini you are good at communication." I actually think the task is to constantly work on developing and improving and manifesting more and more of your Sun-sign. I think the premise of the simplistic type of Sun-sign interpretation is incorrect. I would much rather see a Sun- sign column saying, "If you are an Aries, your task or purpose in this life is to find your courage, to be more adventurous and express who you are, no matter what other people will think. And if you are a Gemini, it is not that you are already good at communication or are someone who can make observations through being detached. Instead, you need to develop those qualities. Those are the things that you are here to learn and to do this time around."

If you are born with the Sun in the 7th house, it doesn't mean that you are automatically good at relating. It means that, in order to find out who you are, you have to develop the area of relationship in your life. I don't think we ever finish with the Sun – it always wants to shine more. Someone with the Sun in the 7th could be very good at relating but they probably will think inside themselves, "I still could be better. There is still more to radiate, there are still more clouds to remove which are blocking my solar expression." Someone with the Sun in the 5th house may be very creative, but they will probably always feel they could be more creative, because it is as if you have to fight dragons and do battles to get rid of those things which are stopping you from radiating what you are.

I'm just using the Sun as an example. The real point I am trying to make is that we are here to become what we are meant to be, to fulfil our destiny. And since most of us have to spend so much time at

_____

work, why not find a job or work or employment or a vocation which is the right one to bring out the most positive constructive qualities of your Sun sign, rather than twist yourself out of shape? If you are a Gemini type of person and you need change and variety, why go for a sedentary job which a Taurus might be better able to do? You can see what I mean in general. I will get more specific later.

I am going to talk about the traditional significators before I go into how I would assess the chart for vocation, because the traditional significators do hold water. They are true as far as they go, as you will see when we talk about the earthy houses. But first I have a question for you. We are not going to have to discuss this, but I would like to see a show of hands on this question. How many of you here today feel that the work you are doing is your vocation, your genuine calling, a true expression of what you are inside? Those who feel this is true please put your hands up.

Audience: Can those of us who aren't working put up our hands too?

Howard: That's a question I am going to be answering very soon. Let me see again the hands of those of you who really think you are fulfilling your true vocation and calling. Not a large percentage, I would say. All right, how many of you think you know what your vocation is, but you haven't quite gotten there yet? Nice – more hands up. I see the same people raising their hands! That's interesting, because the myths which we are closest to, the gods and goddesses we answer to inside ourselves, can shift at different times in our lives. The Saturn return is a time when there is often a shift of motivation. The mid-life crisis is another time when there is a shift. Our myths can change. We can change from being a Zeus type who wants to wield power into a Dionysus type who needs a job in which he or she feels emotionally involved and passionate, and power isn't the issue. Things can shift. That will usually be shown by transits and progressions which bring out new things in the chart.

When I was preparing this seminar I was thinking of the kinds of questions people ask me about the issue of work and vocation when they come for readings. But before I get into the astrology, I want to pose some really fundamental questions. Many of them might be difficult to answer. The first one is connected with what one of you asked a few minutes ago. Is the issue of vocation something that

---

everyone is supposed to feel? Why do some people feel a calling or an urge or some sort of summons from God or the Self to do a particular work? Why don't other people seem to feel that way about it? Why do some people know from a very young age what they want to do? They are pretty clear what path they want to follow. They know when they are six or seven that they want to become a doctor or an artist or a teacher – they just know it right from the start. Other people can be in their forties or fifties and they are wandering around still thinking, "What is it I should be doing?" Or they think they have missed it entirely.

Vocation and visibility

Let me add something astrological here. I do think that the issue of vocation may show up more in some charts than in others, especially in terms of how public we are about our vocation. I'll be coming back to this issue later, and I'll be taking questions and answers from you then. But I just want to get a certain bit out. You know that the 10th house is the highest point in the chart – it is the most visible part of the heavens. If you have planets in the 10th, then I definitely think that vocation is an important issue for you, because there is a need to be seen doing something special when you have planets in the 10th.

Without any planets in the 10th, the vocation can still be important, but you don't have to be so public about it. You can do it around your kitchen table when your friends are visiting, if you understand what I mean. You can be doing your work in a private way. You can be following your vocation right within your family, and not publicly. Planets in the 10th, or the ruler of the MC highlighted in some way, require visibility. You can have an untenanted 10th house, but the planet which rules the sign on the MC may be very strongly placed – such as being a singleton, or having a lot of powerful aspects. Then vocation becomes important, because you need to be seen doing it. You need to be public about it.

Someone with many planets in the 6th may have a sense of vocation, but it doesn't necessarily have to be public. They can be happy quietly working alone somewhere. Or someone with many planets in the 12th may be doing tremendous work, but they are content to be behind the scenes. They don't have to be visible when they are doing their work, and they might even prefer to be invisible. Or you may have a very packed 4th or 5th house, which means that what you are doing to express who you are deep inside is very personal. You do it around the home, or you create just because you enjoy creating, and not because you need to share it. In a sense that can be your vocation, but it is not the kind of vocation that we would associate with a public profile.

Vocation and reincarnation

Some of these questions about vocation generate other questions, like the particular question I just put to you: Why do some people just know what they want to do at a very young age? Many people are equipped to do what they know they want to do, but they never seem to find the opportunities. Why not? If you believe in the theory of karma and reincarnation, you can get some pretty neat answers to all this. In fact, it's really great, because all you need is to be slightly intuitive, and you can make up the answers to these questions if you believe in karma and reincarnation. Let me ask you another one. If someone at the age of five or six is really clear about the work they want to do, or shows a definite talent at eight or nine or ten, how would you explain that in terms of reincarnation?

Audience: They've been there before.

Howard: Yes. They've been working on that aptitude. They've been developing it in other lifetimes.

Audience: And they've been interrupted.

Howard: They haven't got as far as they would like, so they come into this lifetime with a lot of stuff on the credit side of their account in terms of that profession, that vocation. Maybe they didn't achieve it completely in a previous life, but they have done so much toward it that now they are ready to come in and do a really great job of it. There has been a preparation for it, which may be why some people seem to know so clearly what they want to become. It has been developing towards that point in other lifetimes. The Capricorn Ascendant side of me finds that very reassuring and very nice.

Let's say you're doing work which you don't feel is your true calling. Then you retire or you get older, and you start to leave more time in your life to do those things which really do interest you and excite you, like gardening or taking up astrology or learning to be a therapist. But you start it late. If you start something late, it is unlikely that you will become great at it in this lifetime, because you haven't had enough time to get experience at it, to become adept at it.

But it is not a waste of time. This is what I love about the idea – it is not a waste of time because you have started it already, and when you come in next time you will be a little bit further ahead. If you believe in this theory, it can help a lot. If some of you feel that you are not as good an astrologer as you would like to be, not as good an artist, not as good a therapist, or whatever, it may not mean that you shouldn't be doing it. It may mean that you are still apprenticing, and that this life is really about gaining the skills and the practise, and then you will come back next time with that already in place. It is called the continuity principle of karma. It is the nice side of karma. It is not the retribution side of karma. You will come in equipped with what you were developing, and therefore you may do more at a younger age and achieve more in terms of your calling, because of what you have done in the past.

Then there is the question, "Why are some people very confused about their vocation?" There can be several different reasons for this. Again, I am talking about karma and reincarnation here, and you need to accept this or at least be open to the idea for these sorts of answers to make sense. I am also drawing on the work of Edgar Cayce, and I am thinking of a book which was written by one of his pupils. The book is called *Many Mansions*,[2] and it is by a woman called Gina Cerminara. It is actually a very readable, inspirational book about Cayce's work. There is a chapter called "A Theory of Vocational Choice". Cayce spoke about lifetimes where you are having a vocational changeover. This means that you have had previous lives in which you have done as much as you can in terms of one vocation. The idea is that, in order for our souls to merge again with the greater spirit, we have to try a lot of different things.

---

[2]Gina Cerminara, Many Mansions, *New American Library*, 1990.

Maybe you have to be a scientist one time and something more creative another time – or something very manual and then something very cerebral. You have to try it all. You probably have to be an American Indian in one life and an Eskimo in the next. You have to do all sorts of things. If you have finished one whole vocational path, you may come in and have a life where you are exploring different paths to discover the one which you have to move into next. So you can have a vocational changeover lifetime, which means that it is not really your responsibility to become adept or succeed at one particular vocation. You are experimenting with different ones to see which one you are going to work on later.

I have other interpretations for these things besides a philosophical one. We can give psychological reasons for problems around vocation issues, and look at the deeper reasons why someone doesn't find their right work. It can be a family issue, which I will talk about soon. I'm just kind of spewing things out right now. We will have more interaction soon. I am really sharing with you all the questions that went through my head as I was getting this seminar together.

It may be that we have too many talents because of things we carry over from other lives, and we may not know which one to focus on. We are attracted to something because we can get into it easily, and then we are attracted to something else. It is almost like a Gemini issue, or maybe a Sagittarius issue. There might be a fear of making a choice, because if you make a choice, what about all those other things that you are going to miss out on? So it may be that if you are not settling on one vocation, the problem is that you actually have too many resources and you can't choose. I would probably work psychologically with this as an issue around fear of commitment, because I actually think more psychologically. The reason why some people never really make it in something they feel is their calling, or never even really define it, might be that they are afraid to commit themselves to something. That fear of commitment can also be why we don't get a relationship together. The whole issue of fear of commitment is what Liz would call an aspect of the *puer aeternus,* the eternal youth, who doesn't like to be trapped in matter.

Then there is the difference between a vocation – a summons or calling from your deeper Self – and a job. There are instances where someone's calling, someone's urge to do a particular kind of work, may

---

be very strong, but it is not financially viable for them. "I want to work as an astrologer, but there is no way I can earn enough money to support myself by doing it – even though I know that is what I want to do." The opposite can also happen. You could be doing something which is great financially, which gives you enough money for your mortgage and extra money so you can take a holiday every year, but it is not rewarding or fulfilling in the vocational sense.

Then you get astrological questions. A person will come, very often around the time of the Saturn return, sometimes around thirty-five when Saturn squares Saturn, and even more often around midlife. They say,"Do I throw away my material security in order to pursue my vocation? Do I disrupt my stability and go after the thing that really engages my heart?" I must admit that I sometimes give different answers. Sometimes I will say, "Yes, you have to follow your heart." Joseph Campbell said, "Follow your heart." I never quite know what that means, because my heart wants to lead me into a hundred different things. At other times I am not so sure about following the heart. I am inclined to say, "Keep your job, keep the thing that gives you stability, but make a little more room in your life for spare time to explore your vocation as a hobby, at least in the beginning."

We can look at 5th house issues here. The 5th has to do with the things that make our hearts sing, and it is also the house connected with hobbies and spare-time amusements. If you are not doing a job which you feel is your true vocation, then at least please try to do it as a hobby. It may be that this hobby can ultimately develop into something that you can make into a real vocation later. It may not ever be financially viable, but at least you can have something in your life which is really engaging you, which is really giving expression to what you are inside. "Set me a task in which I put something of myself, and it is no longer a task. It is a joy, it is art."

If you are fortunate enough to have something like the ruler of the 5th house in the 10th, then that is a good indication that your hobby, or some heartfelt interest – the 5th house – could become your career. If you have something like the ruler of the 5th in the 10th, or the ruler of the 10th in the 5th, you need to have the two houses linked. Let's take a musician who has a Pisces MC and Neptune in the 5th house, and let's say he is working as a civil servant. That's what his parents talked him into becoming – doing science at university – but he has Neptune in the 5th house and Pisces on the MC. I would say,

---

"Wait a minute, I am not so happy here, because this chart shows a strong creative urge." I might even say, "Because the ruler of your 10th is in the 5th, it is possible for you to make a vocation of creative work." Or you might get something like a good tie-up between the 6th and 10th, like the ruler of the 6th in the 10th. Then something which is an aptitude or a skill could be made into a profession, and if there are good aspects from the 2nd, you could earn money from it. But if you have something in the 5th which isn't linked to one of the vocational houses, then it may be a deeply felt urge that has to be a hobby or spare-time thing, and then you have to do something else for stability or money or recognition. Do you see what I am saying?

Please remember Cayce's views on karma and reincarnation. It might help. If something interests you, it may not necessarily become a vocation, but you might need to make some time to develop it because it could become your vocation in another lifetime. Or it may have been something that you loved deeply before and still want to do, but as a hobby. Let's say someone has a fascination for Spanish cooking. They couldn't make a job out of it, but they have a love of it, and if they go to evening classes in Spanish cooking, they will meet like-minded souls. It may be that, in a previous lifetime, your work had something to do with the culinary arts. Even though it is not your career now, you can still have it as something which gives you pleasure, something which you love. If you go to a class, you are likely to meet other people whom you might have known in a previous lifetime who shared this thing with you. Of course, if you don't believe in karma and reincarnation, this is an intuitive's fantasy.

Discipline and commitment

I mentioned the problem with discipline or commitment. That can be a big issue. You may feel there is something you would really like to achieve, but do you have the discipline and commitment to get there? Let's say you have the Sun conjunct Venus conjunct Neptune in Libra in the 10th house, and you feel very strongly that you want to do something creative. You feel that, in order to give expression to yourself, you need to bring Venus and Neptune in. If you have the Sun conjunct a planet, you have to bring that planet in as well in order to be who you are.

You have to bring in all the planets which the Sun aspects. I am very happy when I see someone who has a career which reflects a close aspect to their Sun-sign. It is not just the Sun's sign or house – the aspects to the Sun can also be clues to vocation. I have seen a lot of people with the Sun aspecting Neptune who are artists, or in a creative profession. I have seen people with Sun aspecting Uranus who are in a career to do with technology or computers. You can see people with Sun-Pluto who work with the dying, or are psychotherapists. Do you see what I am saying? With any planet which aspects the Sun closely, you need to bring that planet into your life in order to be who you are. And in making a vocation of it, you are really getting a lot of time to practise bringing it into your life.

Let's say you have the Sun, Venus and Neptune in the 10th house in Libra, and you would really like to be an artist. But you have Uranus in Cancer squaring that group of Libra planets from the 6th. Uranus in Cancer in the 6th may mean that you are so erratic and changeable that you have a really hard time getting the discipline or the commitment or the steadiness to realise your 10th house ambitions. I often look to see whether there are good aspects between the 10th and the 6th, because it means that your attitudes about working are conducive to fulfilling your vocational urges. But if there are difficulties between the 6th and the 10th, or between the ruler of one house and planets in the other house, then you may not have what you need to get where you want to go in terms of the 10th. The 6th house is how you go about working at something. The 10th house is more the professional goals.

Blocks and obstructions

There are a few more general issues before we go further. There is the problem of talent, which can be a bit painful to talk about. You may have an intense desire or aspiration to write – many people have an intense desire to write novels or stories – but do you actually have the talent, do you actually have the gift? Cayce would say, "Keep trying to develop that talent. It may not come to fruition now, but you may come to it later." Another thing which can be quite painful is the interference of apparently fated issues around vocational things. I have seen this again and again. You have a burning desire to pursue a

---

vocation and something gets in the way. A dancer has trouble with her knee, or a musician gets multiple sclerosis. An athlete gets an Achilles tendon problem which cannot be healed. Or you get burdened with family responsibilities which just won't give you the time to do what you want to do. The vocational dream is thwarted and you can't pursue it, or you can't go back to it because it's too late. What's going on here? What are you running into when that happens – when you have a vocational urge and you really could be good at it, but you get injured and you can't do it and then you have to go and do something else?

There are different ways of looking at it. You might be familiar with John Addey. He conceived the idea of harmonics in astrology. Around the age of twenty-two or twenty-three he developed a severe form of rheumatoid arthritis, or some sort of neurological spinal problem which left him crippled. He himself said, "Before that I would have been really happy to live my life playing golf and riding horses." But because the illness wouldn't let him do that, he said, "I turned to the things of the mind." This all happened when transiting Pluto was going over his Leo Ascendant, and that's when he started to study astrology and philosophy, and contributed a lot to the field in terms of the theory of harmonics.

What I am saying is that some people get pushed into something, and other people get pushed out of something. Something is going on which isn't the person's choice – that's what I mean by "fated issues". I remember hearing an interview on the radio with a well-known radio presenter and media person. The interviewer said, "How did you get into this?" The radio presenter said, "Well, I was in the army, and I had never done radio announcements before, and someone came up to me and said, 'Okay, your job is to do a local radio show for people in the army.'" He didn't really want to do it – he was forced into it. But it was through becoming an announcer while he was in the army that he found his career as a radio presenter. He was pushed into it. He didn't chose it, but he found his true vocation that way. But someone like Jacqueline du Pré, or athletes who are really gifted and are then cut down at some point, are pushed out of what they want most, or it's made incredibly difficult for them. What's going on? Why are they not allowed to follow their vocation? What other things are they meant to be developing? What's the karma here?

I have a theory about it. Jacqueline du Pré had a Jupiter-Saturn square in her chart, and I think this has something to do with

---

it. A Jupiter-Saturn opposition or inconjunct can do the same thing. These aspects seem to say that you have to work extra-hard to fulfil your dreams or realise things. If you look at Jupiter as the planet to do with your vision of possibilities, and it is in difficult aspect to Saturn, this says, "You are not going to get there without work. You are not going to get there without blockage." Probably Cayce would say that you have to work harder than other people because in a previous life you had lots of opportunities to do what you wanted to do, and you turned your back on them. You didn't want to take up the responsibility. Now, when you have a burning desire to do it, it eludes you because you avoided it before. Do you understand what I am saying? You have to work extra-hard to get the expression of your vocation, or you are delayed in it, or it comes late in life, or you keep running into more blocks than other people, because in some other life, when doors were open to you, you didn't go through them.

You can't get growth without Saturn, if Jupiter and Saturn are connected. When you have an aspect between these two planets, it means that when you pull one, you get the other. It also means that hard work opens up growth for you. You can't have growth without hard work – it operates both ways. Saturn can also manifest as blockage, as in Jacqueline du Pré's case. Or you can run into a brick wall which prevents you from going on with what you want to be doing. I remember seeing the same aspect in a musician who got arthritis of the fingers. Jupiter-Saturn people have to work extra-hard – they have to work against the odds this time around. Maybe it is because they had every opportunity before, and they turned their back on it.

I was thinking about this in psychological terms, too. It can also be an issue of commitment, of putting your money where your mouth is. For instance – and this is just a generalisation – I have known people with a strong Virgo component in their chart, such as the Sun in Virgo or Virgo rising, who could be excellent astrologers, but they never feel they are good enough yet. "Oh, I still need to learn more. What if I make a mistake and say the wrong thing?" It is as if they are waiting to be perfect before they do it, and this bothers me, because you learn by doing. You learn by making mistakes. You learn by messing up. You don't have to be perfect right away – let me tell you Virgos this. It is a message from the divine. I'm channelling!

Someone once said that all writers are rewriters. You don't just sit down and write brilliantly. You write, and then you throw it away and you change it. I also heard a rather disturbing thing. When a plane is flying to a destination, I was told that it is off course about 90% of the time, which is a little worrying. It only gets on course by readjusting every once in a while. I know that there is something which experience gives you which no other form of teaching can give. So what if you are not going to be perfect right away, and you make a few mistakes? That judge in you – it might be Virgo, but sometimes i t can be Capricorn, or a strong Saturn – watches you all the time. "Why aren't you perfect?" it keeps whispering. I would say to that voice, "Wait a minute, give me a chance!" because you learn by messing up and getting experience.

This issue of putting your money where your mouth is comes up for Leo as well, and to some degree for Sagittarius – but especially for Leo. I am thinking of the Sun in Leo or Leo rising, in particular. They have an inspiration to be great at something, to really shine at something, but they are afraid. "What if I do it and I fail? What if I do it and I am not as great as I think I could be? Maybe it is better not to do it than to try to do it and risk failing. Maybe it is better for me to imagine how great I could be at it, better than everyone else who is doing it, rather than actually attempting it and risking not being brilliant right away."

As far as I am concerned, not doing something because you are afraid you will be a failure is a nowhere philosophy. I would say to Leo, or Leo rising, "You've got to take a risk. Fire signs have to take a risk, and you also have to be prepared to earn your recognition." Leos may want recognition, but they need to be prepared to do the work necessary to earn it, and not just expect that it should be given to them on a plate. You can get Leos who are a bit like Billy Liar, who fantasised greatness. The Leo sees someone giving a speech, and imagines how much better they could do it, or they see someone teaching a class and fantasise how much better they could do it. They may be very envious, unless they really try themselves to make those dreams real.

There is another side to this. It doesn't apply just to Leo. If there is some talent or quality someone has that you truly admire, that really excites you, then I would say that you probably have it in yourself, because you wouldn't be so excited and so admiring and such a fan unless it was touching something in you. You have given it to the other person, projected it, and you really admire the person who is doing it. If you have that degree of charge when you meet somebody who is very adept at something, it could mean that the potential is there in you, if you are willing to do the work to get it. It wouldn't excite you so much unless it was there in you. In the same way, something you don't like in someone wouldn't bother you that much unless there was something similar in you. What we dislike in others is what we dislike most about ourselves.

Erica Jong said, "Everyone has talent. What is rare is the courage to follow the talent to the dark place where it leads." I really believe that. I'm going to be a little personal here. When I was under contract to write *The Twelve Houses*,[3] which was my first book, it was a horrific experience to have to face the writing. I wanted to break the contract many, many times. I used to say to myself, "I should accept the fact that I can't write. This shouldn't be so hard." I had to face an awful lot of blocks. I realised that part of the reason the writing was difficult was that I had it in my head that, in order to survive, everyone had to love the book. It was a childhood thing. Our sense of survival is very much reassured if we feel we are very special to a parent. If you feel mother really loves you, if you can do things that you know will win her approval, then it reassures your survival instinct because you know she wants to keep you around. But if you don't feel loved, then you might be abandoned, or she might go off to help someone else when you are in dire need, because she doesn't love you as much.

Not to be great and special, not to be loved, can be equated with death. When you start writing and your work is going to be out in print, you can't change it once it is out. You can get away with an awful lot when you are lecturing, believe me! But when you have to start putting it into words that are going to be printed, you have to face all those nagging thoughts: "Is this right? Wait a minute, what am I saying here? This is a bit woolly." I found that I had to get over that hurdle. I got so worried about it being good that I got blocked. I just couldn't write. It crippled me. The reason I was worried about it being good was because I thought I would die if it wasn't. If I wasn't appreciated, then I would be abandoned and die. It is infantile stuff. A big change happened when I said, "This is no good, to go on like this." I made a shift from the first person to the third person.

---

[3]Howard Sasportas, *The Twelve Houses*, Thorsons, 1985, and Newcastle Publishing Co. 1989.

I am sharing this because you may be familiar with the problem. I thought, "Wait a minute, this isn't about me getting recognition, this is about the fact that there are people out there who would like to know some information, and maybe I can be a medium through which this information is passed." Do you see what I mean about shifting from the first to the third person? The way I ended up writing the book was by imagining a class in front of me. The need for them to know more about the houses elicited stuff through me. I stopped focusing on what I was supposed to give, or on being good and winning approval and being brilliant. That really did help. I do think, in general, that if you are doing something just to bolster your own identity or your own ego, then you are going to have more trouble with it than if you are doing it out of a sense that there is a need for it out there and that you may be a vehicle to fulfil this need. There will always be some ego involved. "Hey, look how big it is, and look how much the book has sold!" And you think, "I did that really well." The ego will always grab something. But if it is grabbing too much, then you can get into trouble.

Let's say you are opening a restaurant only because you are going to show how great you can be, and prove to your parents how brilliant you are and what a great business person you are. You might have a lot of trouble making it work. I have seen this kind of thing a lot, especially if you have Neptune close to the Sun or around the Ascendant or in the 10th house. If you are doing it for mostly personal motives, it messes you up – it just doesn't work. But if you shift it away from the personal, and you say to yourself, "Well, there is a need in this area of town for a restaurant that can cater to people who want good, healthy food," your idea may be the mediator or the medium through which this happens. You are not doing it just for yourself, you are doing it for others, and you will succeed better at it. Neptune is anti-ego if it is tied up with vocational issues.

Psychological factors

In addition to the things I have been talking about, I think there are more directly psychological or family issues which affect our vocational choices and how well we do in terms of the pursuit of a career. Let me highlight some of these issues, which I will talk more about later. Was your father a success or a failure? Father is a role model, especially for a boy child, of what it is like to be a man. He is the first model of masculinity. If he has succeeded, then you have an image that it is possible to be a man and be successful. I'm saying it very simply. If your father missed the mark, or if it was pretty obvious to you that he was very frustrated in terms of his work or self-expression, then you are left with an image or picture of a man being frustrated. We carry these things around with us. If you make a little scratch in a sapling and it grows into a big tree, it has a big cut in it. You can also get a situation where your father was a failure and you want to redeem him by becoming successful. So you try really hard to be successful for the sake of redeeming your father, but you are likely to be less cool about it that way, because it becomes an infantile issue. "I must save my father, therefore I have to be successful." When you are that intense about something, you often get in your own way. Do you see what I mean? If I was trying to write to be recognised as brilliant, I would get in my own way much more.

I am finding an interesting thing. Earlier this year, in June, Liz and I did a one-week seminar in Zürich on the personal planets. It went very well, so we had the tapes from the seminar transcribed, and then we took our different sections and we edited them into a book.[4] It is much easier than writing from scratch because you already have a structure, but I still found myself quite slow at it and quite uptight about it, because I really wanted to edit it well and make it more flowing. I was working on that and it was quite hard, even though it was easier than sitting down and writing *The Twelve Houses* and *The Gods of Change*,[5] which I just wrote from scratch. The seminar book was more fun, but I was still conscious that this was my stuff and my name was going to go on it. It had better not be stupid and it had better make sense. So it was still a struggle.

More recently, I took on editing someone else's transcripts. There was an astrologer called Richard Idemon, who was from California. You may not know of him. Richard and Liz used to run a lot of courses together, very successful week-long intensive seminars in

---

[4]In fact two books resulted from this seminar: *The Luminaries: The Psychology of the Sun and Moon in the Horoscope*, Seminars in Psychological Astrology, Vol. 3, Samuel Weiser Inc., 1992, and *The Inner Planets: Building Blocks of Personal Reality*, Seminars in Psychological Astrology, Vol. 4, Samuel Weiser Inc., 1993.
[5]Howard Sasportas, *The Gods of Change*, Arkana, 1990.

lovely ski resorts in the States and exotic places like Orvieto in Italy. But then Richard got AIDS. He got very sick around 1985 or 1986, and then he died. He helped his death along a bit, because it had reached a point where the quality of life was just unbearable, and they really didn't have much to help at that time. He died without ever having been published, which was something he had really wanted to do, and he left behind all these marvellous tapes of the workshops he had done.

What happened was that the responsibility fell on Liz and me to do something about it. We had his tapes transcribed, and because Liz is very busy, I am working on it now. I am turning his lectures into a book of edited transcripts.[6] It is a great pleasure to do, because you know that wherever he is, he is going to really appreciate the fact that he is going to be published. Also, his material is very, very good psychological astrology. I am learning from doing it. I am really getting a lot of new ideas. Transiting Pluto is still in my 9th house, so I'm learning from the dead! But the thing I noticed is that I can sit down and tear through editing it, because it is not my stuff. I am less self-conscious about it, and I can do five to seven pages an hour, while it would take me a whole day to do that much if I was editing my own material. This is because I am less uptight about it – my name isn't on it, and it's coming out better than if I was neurotic about it. Do you see what I'm saying? These psychological issues that have to do with being special get in our way, because we are afraid that if we are not perfect, or if it doesn't come out brilliant, we won't be loved and we will die. It is the irrational infant in us.

There are also mother issues. Did your mother fulfil her vocational needs, or did she sacrifice them in order to raise the family? Let's say you have Moon conjunct Uranus in the 10th house. The 10th house is mother, and Uranus in the 10th describes a mother who really wanted to have some life other than just the maternal one. If you have Moon conjunct Uranus, you need to do other aspects of the feminine besides the maternal – you need to do something less conventional. Maybe your mother didn't live that out because she

---

[6]Richard Idemon, *Through the Looking Glass: A Search for the Self in the Mirror of Relationships*, Seminars in Psychological Astrology Vol. 5, Samuel Weiser Inc., 1992. A second volume of Richard's transcripts was published after Howard's death, edited by Gina Ceaglio: *The Magic Thread: Astrological Chart Interpretation Using Depth Psychology*, Samuel Weiser, Inc., 1996.

raised a family. She had an unlived need to achieve something in the world, and you picked that up. Therefore are you living out her unfulfilled stuff, which may be right for you, but it also may not be right. If you are living out something unfulfilled for someone else, it is not as clean as if you are doing it just for you. It may motivate you, but you should be aware of your hidden motivations.

There is another issue which is a bit harder to accept, and which you may have to look at psychologically if you are being blocked in terms of vocational achievement. Some parents feel envious if their children are more successful than they are. We don't like to think that. A father has a first child, and let's say it is a boy. This father says to himself, "How wonderful! This boy is going to carry on my name and be successful, and I'm so proud." No father sits down and thinks, "I'd like my son to be a great failure." Consciously they don't think that, but unconsciously it can be a real threat. Unconsciously the father is thinking, "This child is going to come into his prime when I'm losing mine. I have to share my wife or partner with him." There can be envy, there can be competition, there can be a fear of being toppled by your own offspring.

Saturn swallowed his children because he was afraid they would overthrow him. He couldn't allow them to exist. Saturn also castrated Uranus, so he overthrew his own father, which is why he was afraid his children would do it to him. And they did – Jupiter overthrew Saturn. It happens. Then Jupiter had a consort called Metis – she was the goddess of wisdom – and he was warned, when she was pregnant, that if Metis gave birth to a boy child, that child would overthrow him. So he swallowed Metis. He ate her and then actually gave birth to the child by himself. It turned out to be a girl-child, the goddess Athene. That wasn't such a problem. In the Oedipal sense, we think of the child wanting to get rid of the parent in order to have the other parent to himself or herself. But there is this other thing – a father actually not wanting his son to achieve, because it makes him feel he is overthrown. Or there is the mother who, on the one hand, encourages her daughter to be successful, but on the other hand, really puts her down, because unconsciously she doesn't want her daughter to have more fulfilment than she had. It is very painful to see someone having more fulfilment than you did. We get double messages from parents.

Audience: Can that happen across the sexes?

Howard: Yes, it can happen across the sexes as well. It applies both ways. But you can see it very clearly with father-son and mother-daughter issues. The mother gives double messages. "I want you to achieve, but why don't you have a family?" Or, "I want you to look good, but you had better not look as good as me, so why don't you eat more and get a bit overweight?" Then the child becomes bulimic. The Oedipal conflict is quite interesting. Normally we think Oedipus is the baddie, because he killed his father and married his mother, but actually the reason he killed Laius was because Laius was standing in his way, and he didn't even know it was his father. He got to a crossroads and there was a stroppy old man who wasn't letting him progress. I have seen many cases of father-son chart comparisons, where the father is actively standing in the way of the son progressing. He is envious of the son becoming greater than he is, even though one part of him wants to be proud of his son. Laius is just a stroppy old man who won't get out of the way, and he goads Oedipus, so Oedipus finally kills him. It is really Laius who starts the problem. Some fathers can have a Laius complex, which is like a voice inside saying, "Why don't you get rid of your son?"

What did your mother do with her life? Was your father successful? This is an issue of envy and double messages. There can also be competition between a mother and a father for the love of a child. It is hard to admit. But sometimes the mother wants the child to love her more than the father. She may be working out her own Electra complex through her child. I have seen situations where the mother wants to woo the son and win him over, and will do it by putting down the father a lot in front of the son. This is very difficult, because the father is meant to be a role model of what it is to be a man, but the mother is saying, "Don't be like that." Every family and situation is different. But ideally father is meant to act as a bridge to the outside world. It doesn't always happen that way, but how he behaves in the world, and what we learn from him about work, often take us beyond the personal sphere of our life with our mother. Father opens up ways to behave in the world.

Let me share something personal again. My father was a labourer – he worked with his hands. He was a wallpaper hanger. He was a first generation American, and he did painting and wallpaper hanging, which I am hopeless at. He worked very, very hard, and he became quite successful. They used to call him the Rembrandt of wallpaper hanging, and he did the best homes and the Governor's mansion. He was very good at it. He was a good model of worldly success. I used to go with him when I was quite young, maybe ten or eleven years old. I used to help him on Saturdays. Sometimes he would go and estimate a job, and I would come with him. He would do his thing with the prospective client who wanted to hire him, and then we would go back to the car and drive home, and my father would explain what he was really up to. I am grateful to him, because he did take time to teach me a little bit about it.

There are a lot of similarities. I'm self-employed, and he was self-employed. There are certain similarities which are uncanny. My father is retired now, but during his working life, when he was at home and the phone was ringing, he would say to my mother, "Take it off the hook during supper." The same thing happens at my house. The thing was, if I had decided to become a wallpaper hanger, they would have thought I was a failure. It is a first generation immigrant thing – I was meant to become a doctor or a lawyer. In fact my parents gave me three choices. They said I could be a corporate lawyer, a supreme court judge, or a bone surgeon. Those were my choices. When I was six I said I'd like to be a movie director or a psychiatrist, which sort of fits with astrology. Even when I went to college, I was pre-med for the first couple of years, and then, without telling my parents I changed my subject. I was afraid to tell them that I wasn't going to be a doctor, and I thought I would have to get doctor's licence plates for my car and pretend. Do you see the dilemma? "Be like your father, but if you do what he does, it is not good enough." That is very common for a lot of people. We have questions about fate around vocation. But we also have psychological issues. We are going to go first into the traditional astrological approach, but my heart is not really in the traditional thing – I am more concerned with finding your myth, and what god you answer to as a reflection of your true vocation.

Astrological significators

I want to mention something called the Smithers study. It appeared in *The Guardian* in 1984. Professor Alan Smithers of

Manchester University collected the birth dates of about two and a half million people and examined their careers in relation to the month of birth. He said there was some link between the time of year when people were born and the careers they got into. Some of these make sense. For instance, the majority of artists studied in his survey were born in late April and May, which is Taurus, the sign ruled by Venus. A lot of secretaries were born in late June and July, which is Cancer, a sign traditionally known for its ability to serve others, so secretaries are often Crabs. A lot of show business entertainers came in under Aries, which is an extroverted sign. Some of it is sort of odd, though. For example, they got a lot of dentists born under Aries. I guess it's just a sadistic sign! A lot of radiographers were born under Aquarius, but so were barmen and barmaids. Maybe it's to do with the Water-bearer. Anyway, it is worth looking at.

The other important study is the Gauquelin study, which you probably all know about. He noticed that Mars was just rising or culminating or descending or hitting the nadir, always in the cadent houses, in the charts of successful athletes. He also saw Jupiter in the same positions in successful actors' charts, and also in the charts of politicians. Maybe they are the same? When something is rising or culminating, moving from the 1st to the 12th by daily motion, or the 10th to the 9th, or descending from the 7th to the 6th, or going from the 4th to the 3rd, it seems to be connected with vocation. Saturn happened to be in those positions in the charts of scientists. The Moon was in these four important sectors for writers and artists. I have a little more to say later about why the cadent houses might be a significator for vocation.

The traditional indicators of vocation

Let me do the traditional indicators first. The main book I am taking this from is out of print. It is called *Vocational Guidance by Astrology,* and it's by Charles Luntz.[7] The first edition was published in 1942, and there was an update in 1969. It is not a bad book for the time it was written, although he does say some funny things. In the 1969 edition he included the chart of President Nixon, who was

---

[7]Charles Luntz, *Vocational Guidance by Astrology,* Llewellyn Publications, 1962 and 1969.

President at that time, and he does an interpretation saying what an honourable, wonderful man this is. In the 1942 edition, which must have been written about 1941, he does Hitler's chart.

Audience: Does he say that Hitler was also honourable?

Howard: Well, actually, Luntz said what a good example Hitler's chart was of vocational aptitude. He said quite definitely that Hitler did use astrology, and that when Hitler wrote *Mein Kampf* and it was published, he timed the publication to coincide with a good aspect bringing out his Moon conjunct Jupiter in Capricorn in the 3rd house of writing. Luntz then said what a good example this was to us all, about using astrology to achieve things.

Luntz lists all kinds of suitable vocations under each planet. For instance, under the Sun he has lion tamers and gin manufacturers. The lions are obvious, but you might not have known that the Sun rules juniper bushes, and gin is made with juniper berries. When I read this, I thought, "Who am I to say that lion taming might not be someone's true vocation?" Luntz looks to the 10th house for an indication of profession. So if you had the Sun in Leo in the 10th house, maybe you could consider being a lion tamer.

Audience: While you are making gin at home in the bath!

Howard: Then I started to think, "What if you had Pluto square that Sun in the 10th?" I don't know whether I would suggest lion taming in that case. But you could also be a walnut grower.

Audience: Why walnuts?

Howard: I don't know. The walnut must be a nut associated with the Sun. Each archetype is like a spectrum, so you can get the Moon representing mothers, and women in general, but the Moon also rules melons and night-blooming flowers, and also coffins, vases, and anything that contains. You get a whole spectrum of things. This used to be called the Law of Correspondences. The one I like for the Moon – and I hope some of you are inspired to do this – is a cabbage and cauliflower grower.

Audience: How about a bathhouse proprietor?

Howard: There used to be more money in that once than there is now. There are some other good ones. Mercury in the 10th could be a juggler. I thought that was quite nice – it fits. Jupiter could be a whale hunter, which would make you very unpopular nowadays. Saturn could be a tombstone maker. Anyway, they're all in the handout. When we talk about Luntz' traditional significators, if there is a planet in your 10th house – which he says is an indication of your vocation – you can look up the different things associated with that planet, or with the sign on the MC, and think about it.

A different approach

I can't emphasise enough that my emphasis is not just on the earthy houses. It is about looking at the whole chart, and particularly the Sun by sign and house. These are my own points of reference. Let me list them now, and we will come back to them later. I do consider the 2nd, 6th, and 10th, but I think the Sun by sign, house, and aspects is just as important, or maybe more so. I would also take the Ascendant into consideration, as Liz does. I believe the qualities of the sign on the Ascendant are things that we are really meant to be developing, so it would be ideal if you could find work that reflected something of the qualities of the sign on the Ascendant and its ruler and ruler's house placement.

Another important thing is any house that is packed. For example, if you have five planets in the 11th house, your work probably should involve groups. If you have five planets in the 3rd house, your work probably should involve communication or teaching or distribution of information. I look at the packed houses. Also, I would look at the missing element, funnily enough, because sometimes we are propelled in the name of wholeness to develop what is missing. You get a lot of therapists who have no water in their chart. It is as if they need to work with feeling. Funnily enough, I have noticed I do a lot of charts for body therapists, such as neo-Reichians, who have a lack of earth, and writers with a lack of air. You can turn your missing element into a career.

Also, I give relevance to Saturn's sign as an indicator of career, because whatever sign or house Saturn is in, this is where we feel weak or limited, and therefore spurred on to master things. Goethe said, "It is in limitation that the master first shows himself." If we feel insecure or inadequate at something, we try to compensate, and we can get very good at it. Let's say you have Saturn in Gemini, or Saturn in the 3rd, and you are not sure about your ability to communicate. You may try very hard to improve that, and you might become quite masterful at communication. Where you are weak, where you have problems, can be what really interests you in terms of developing that area, and that might be something which forms a vocation for you.

Look at the chart and say to yourself, "What is the myth here? What god do I answer to?" Try to find work which enables you to live that myth. For instance, if you have Pisces rising, you need some sort of work which brings in the theme of victim and saviour, where you are redeeming something or saving something. Or you need some sort of work where you are being a medium for the creative imagination, where you bring something through which needs manifestation. There are lots of different things you can do that describe those themes. But if you are not doing something that is satisfying the need for rescuing or saving or comforting or channelling some creative thing for people, then you are not fulfilling that Pisces Ascendant, and you won't feel complete.

I love it when someone has something like the Sun in the 9th house and he or she is a travel agent. I love it because it is true. The house the Sun is in shows the area of life where we find ourselves. When we are doing work which relates to that, I am glad to say that we may change levels at some point. But the theme needs to be the same. You might see someone with the Sun in the 7th who is a marriage guidance counsellor, or someone with the Sun in the 8th who works with other people's money. It satisfies me when I see that – I'm happy with it. Of course there's much more to look at than the traditional significators, but they do have their place.

Let me go back to Luntz. This is actually Liz' book, which she loaned me for the seminar. Luntz gives all the different things you can be with Mercury in the 10th or ruling the MC: a clerk, an accountant, a bookkeeper, a mail carrier, a bee keeper, and so on. He gives others which obviously fit for Liz: writers, teachers, and lecturers. But when she gave me the book she said, "I've missed my vocation. I wonder if

it's too late to start again. Luntz says I should have been a bus driver."
A funny thing happened at the Zürich seminar in June. Someone asked
me what sign Liz was. First I said she was a Pisces with Venus in
Sagittarius square Mercury in Gemini. It took a few minutes for the
person to work that one out, but then he said, "No, really, what sign is
she?" I said, "Okay, I'll tell you her sign. 'Please do not disturb.'"
Then Liz got back at me. She said to the group later, "During the break
one of you asked me what Howard's sign was. All right, I'll tell you.
'Out to lunch!'"

The 10th house

Let's go through Luntz more carefully. Here are real
traditional rules. Rule 1: You look for any planets in the 10th as a
significator for what profession you should be in, particularly the one
nearest the MC. We are assuming a quadrant house system here, not an
equal house system, so the MC would be the cusp of the 10th house,
which you would get with Placidus or Koch. You give a lot of weight
to the most elevated planet in the chart, which makes sense because it
is the one which is most visible. If you are born at noon, then you are
born with the Sun directly overhead, and who you are is shining down
for everyone to see. I have noticed that, unless there are difficult
aspects to it, people with the Sun in the 10th often do come into their
profession earlier than someone who has, let's say, the Sun in the 4th,
who might take longer to access what is deep inside them.

Audience: Do you give precedence to a planet which is more elevated
from the 9th house side?

Howard: Yes. Luntz, to give him credit, actually said that you would
look at a planet in the 9th which was within 5° of the 10th house
cusp. Gauquelin's studies highlighted planets that had just
culminated, that were in that sector, and Luntz is corroborating that.
In my work as an astrologer, I've noticed that, with people with
planets in the 9th but near the 10th, even as far as 9° degrees away,
often their vocation reflects the 9th house planet.

We'll call the next rule Rule 1a. After you look at the planet, you look at the sign it is in. If there is no planet in the 10th, you look at the sign on the MC, and then you look at the ruler of that sign in terms of its house, sign, and aspect. Okay, let's do a little bit of work with the chart which I've just put up. I won't tell you who it is, but it's a woman. You may know the chart, but if you do, don't say so. I don't want to make a guessing game out of it.

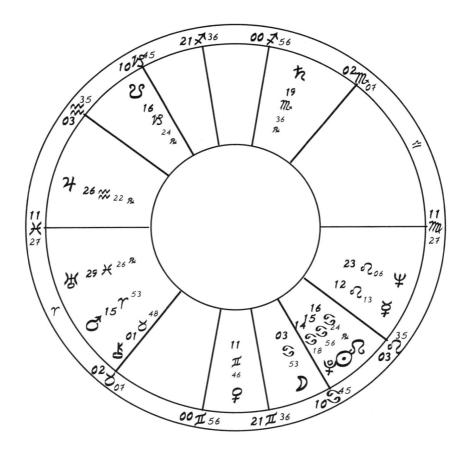

Elisabeth Kübler-Ross
8 July 1926, 10.45 pm, Zürich
Placidus cusps
Chart source: Hans-Hinrich Taeger, *Internationales Horoskope Lexikon*

The MC is 21° Sagittarius, and there aren't any planets in the 10th. If we were doing things according to Luntz, we would be looking for a career which reflected the sign Sagittarius. So she could be a whale hunter, or any of the other careers that go with Sagittarius. She could also be a lawyer, a clergyman, a travel agent, or a chiropodist. Then you would look at the ruler of Sagittarius and see where it was by sign and house, to get more input about vocational leaning. What's the ruler of Sagittarius?

Audience: Jupiter.

Howard: Where's Jupiter?

Audience: In the 12th house in Aquarius.

Howard: So what do you think? If the ruler of the 10th is in the 12th, where might she work?

Audience: Hospitals or institutions.

Audience: With groups in institutions.

Howard: Yes, with groups in institutions, which is actually what she does. I think it comes from other parts of the chart even more, but the placement of Jupiter refines it. The next thing Luntz would say is that you look at the planet ruling the sign at the MC according to what planets aspect it. So you look around for aspects to Jupiter. Well, it opposes Neptune. Somehow, through her career in institutions, she should bring Neptune in, which might be some sort of healing work. You might think, "Well, maybe she is a healer." Jupiter is also trine the Moon. It is an out-of-sign trine but still a trine, so you might consider what that brings out.

Audience: Contact with the public. Something to do with the caring professions.

Howard: Good. Then Luntz would say that you look for any planet which is very closely aspected to the MC itself. This is Rule 1b. We are getting a slightly different thing here. Her MC is 21° Sagittarius and we are looking for something which is pretty closely aspecting it. Neptune trines it from the 6th. Lunz would consider that important. It is very nice if you get trines from the 6th to the 10th in any form, because it means that the way you work – the 6th house is how you approach your job – the way you work, or the innate skills you have, work well with realising your vocational choice. If she had something in the 6th squaring the MC, one would be worried that the way she approached her job didn't really help her in her work and her profession. Uranus squares the MC by 8° degrees. That might mean something, even though the orb is wide. Maybe there is something a little shocking about her work.

Then Luntz gives another rule. Let's call it Rule 1c, which says that you examine the sign that Saturn is in. The reason he gives for this is that Saturn in the natural zodiac is the planet which rules the 10th house. He isn't being psychological about Saturn. He says Saturn's sign, and maybe Saturn's house, might give you some information because Saturn is the natural ruler of the 10th house. This chart has Saturn in Scorpio in the 8th. Do you think the people she is working with are particularly happy all the time? It sounds pretty deep and intense. I was saying earlier that you should look at Saturn, not because Saturn is the natural ruler of the 10th, but because Saturn shows where we have fears. We want to face those fears, and therefore we can try to do work which involves them. Maybe her fears of the 8th house – her fear of death, or fear of deep emotion, with Saturn in Scorpio – have made her create a vocation out of facing those fears. Someone with Saturn in Sagittarius may make a vocation out of something to do with travel or philosophy, because they are battling with it, they are grappling with the future and with ideas and meaning. Wherever Saturn is by sign and house is either where we try to deny the whole of what we are, or where we compensate to become good at it because we feel insecure.

Then Luntz says something which I wouldn't think of doing. This is all under Rule 1 – all 10th house stuff. He says, "Look to see if there are any planets in Capricorn," which is the sign of the natural zodiac associated with the 10th house. If you have planets in Capricorn, even if it is not connected to your 10th house in any way, then this could tell you something. If you are really stuck – if you have come up with nothing yet for the 10th house and the ruler of the 10th and Saturn – then maybe there is something in Capricorn. If Venus is in

Capricorn, maybe you will work at something artistic. If Mercury is in Capricorn, you'll work on something to do with writing or teaching or communications. That's what Luntz would say. It's not something I would think of immediately. This exhausts the 10th house factors. Later, after we have done his straight rules about the 6th and 2nd houses, I want to talk about them from a more psychological point of view and give you another dimension.

The 6th house

The next thing Luntz would say, if you are assessing the chart for significators for aptitude or calling, is that, if you can't get anything out of the 10th house for some reason, go to the 6th. Now, let me say something more here – something he does which I can't really agree with. Let's say there is a planet in the 10th house, and let's say the planet is Venus, which could mean any of the careers associated with Venus. This could mean artistic careers, the legal profession, or something to do with diplomacy or liaison work. Luntz says, "Count up how many good aspects there are to Venus, and how many bad aspects there are." "Good" in Luntz' terms means trines, sextiles, and easy conjunctions like Venus conjunct Jupiter, and "bad" means squares, oppositions, and difficult conjunctions like Mars conjunct Saturn. He would say that if there are more bad aspects than good aspects to a 10th house planet, you should ignore the 10th house planet completely and go right to the 6th. Do you see what he is doing? I don't agree with him. It's a cop-out. It's as if he is saying, "Oh God, your 10th house Venus, which could be a significator for career, is badly aspected – therefore avoid it." This ignores the fact that you might learn something through the challenge.

Part of the value of vocational work is that it can provide us with a transformative experience. You can grow and learn as much from the issues that come up in pursuit of career as you do through relationship or through meditating with a guru. Work provides a framework from which you get lessons in life, from which you learn more about yourself, but you have to do battle with your complexes. Work can be the appropriate "other" that you need in order to evolve through something outside yourself. It is your testing ground, which suits Saturn as the natural ruler of the 10th house. But Luntz didn't buy into this. He says that if there are too many difficult aspects to a planet in the 10th, don't follow that planet, because you are not going to succeed or it is going to be hard for you. I would say, "Try it, because it is going to bring up issues which you need to work out anyway, and which will come through the area of life which is your vocation." Of course, if you had the Sun in Leo in the 10th and you were considering being a lion tamer, then I would count up the good aspects! And if you had the Moon or Neptune in the 10th and wanted to go to sea, but you had Moon square Pluto in the 8th, maybe you should worry a little about pursuing a vocation on water.

One of the things Richard Idemon makes very clear in the material I am transcribing is that he didn't like the words "good" or "bad" in relation to aspects. He didn't even like "easy" or "hard", or "flowing" or "dynamic". He felt that squares and oppositions are aspects of resistance – the two planets brought together by these aspects will try to resist each other, whereas with trines and sextiles, the two planets are brought together by acceptance. The two planets blend together and work with each other comfortably. I think it's quite good to talk about aspects of resistance or aspects of acceptance, rather than good, bad, or flowing aspects. He also said another interesting thing. He felt that the opposition is wrongly named. Richard was American. He said the opposition should be called complementarity, because opposites often complete one another. He said the inconjunct is more like an opposition, because you are getting a planet in a contrasting element. Also, the planets are in different sectors. You have a planet in a personal house inconjunct a planet in a social house, like something in the 1st inconjunct something in the 8th. The 1st house is a personal house, but the 8th is a social house because it is concerned with shared resources. Inconjunct planets have nothing in common, whereas signs brought together by opposition often turn into one another. So he felt the inconjunct is more like an opposition. It is an interesting way to look at it.

Anyway, back to Luntz. When you have exhausted the 10th house, you go to the 6th. I believe the 6th does show skills which are unique to you, resources which you have which are worth developing. They are resources which could define you as a separate person, as an individual. The 6th house has to do with how you approach a job. And it also has to do with inequality – I call the 6th house "relationships of inequality". When you are a boss, someone who works under you will be shown by the 6th house, and when you are the server working under someone else, that person will be shown by the 6th. If you have Saturn conjunct Pluto in the 6th house with difficult aspects, you may have trouble with people who serve you. For example, your *au pair* may run off with your husband. You might have problems with the man who fixes your car. Or if you are fixing cars, you might have problems with the person who hires you. The 6th shows how you get along with people who serve you, what you are like as a boss, and also what you are like as a server.

The 7th house has to do with relationships of equality, but the 6th house shows situations where there is inequality going on. Karma with co-workers also shows up in the 6th. If you have Venus in the 6th, you may fall in love with a co-worker. If you have Pluto there, there may be heavy undercurrents between you and co-workers. As I said, the 6th house is how you approach a job. It is different from the 10th, which is more visible – how you like to be seen, what you like to be seen as, can be different from how you approach what you do. I'm going to come back to the 10th house and talk about it more psychologically later. Essentially, Luntz does the same things with the 6th house as he does with the 10th. Let's call this Rule 2. Look at the planets in the 6th. What's there which could give some indication of skills? With Saturn there, for example, the fact that you can be methodical and persistent and disciplined would describe what kind of work would suit you, because your approach to work is Saturnian. Uranus in the 6th doesn't like to work with someone looking over its shoulder. Uranus doesn't like to punch a clock. Mars in the 6th may prefer to be left alone to be in charge of it's doing without having to answer to someone. Neptune in the 6th may fluctuate about how to do a job – sometimes the person is into it, sometimes they are falling asleep at the job, and sometimes they are feeling inspired.

Next Luntz says we should look at the sign the planet is in. We'll call this Rule 2a. If there are no planets in the 6th, or even if there are, you also consider the sign on the cusp. Then you look at the ruling planet of the sign on the cusp by sign, house, and aspect. Remember Rule 1b, where we look at planets aspecting the MC? Well, Luntz says don't bother about planets aspecting the 6th house cusp. Then he gives Rule 2b, which is like Rule 1c – look at Mercury in the chart, because Mercury is the natural ruler of the 6th house. I never thought of that, but it's true – you might get a clue about vocation from

Mercury because it is the natural ruler of the 6th. I usually look at Mercury aspects in terms of how you get along with brothers and sisters, but aspects to Mercury may also suggest how you get along with co-workers. Very often there is a relationship between how we experience brothers and sisters and how we experience co-workers. The 3rd house squares the 6th, so if you had sibling rivalry, that could carry over into rivalry with the person working next to you. Let's say you are both trying to please the boss – that's the same thing as trying to win love from Mummy or Daddy. Unfinished business with siblings can crop up with co-workers. After you look at the sign Mercury is in, Luntz tells you to look at Virgo to see if there any planets there. If you are really stuck, you can go to planets in Virgo to look for things about vocation. Let's play around with the chart I've put up, and look at the 6th house. What aptitudes might she have in her work, with Mercury there? Obviously she would have communication skills.

Audience: She would be very discriminating.

Howard: Mercury is in Leo, so she would be good at speaking from the heart to people. Neptune is also in the 6th. What quality would come into her work from Neptune?

Audience: Healing. Imagination. Caring. Inspiration.

Howard: Good. Next Luntz would look at Mercury sextile Venus, so that makes how she speaks graceful and nice. That's going to help her to be successful. Mars trine Mercury is going to add power to her ability to communicate. You see, these aspects tell us a lot.

Intercepted signs

Audience: May I ask a question? Does Luntz say anything about intercepted signs? I am interested in what it means if a sign is intercepted in the 10th house.

Howard: I'll tell you what I feel about intercepted signs. I feel planets in intercepted signs are just as powerful.

Audience: I was thinking more about the sign, not so much about the planets.

Howard: I think the sign on the cusp should be looked at first, but I find an intercepted sign is equally important in terms of the interpretation of the house. Let's say you have 29° Pisces on the MC. The sign on the cusp is most influential, but if the last degree of Pisces is on the cusp, you have a lot of Aries in the 10th, even if it is not intercepted, and so Aries is important as well. In terms of vocation, you might think of a blend of Pisces and Aries, like being a fisherman who dares to take his boat into dangerous waters where no one else goes to bring back very special fish. Or you might be an artist who develops a controversial new technique or style. I looked into this when I was writing *The Twelve Houses.* Also, as I said, planets in intercepted signs can be as powerful as planets in a sign which is not intercepted. That's my feeling. Other astrologers may say something different. But having three planets intercepted in Leo in the 7th, I know they are there, and so do my partners!

The 2nd house

Next we go to the 2nd house. Luntz says the 2nd isn't so much an indication of what career you can do, but it can tell you whether you will make money, or whether you will gain or lose through your career. I don't completely agree with this. I believe the 2nd house has to do with resources which, if you develop them, make you feel more confident and give you self-worth. Self-worth may be measured in how much money you are worth. So I would consider the 2nd house to be a bit like the 6th in terms of aptitudes – if you develop them, you feel more substantial, more worthwhile.

Psychologically, the way I look at the 2nd house is that it is what constitutes security and safety for us. It is Taurus' house – what makes us feel more solid. By developing in a constructive way the planets and signs in the 2nd, you feel safer, you feel more secure, you feel of more worth and of more value. It is the house of values. If you have Mercury in the 2nd, then by developing your ability to communicate or think, you get a greater feeling of self-worth, and also, you can earn money through Mercurial work. It is something that is of

---

value. People value different things. Some people like to travel light. They value independence, so that is what they go for in their work. What you value affects the kind of choices you make in vocation. Some people value security. Some people really care that the house is decorated nicely. Other people don't care what it looks like. The 2nd house describes what gives you safety or security, what makes you feel good, and therefore you will try to develop it because it makes you feel good and makes you feel worthy.

Audience: The second house could be interpreted as talents.

Howard: A talent has two meanings. It means a gift, something you are naturally good at. But it's also a kind of ancient coin, an old type of money. Talent is another word for money. I have seen a lot of people turn their 2nd house planets into a vocation. I have seen people with Neptune in the 2nd earn money through music or healing. People with Pluto there might earn money through mining, or working for the London Underground, or working as therapists.

Audience: I have got Jupiter in the 2nd, and I work in publishing.

Howard: I differ from Luntz about planets in the 2nd. He just sees the 2nd as how you might make money, rather than as your true vocation. If there is a nice link between the 2nd and the 10th, you will make money at your career. If there isn't, there may be a problem getting money and career to work together. But a planet in the 2nd can describe a true vocation. Here we are in the 2nd house, and by now you should be able to work this out by yourselves. The procedure is the same as for the 10th and 6th houses. What's the first thing you look at?

Audience: Planets.

Howard: Yes, any planets in the 2nd. We'll call this Rule 3. If there are no planets there, the next thing you would look at is the sign on the cusp. Then what would you do? You would look at the ruler of the sign by house, sign, and aspect. I hope everyone is following this.

Audience: Oh, yes.

Howard: Thanks. I am glad I am giving you such new information! Here's one bit of information you might not already know. I love this one. Luntz says that if Venus has not appeared yet (which means if you are really hard up and can't get any insight into planets in the 2nd, or the sign on the cusp, or the ruler), then you should look at the sign Venus is in, because it is the natural ruler of the second. I would not necessarily base my advice about someone's occupation by just their Venus sign, but it is a supplement. That's Rule 3b. Then Rule 3c would be to look for planets in what sign? Taurus, because Taurus is the natural ruler of the 2nd house. Then Luntz says we should look at the aspects between the planets concerned with the 10th, 6th, and 2nd houses. For example, the ruler of the 2nd might trine something in the 10th, or the ruler of the 2nd might trine the ruler of the 10th. That's a good indication of money through career. Or the ruler of the 6th might make a good aspect to the ruler of the 10th or a planet in the 10th. That is a good indication that the way you work is favourable towards your achieving what you want to achieve.

I don't want to put Luntz down, because the book was written fifty years ago, and he actually has some pretty insightful things to say in it. Some of it looks a little funny now. I was trying to think of someone fifty years from now reading *The Twelve Houses* and laughing at it. "Look at what he said here!" So I don't want to be too mean to Luntz. If you can find a copy, some of it will make you laugh out loud, though, because the language is a little archaic.

Audience: What does he say about Uranus in the 2nd?

Howard: Become an astrologer. Let's go back to the chart I put up. We haven't done her 2nd house. Are there any planets in it?

Audience: Chiron.

Howard: What do you think her resources might be?

Audience: Healing.

Howard: Yes, doesn't the theme keep showing up? And Chiron is in Taurus, which is the natural ruler of the 2nd. Let's look at its aspects. It's sextile the Moon, trine Neptune, and sextile Jupiter. Jupiter rules the 10th, so there's a good aspect between a planet in the 2nd and the ruler of the 10th – she would be materially successful at what she does. And Neptune is in the 6th. There's a good link between the way she works and her prospects for making money. All three houses are nicely linked. Venus is in Gemini in the 3rd. But it rules the 2nd, so what does that say about some quality she has which would be beneficial in terms of work and money? Communication and teaching. That theme also showed up through Mercury in the 6th, didn't it?

Audience: Does Luntz say anything about the rule of three – that, to be significant, something has to show up more than once?

Howard: He doesn't, but I would. Anything that is important in the chart will show up three times, in different ways. It is a repeating theme that runs through the whole chart.

Audience: Is there a way in which the darker side of Chiron might be shown, as well as the teaching part?

Howard: I tend to see people with Chiron prominent as often having some kind of wound. The wound may be obvious or it may not be, but it is not really able to be healed. But because of it, these people have developed a kind of wisdom or creativity which can be very inspirational or helpful to other people. I don't know enough about this woman's life, but she may have some deep woundedness which has made her very good in her work. Is that what you mean? Chiron is an educator as well – it is a teacher as well as a healer.

Audience: I was thinking of the 2nd house and what sort of wounds might be suggested by that.

Howard: Maybe it describes a wound to her body, or to her body-image, or to her sense of survival. She was a triplet, which I imagine would be a bit weird because you have to wait in a queue. Very early on, you must feel, "Is there enough for me? When is it my turn?" Also, she was the strongest of the triplets, so she probably got the most neglected, if you see what I mean, because the other ones needed more. These are body and survival issues which might have created a kind of wound. I don't know about early money problems. I don't think there were early wounds around money, like the parents being poor. I think the wound was more to her sense of value, or to her survival in the physical body.

I'll tell you who she is in a minute, but I want to wait a little longer because I think her vocation shows up more through her Sun and Ascendant, and her Saturn sign, than through anything else. Even though Luntz' rules work, they really confirm and refine what the Sun, Ascendant, and Saturn say. She has been very successful, as you will see, because she has found something to do that brings in so much of her chart. Our true vocation is to be ourselves. Mark Twain once said, "The secret of success is making your vocation your vacation." And Noel Coward said, "Work is more fun than fun." If something is really engaging you, you can enjoy it more than something that is more obviously supposed to give you pleasure. I have had one or two moments when I have been working when I felt that. Do you see what I am saying?

Untraditional significators

The Ascendant

Let me list my significators here. Liz and I have discussed this quite a bit, so these are things that we have both thought about. We differ to some degree in the order in which we look at things, but we look at the same things and come out in the same place. Liz would go first to the Ascendant as a significator, and the whole Ascendant complex, which means not just the sign on the Ascendant but any planets near, as well as the planet ruling the Ascendant and its placement by sign, house and aspect. Also, she would look at any aspects to the Ascendant itself, such as an exact Saturn square. She would go to that first to build up a picture of the vocation, although she also thinks the Sun is a necessary part of it, because she believes the Ascendant has a lot to do with the journey that we are meant to be on. She would say the Sun describes what kind of hero you are, but the Ascendant is the journey the hero has to take in order to become what he or she is.

I also believe that the Ascendant is the path to the Sun. The vocation you pursue is the outer means through which you become what you are – or, as Liz would say, what kind of hero you are, or what kind of myth you are following. By developing the qualities of the sign on the Ascendant, you become better at being your Sun-sign. That can sometimes be very paradoxical. If you are an Aries with Capricorn rising, then by learning to be disciplined and to structure your time – and to stay in one place long enough – you come into your ability to lead and inspire and initiate. If you are a Pisces with Libra rising, then through relating to people, through being creative in the arts, or by getting your life better balanced, you come into your Sun-sign, which might mean that you find the kind of healing you can do, or the kind of spiritual path you are seeking. The Ascendant is the ground for the Sun flowering into what you are. I don't need to go through all of the Ascendant signs with you, but we could look briefly at a few. If you have Aries rising, what myth do you need to live out?

Audience: The hero.

Howard: A certain kind of hero, yes, a hero who has to battle with something. Aries has to be a champion, to fight for what you believe. That's how Liz sees it – Aries is very much the knight who is battling for a cause. So to find something which is a vocation for you, you need work which involves fighting for what you believe in – a crusade or a mission.

Audience: You need something to believe in.

Howard: You need a quest, like Jason going after the Golden Fleece. You need to feel you are championing something, changing the world to make it better in some way. What if you have got Gemini rising? What is the myth associated with Gemini, or with the god Mercury? What did he do in myth? What was he?

Audience: Messenger of the gods.

Howard: Yes, Mercury was Zeus' personal fax machine. He was the messenger of the gods. That is one aspect of him. So your myth, if you have Mercury ruling the Ascendant, has to do with work which involves some sort of exchange of information, or distributing goods from one place to another. If you can get work which is all about that, then you are getting close to a true vocation, because you are living out your myth – you are being true to the god in you.

Audience: How about Sagittarius?

Howard: What do you think one of the myths of Sagittarius might be?

Audience: Is it to do with philosophy? I was thinking of Jupiter. Or with the Archer who shoots an arrow at the bull's-eye?

Howard: It is something about sharing your belief system or your philosophy, or expanding others mentally, spiritually, or materially. I sometimes see Sagittarius as the coach who says to the team, "Come on, team, look what we can do!" Or it might be the literary agent or the artistic agent who says, "I see great things for you." It might be someone who wants to go further and faster – the racing car driver, or the traveller. Sagittarius needs work which involves seeking something out there – something which you want to get to but which keeps changing and getting bigger every time you get to it. Also, you need to share your enthusiasm with others. I don't care what you do as long as you are doing something which is expanding others' vision, or sharing your beliefs or philosophy, or educating yourself and others in terms of the wisdom and meaning of life. Then that career is getting close to a vocation, to a true calling from within yourself.

The Sun

Liz would go to the Ascendant as a route to the Sun. I go to the Sun directly, before or at the same time as the Ascendant. The Sun is at the heart of the chart. Everything is ultimately meant to revolve around the Sun, and as we get older we can often use the other planets in our chart to serve the Sun-sign. If you have the Sun in Aries and your mission is to initiate or to lead, and you have the Moon in Cancer, you can use your sensitivity to others to be a better leader. Or if you have the Sun in Aries and Saturn in Capricorn, eventually you can learn

---

about the right proportion of energy to use in order to lead well, so that you are not overdoing it. I think that ultimately the idea is to get all the personal planets to serve what the Sun represents, because things revolve around it.

When we are younger, we are not like that. We are our Mars for a few years, then maybe we are our Jupiter for a few years. The Sun doesn't have a pull over them at first, but as we get older it does. Liz would also say the Ascendant doesn't come into its own until after you are thirty, until you have experienced a Saturn return. She says we often fight against the Ascendant sign when we are young. So you get people with Capricorn rising who are real rebels, who don't want to settle down, and who kick against restriction. I have often seen younger Capricorn Ascendants, even younger Capricorn Suns, who are very rebellious, at war with the father, at war with authority. And later on they become more accepting of it. Then they discover they want authority themselves. Or you can get a Gemini Ascendant who feels very awkward about communication until later on, when they see the importance of it. Or you might see an Aries Ascendant who is a bit meek until later on, when they see the importance of taking risks and asserting who they are, even if others don't agree. Liz says that sometimes we don't like our Ascendant, but very often we will be forced into it by life as we get older.

I am very happy if someone has a career that reflects the house the Sun is in. When I see someone with the Sun in the 12th who works in an institution, I think that's good, because it fits. It is music to my astrological ear. I like the sound of it. And I am happy if the career reflects the aspects of other planets to the Sun, as I was saying earlier. I like to see someone with Sun conjunct Neptune who is in a profession which involves either healing or something creative. Someone with Sun conjunct Uranus may be in some sort of unusual work – an astrologer, or someone who works with computers, or someone who is doing something to change or enlighten society. Someone with the Sun conjunct the Moon might work as a nanny. You find yourself through the planets aspecting the Sun. They need to be included in your identity. I often find that we are drawn to do work connected with planets aspecting the Sun.

Other chart factors

The next thing I think is important is the Moon sign, although the Sun and Ascendant are more important as significators of your myth. But the Moon is important because we feel happy when we are doing things connected with the Moon-sign. We feel content and satisfied. And Saturn is also very important. I have known people with Moon conjunct Saturn who have made a vocation out of things Moon-like. For example, I know a midwife with Moon conjunct Saturn – she has made a career out of the Moon, but I think it is because Saturn is there. Sometimes we make a vocation out of the sign Saturn is in, or out of any aspects to it. Venus conjunct Saturn could be a model. I have seen a lot of top models with Venus-Saturn. Or Venus-Saturn might be an artist, and so might Saturn in the 5th house.

I mentioned packed houses before. I think this is obvious. You have six planets in the 8th house and you work as a bank manager who deals with other people's money, or you work as a funeral director, or you are in insurance. You have six planets in the 5th house, and you do something creative, or you work with children. I am happy with that as an indication that you are using a lot of your chart in your work. Do you know what I mean by a singleton planet? This is a planet that is alone in a quadrant or a hemisphere, like the handle to a bucket chart. If you have Mars as a singleton and all the other planets are somewhere else, in the other hemisphere, a lot can get funnelled through that Mars, so you may be in the military, or you may be an athlete, or you may be a firefighter. I would look for any planet that stands out as a singleton. Funnily enough, an unaspected planet can also be important. I remember being told that Shakespeare had a virtually unaspected Mercury. I have seen women with an unaspected Moon making a career out of working with children. It is as if that planet can function on its own.

Audience: By an unaspected planet, do you mean no major aspects?

Howard: No major aspects – and not even any really close minor ones. Sometimes you really do get an unaspected planet, and that may be a significator for career. But I've seen it more with a planet that stands out by being a singleton.

Audience: I am thinking about an unaspected planet as something that needs to be integrated.

Howard: Yes, that's what I meant. That's why it's so important. It needs to be integrated, and if we do work which involves that planet, we are integrating something important in the personality. Missing elements can also work like that. Do you know the different chart shapings, like the "bowl", where everything is contained within an opposition? Very often the leading planet of the opposition containing the bowl is a significator for career. If you had a Venus-Neptune opposition as the delimiting opposition to your bowl, and Venus was leading, your career may very well have to do with Venus. Or if you have a "bucket" chart, which is really a bowl but with a single planet standing outside the bowl, the planet which stands outside may be a key to your work. I have seen Saturn as a singleton where someone became a scientist, because of their love of research and classifying. I have seen Jupiter as a singleton become a philosopher or teacher, because so much gets channelled through a singleton. The leading planet in a bowl chart, or the handle of a bucket chart, or a singleton planet, can all be vocation indicators.

Audience: Which is the leading end? I always get that mixed up.

Howard: The leading end is the one which rises first, going clockwise. You look at the delimiting opposition and then you look at which one leads going clockwise.

Audience: Suppose it is an upside-down bowl.

Howard: It's still the same – if you look at the planet in the delimiting opposition which has risen or will rise first, going clockwise, that is the leading planet. The one that leads or rises first is the engine, and the one which follows or rises last is the caboose. Let me just finish this chart with you. The Ascendant is Pisces, so what needs to happen in her work?

Audience: She needs to give something of herself to others, in order to become herself. She needs to be involved in healing work, or some kind of spiritual journey.

Howard: Good. Let's look at the aspects to the Sun. How about Sun conjunct Pluto?

Audience: A therapist.

Howard: Yes, she could be a therapist. Let's look at the Saturn sign. If you have Saturn in Scorpio in the 8th, the fear of deep emotions may lead you into work exploring the emotions. Or maybe the fear of death might lead you into work exploring death. Do you know who this is yet?

Audience: Is it Elisabeth Kübler-Ross?

Howard: Yes, it's Elisabeth Kübler-Ross. She pioneered working with the dying, and she has done very good work. Isn't it perfect – someone with the Sun conjunct Pluto in Cancer and Pisces rising, who cares for people who are dying? I told you she was a triplet, so I think it was a personal issue. I also heard that she helped clean up Auschwitz after the war – she was one of the people who mopped up. The family were Swiss, and her father was a doctor, and she became a doctor. There is something about Sun-Pluto which describes the father. Pluto often has to do with the medical profession, because it tries to bring to the surface diseases that are hidden. Pluto tries to regenerate, to cleanse. Also, Pluto is conjunct the Moon's north Node. If something is conjunct the north Node, it is very favourable to follow it.

Audience: She has a very creative way of working.

Howard: Well, so much of herself comes through. If you have ever heard her speak, it is her as much as anything she says that inspires. It is quite remarkable. Look at how apt it is, to work with death and have Saturn in Scorpio in the 8th. I am sure she was terrified of death, maybe partly from being a triplet. Saturn is what you are really afraid of. Scorpio is connected with death, with the hidden. The 8th house is connected with death. Do you see how you can turn your Saturn sign into a career?

The traditional significators give us more details. The ruler of the 10th is in the house of institutions. The 12th house is one of the houses of death as well, because it is what is beyond the corporeal.

There are other examples of this repeating theme, but it is really described by the Sun conjunct Pluto. In this case the Ascendant works very well too. I think you really get her vocation by looking at the Ascendant and the aspects to the Sun, much more than by just looking at the 10th and 6th and 2nd houses.

The personal myth

So you should know what you are doing now. Someone comes to you for a reading, and you then ask yourself, "What god does this person listen to? What god is the individual responsive to? What work, what kind of career would best give this person a chance to connect with that god, or with the myths associated with the deeper levels of his or her psyche?"

You can do a lot of different kinds of work and still bring in the essence of your myth. Some are really obvious – if you are a Gemini and you are a taxi driver or a journalist, that's really obvious. But you can bring your Gemini myth into lots of other kinds of work where it isn't so obvious. With Gemini, the career you are doing, or the aspect of career that you focus on, should be one which has to do with networking. That's what I listen for. If someone is asking for advice, I would look at the traditional significators, but I really want to get to what god this individual answers to, which may change at different points in life. You can get shifts. You can get Zeus for a part of life, and Zeus likes to wield power, but he could turn into Hephaistos, who finds out he is quite happy working alone quietly at something for hours and days and months and years. Maybe you have Jupiter aspecting the Sun, but there also might be a lot of planets in Virgo, and then you might need to change direction at some point.

If you are a Hephaistos type – that's Vulcan in Roman myth – it might show up through having a lot of planets in the 6th house or a lot of planets in Virgo, where you are happy just to work at some specific craft or detail alone, and you don't need other people around. You don't even need to get praised for it, because you just enjoy craft for itself. But if you are a Dionysos type you need work you are passionate about. If you are doing something which you are not passionate about, you will be miserable – you will be an alcoholic or a drug addict, or you'll be going away as much as possible to meditate. But what if you are a Dionysos type who is a bit sensitive and emotional, and your father is a Zeus type? Is he going to like your Dionysian side? Your myth might be clear for you, but it might not be acceptable to your family.

In myth there is something called the bed of Procrustes. When travellers were going to Athens and were waylaid by the bandit Procrustes, they were put on this bed, and if they were too tall for the bed they were cut down to size. If they were too short they were stretched to fit. Sometimes we do that to ourselves, if our family or our culture doesn't approve of the divinities which are strong in us. If these divinities are not popular with our family or culture, we cut off parts of ourselves to win their love. Or we take the parts which are favourable and we stretch them out at the expense of other bits, to conform, to fit the bed. Even if you succeed at what you are doing in that way, you probably won't feel a great deal of benefit from it, because it is not who you are. If you are a Hephaistos type trying to be in a position of public power because your parents wanted you to be somebody important, you won't be very happy.

Family issues come into how we deal with our myths. Zeus definitely had favourites. He loved his son Apollo. Apollo was the golden boy, because he was so clear and rational. But Zeus hated the god Ares, who was also his son, because he was too brash and impulsive. Zeus didn't really like his son Dionysos because he was too effeminate and emotional. He hated Hephaistos because Hephaistos stood up to him when Zeus was quarrelling with Hera, so Zeus threw him out of heaven. Hephaistos was born lame, and being thrown out of heaven messed him up even more. Zeus thought he was too ugly to be a proper Olympian. Zeus is like the planet Jupiter – you want to shine brilliantly, to wield power and authority. If you have Jupiter in the 10th house you want to be brilliant at what you are doing, dazzling to the public. That doesn't interest Hephaistos. Hephaistos works quietly alone, making beautiful things, just trying to get it right, not concerned with dazzling others.

You must own these kinds of things. If you have a lot of planets in the 10th, there is ambition there. If you have Sun conjunct Jupiter in Leo in the 10th and you tell me that career isn't important to you, I wouldn't buy it, because I believe the chart more than what the person sitting there says. People aren't always conscious of all of themselves. I would say, "Look, didn't you know that part of you wants to dazzle

---

others?" That's part of being an astrologer, helping people to see what they don't know, or confirming what they suspect.

Audience: What would you say about vocation when the Sun is conjunct the south Node?

Howard: The Sun conjunct the south Node is a little weird, because the south Node is what we have already done and what we shouldn't be doing too much of now – otherwise we are not evolving. If the Sun conjuncts the south Node, it might mean that you've done certain qualities of that Sun-sign before, and now you have come back under the same Sun-sign, but you have to do other levels of it. Let's say you have Sun in Libra conjunct the south Node. Maybe you have been very good at being an artist in the past, but now you have to learn about the relationship side of Venus. So there are some aspects of Libra you have done before, but because the Sun is there, which is what you need to develop, there are other facets which now need to be worked on. That's how I would interpret it. It may therefore be right to have the Sun-sign as a career, but I would still say you must balance that with the north Node, by house and sign. You must find room for both.

Let's move on now. I want to look at a few charts from the group. Some of you who are really confused about vocation have already given me their charts. Obviously I won't be able to get to all of them, maybe only a few, but I would like to do a few. Also, I have some charts of my own which I would like to show you, and you can guess the careers.

Example charts from the group

Before we look at the charts, I have some questions which you can all ask yourselves and be thinking about:

- When you were a child, what were the fantasies you had of what you wanted to be when you grew up? I am assuming you did grow up!
- Think about the actual work that you are doing. That's assuming you are in some sort of employ or something you would consider work right now. Is this something that you really feel fulfilled doing?

- How did you happen to get into that work? Did it happen by chance, by synchronicity, or by careful planning? When did you know it was what you wanted to do?
- If you are not doing what you want, is there something stopping you? What's stopping you?
- If there is a vocation you would really like to be doing, then the question is divided into two. First, how realistic is that aspiration? Second, what steps do you need to take to realise the aspiration of doing that vocation?

Why don't you take five or ten minutes now to meditate on the questions? We are all here to learn about vocation. Obviously these are your own personal issues, but the more you understand your own stuff, the more you can understand others.

Audience: I work as a therapist, and I've gone back to learning clinical skills, which is what I was doing at the beginning of my training. There are some big transits hitting my 4th house right now. It's as though I have come full circle.

Howard: I'm intrigued. But I think vocational issues can go in cycles. There is a time when we can put a lot of energy into achieving outwardly, and at other times we need to pull back or pull in, or complete something which we didn't finish earlier. This kind of time can sometimes show up if you are getting very heavy transits to the 4th house, like Pluto hitting the IC, or these current Capricorn transits through the 4th. That may be a time when you need to gestate. You might feel you want to withdraw from the outer world because you need time to go through personal changes which you couldn't go through if you were trying to do your normal work at the same time. If you have always identified with your work, or you have a busy practise as a therapist and are seeing a lot of people, and then you get these 4th house transits, you may feel like you just want to be alone and centred in your own self. Or you may want to refine what you already know, or go back to the foundations to rebuild something, rather than just charging ahead. It can be a difficult thing to do, if you've always been focused on the outside world. At other times, if you are getting a lot of transits to the 10th house – except maybe for Pluto – then it is as if changes are meant to be happening in your work which put you more before the public. It is not really a time to hide or retrace your steps. Usually it is a time to be trying new things or expanding your work. All right, let's see what we can do. All these charts are interesting and I wish we had time for them all.

Chart 1: Karen

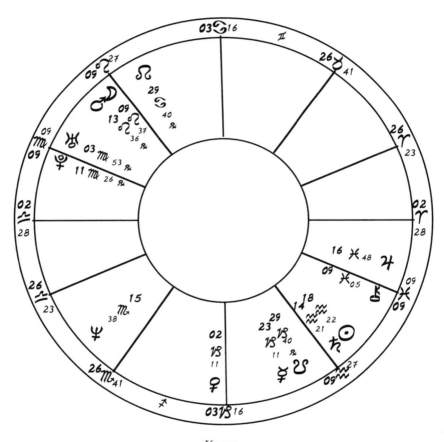

Karen
8 February 1963, 9.00 pm GMT, Norwich
Placidus cusps

The reason I put Karen's chart up is that, first of all, I want to talk a bit about what it means to have the north Node in the 10th house and the south Node in the 4th. Also, this chart has a funny reversal, because the north Node in the 10th is in Cancer, although Capricorn is the natural sign for the 10th, and the south Node in the 4th is in Capricorn, when the 4th is actually Cancer's natural house.

I do invite you all to come in on this discussion. The general interpretation of the north Node in the 10th is that it is actually quite important in this lifetime to have some sort of profession, or to achieve some sort of status or make career important, because the north Node is always what pulls us forward. The south Node in the 4th on its own suggests that just to be a housewife, or just to stay at home, or just to be concerned with the personal and the private, won't offer the most growth in terms of evolution this time around. We really should try to develop the house the north Node is in. So one might say that if you have the south Node in the 4th, if you just stay with your family too much or you don't take risks to become more public and to get out there and go for it in terms of a career, then you are not fulfilling your life purpose. In this case, because the north Node is in Cancer, I would be looking for some sort of career or work which brought Cancerian qualities out.

Let me say something about the 10th house in general. When Liz talks about the 10th house, she says it describes qualities you would like to be remembered for or be seen as having – it's what you would want engraved on your tombstone. If you have Scorpio up there, you want to be seen as shrewd and incisive. If you have Libra up there, you want to be seen as beautiful, or as someone who is very harmonious and balanced. If you have Aries up there, you want the world to see your courage. You want to be seen as an innovator, or as a fighter. If you have Cancer up there, I think you want to be seen for your sensitivity, for your feeling gifts. In your case, Karen, because the north Node is there, it is good to develop that, because the north Node in Cancer says you need to work on the realm of the emotions and the feelings as part of your development.

Let me just babble on a bit more, and then I want to bring everyone else in. I want to say what catches my eye when I am looking at this chart in terms of vocation. I am going to narrow these readings that we are doing here to only vocational issues, although one is tempted to do much more because one sees so many other things to talk about. What's the ruler of the MC?

Audience: The Moon.

Howard: And what sign is the Moon in?

Audience: Leo.

Howard: What's the most obvious aspect the Moon makes? It's conjunct Mars. So if Moon-Mars in Leo rules your MC, this describes you before the public. It's what you would like to be seen as, and also the qualities which are fuelling your career drive. What do you think about Moon in Leo ruling the Midheaven, conjunct Mars? What is there an inner need for?

Audience: Recognition.

Howard: Yes. It may surprise you, Karen. This Moon-Mars in Leo ruling the MC is a need to be admired or applauded or recognised. I think it is all right to own that. Sometimes part of us may think it is egotistical to want to be admired or lauded, but I actually think that, with Moon-Mars in the 11th ruling the MC, there is a need to be recognised as special. We all have it to some extent – it is the solar side of ourselves that wants to be recognised. It looks like you could do it if you work within a group or team setting. If I think of the 11th house in terms of work, I think of working in a group or working with a team, where your power could come out. There is something quite different going on with the Sun-Saturn conjunction opposing it. Even though you have Mercury hidden away in the 4th, and even though you have Saturn holding back your Sun, I would be hoping that you could find some sort of team or group of people, even if it was a group like this, where you wouldn't be too shy to come out and contribute your feelings and ideas. Do you find that easy or hard?

Karen: Well, at the moment, I'm not fulfilled in vocation. I am working in a darkroom, in a photography lab. I really am hidden away!

Howard: There may be reasons, with so much transiting the 4th house right now, and your Saturn return coming up, why you're doing the opposite of the Moon-Mars in Leo. Are you alone in the darkroom?

Karen: Yes, for most of the day. At the moment I feel the issue of vocation is something that has always been very important to me, and it is, but it is trying to find the right direction that I have had difficulty with. Obviously, doing astrology seminars has been very helpful. At the moment I am thinking of maybe doing a counselling course.

Howard: Let's talk about that. First of all, I like the idea of counselling for the Cancer MC. It's a career where you are caring. With the Moon-Mars in the 11th ruling the MC, it may be a good idea for you to think of eventually working with groups rather than just individuals. Do you see how I am getting that? I am drawn from the 10th right to the 11th. Leo can be the facilitator, the guide or group leader. It may even be a women's group – helping women find their power, or whatever. That would fit the Moon in the 11th. Do you follow me? Also, if we are looking at houses which are busy, or packed houses, there are three planets in the 11th, and it is also the house which is ruled by your Sun. Remember, I said I look for the Sun and the house the Sun rules in the chart as a clue to vocation.

Another thing in the chart that says groups to me is that the Sun is in Aquarius. But it is a funny mixture here, because it is in the 5th house, which is Leo's natural house. Let me explain this. The 5th house is the need to give expression to what's inside you, and to have the freedom to express what's inside no matter what other people need or want. The 5th is what you want to do, not what other people want you to do. But Aquarius is the sign that is naturally associated with the 11th, and the thing Aquarius has to learn is not so much, "I'm special!" but more, "What can I do to promote the group or the ideals I believe in, which are not just for myself?" The 11th house is where we are meant to adjust to a group. But if you have Leo there, it is about finding your power by being in a group. Do you see? Leo in the 11th finds its power through groups. Aquarius on the 5th house cusp has to use its creativity, and what it has to give out, not just because it is pleasurable to give it out, but because the creativity has to be used for the sake of others. It is an Aquarian 5th house. Instead of painting a picture for yourself, to give expression to yourself, maybe you design a poster to promote the ideals of a group you believe in. Then you are combining creativity with serving something larger. To have Saturn in the 5th and the Sun conjunct Saturn is a sort of double whammy, because the 5th house is the Sun's natural house. The Sun has a lot to do with our need to be appreciated as someone unique, our need for people to see that we have something which we can give which no one else can give. That's what the Sun is – it is really your uniqueness. When I say "I", I mean something absolutely unique and special. There's no other "I" like my "I". The Sun has so much to do with the development of a sense of a separate self, which is unique from everyone else's separate self.

You know my rap on this. Underneath, we are all one. We are all interconnected. But still, on another level, if you switch channels, we are different. I am different from you and I have different abilities. You are blonde, I'm a brunette. Through developing your Sun-sign you find out what's unique and special about yourself, but when you have Saturn on top of your Sun, that does not come easily. It is as if one is uncomfortable about one's uniqueness, about what one has to give in order to shine. Whenever I think of Saturn conjunct the Sun, I see Saturn as someone sitting on your shoulder judging you. You want to say something and Saturn whispers, "Is it right? What will they think? Maybe you shouldn't. And what would your mother say?" Saturn is a critic. That also applies to Saturn in the 5th, because the 5th house is the joy of being creative, the joy of self-expression, and when you have Saturn there, it is hard to get that joy. Maybe you feel inadequate about what you have to express. As a child your parents might have valued you for certain things and not for other things, and maybe you weren't valued for those things which were most uniquely you. So you felt guilty about being individual or about being creative. You know how we can develop a false self in order to win love.

There is something called sandplay therapy. I don't know if you are familiar with it. It is great. The therapist says nothing at all. Only if you ask do they say anything. You can have dry sand or wet sand, and they have a whole lot of different toys around, little human and animal figures and tiny houses and machines and so on, which you arrange on the sand depending on your fantasies. It is completely visceral and non-verbal. You are left alone and you go for the toys you want and arrange them however you want, and you work things out through that sandplay therapy. When I think about the 5th house, I think of a person as a child – you as a child getting into a sandbox. What comes out is the planets you have in the 5th. If you have Jupiter in the 5th, you get in the sandbox and what happens? How do you feel when you have to create in your sandbox?

Audience: It's not big enough.

Howard: And not showy enough. Or Jupiter says, "I can't wait to get in there! I'm going to build the biggest, most wonderful sand castle in the world!" If you have Venus there, when you get in the sandbox you are going to create beautiful things, and you won't mind sharing the sandbox with your friends, either. But what happens when you get in the sandbox and you have Saturn in the 5th? "I've got to make something. They expect me to make something. But am I good enough? What if I make a mess? What if they don't like it? Maybe I should take a course in sand castle building so I don't get it wrong." A tension can come up, which seems to me to be shown by the Sun-Saturn in Karen's chart. It's so different from having Moon-Mars in Leo, which is instinctively so spontaneous and creative. Moon-Mars would seem to free your creativity. By creativity, I don't just mean being an artist. I mean what you have to express, and your power to re-parent yourself and give yourself permission to be the spontaneous, playful, rumbunctious, individualistic child that your parents may not have approved of.

Karen: I find what you are saying very relevant. I grew up in a household where both parents were alcoholic.

Howard: Can any of you see that in the chart? Neptune is in a T-square to the Sun and the Moon. That's a perfect description. It isn't a perfect thing to grow up with. But astrologically it's absolutely right. Neptune is a significator for drink, and Neptune squares both the Moon and the Sun, the Sun being a paternal image and the Moon being a maternal one.

Karen: Both my parents are dead now. My father died earlier this year, and I feel it is important for me to do something for myself.

Howard: Now that your parents are dead, you really have a chance. That may sound hard, but it's often like that. I was wondering about the transits through the 4th house, if you take the 4th to be the

----

father. And Pluto has been squaring the T-square, and your father died when Pluto squared your Sun. He was right on time. Did they leave you any money?

Karen: Well, I will get some from him, yes.

Howard: So that will help you.

Karen: That will help with the fees if I do a counselling course. But I do have some need to do something gainful, and I feel at the moment I would like to maybe combine astrology with the counselling.

Howard: I think the first task is your training. You are having the Saturn return, and when it gets to your Saturn-Sun it is a time to learn, to start really defining yourself – "This is what I want to be!" – and also giving your vocation more definition. I remember my Saturn return very clearly. I was mostly teaching meditation, but I really loved astrology, and around the time of my Saturn return I thought, "I am going to get serious about astrology. I am going to take psychology courses and study more astrology." That was around the time I did the Faculty Diploma. It was a feeling of having to define myself and what I wanted, and doing something to concretise it and manifest it and get serious about it. Training and working on yourself will somehow lead into the kind of career you are talking about. The creative drive is very strong here. Why do I think the creative drive is strong? Give me a few other reasons besides the 5th house.

Audience: Venus is on the IC.

Howard: Yes. Any planet on the IC describes what you are like deep down inside. And what does Venus rule in this chart? The Libra Ascendant. Sometimes, with planets in Capricorn, or a Capricorn IC, people don't come into their own until they are a bit older. That's even true of Sun conjunct Saturn. The Sun has to do with forming your individual identity and radiating it outwards. With Sun-Saturn it is a slower process than what other people might have. It slows down the process of building a healthy, solid sense of self. And with Neptune square your Sun and Moon, and coming from an alcoholic family, a healthy, solid sense of self would not have been easy to get. There are just a few other things I wanted to mention. Pisces on the 6th house suggests work which is creative, or work which involves healing. Was working in a darkroom with photography something you thought about and choose, or something you just fell into?

Karen: It was a conscious decision. It was a question of finding an area which I was actually interested in.

Howard: Neptune does rule photography, and it aspects both your Sun and Moon. All right, let's finish with this one. Are there any more questions or things you might have to add about vocation, in terms of both traditional significators and the personal myth?

Audience: I was thinking of some sort of occupational therapy work for Karen.

Howard: Tell me how that spoke to you from the chart.

Audience: Venus in Capricorn, ruling the Libra Ascendant. It would mean using Venus practically.

Audience: Perhaps Pluto in the 12th house says something about working in institutions.

Howard: You could get into some interesting work with your background, Karen, working with other children of alcoholic parents, and using your creativity and your astrology as part of the work. I wouldn't say that your task was to be an artist for the sake of your own self-expression. Your creativity needs to be used in some sort of practical way. If you had Sun in Leo in the 5th, you could be an artist, but because it is in Aquarius it is for others as well as yourself.

Audience: We were talking in the break about the possibility of Karen doing a photograph for a women's group that I'm participating in. I was thinking it would be brilliant if she could do some photographs for the group.

Howard: You see, with Karen's Moon in the 11th, you also thought of women's groups.

Transits over the MC

Before we look at the next chart, I wanted to say a few things in general about transits to the MC, in terms of work. This may not apply in all cases, but it does apply in a lot. With Pluto coming up to the MC, it would strike me that if we are in a particular sort of work, it can't go on in the same way as it always has. This is because Pluto shows where there is going to be death and rebirth. A tearing down of the existing occurs, so that something new can happen. I have seen i t work in a few different ways. One is that, if you really haven't found what you think is your true calling, then, if you have Pluto going over your MC, it may be the time that you do find something to become passionately engaged in.

I use the word passion with Pluto because ultimately, where Scorpio is or Pluto is in the chart, we need to feel passion. We do best at something if we feel passion about it. One can do other things, but i t won't really click – it is best if it is something that one is really intense about. When I think of Pluto, I think of drama and intensity. So if you are born with Pluto in the 10th, you need work that you feel passionate about. However, I have to tell you that I have seen a number of people born with Pluto in the 10th house who do what seem like quite wimpy jobs, or who really haven't found their power. For instance, I remember doing a chart for a man who had Pluto in Leo in the 10th, and he worked in the music department at Harrods, selling popular tapes and records and CD's. Somehow I didn't think that fit Pluto in the 10th. If you asked him what he wanted to do, he was vague. He didn't seem to have any real definition. He didn't feel solid. There wasn't anyone home.

With some people with Pluto in the 10th, there is a fear of owning one's power. Sometimes, whatever house Pluto is in, this happens, and in the 10th it may come out as a fear of going before the public or becoming powerful in one's career. Actually, there is an intense desire to be powerful or to have some sort of control, wherever Pluto is, but sometimes we don't want to let Pluto into the house that i t is in. We try to lock Pluto out because we are afraid of its intensity, or afraid of having passion stirred up. We are afraid of not being in control any more. Oddly enough, even though you might expect Pluto's house to be where one is a beast or one is a tyrant or one is really dramatic, I have seen Pluto in the 10th with people who just didn't feel that way. Either they haven't found their power yet, or for some reason they are afraid of it.

Audience: Could it be to do with an overpowering mother, Howard? They grow up being unable to claim the power for themselves.

Howard: Yes, I think that happens. The mother still has the power. In this client's case, that was definitely the situation. He was still a little boy for his mother. It is like still being small inside. Let me just continue generally for a minute. What I am saying is that there's a good chance you might not even get Pluto over the MC – Pluto has a 248-year cycle, so you are only going to get it over your MC once, if you get it at all. It has to start in at least the 6th house to get to the MC, and maybe in the 7th or 8th or even the 9th to get there when you are young enough to make big changes in your work. In Marianne's chart, the next chart I want to look at, it starts in the 7th. For your whole life it is only going through one sector of the chart. When it reaches the MC, that may be when you really do find your work.

Pluto at the MC may take things away from you, too – it may make you lose interest in what you have always got your sense of identity from, and that's like an ego-death. If you have been very identified with your career and your work, and then it no longer works for you and it goes dead on you, who are you? I have actually seen certain cases where there has been a kind of reducing of everything to ashes – having everything fall apart in terms of your vocation or work sphere, so that you can be reborn in a new way. I have seen cases of Pluto hitting the MC where the person stops working for a while, because there is some sort of restructuring going on in the psyche.

Let's say Pluto is coming to conjunct or square your Mars. Some of you may have Mars in Leo with Pluto squaring it right now, or Mars in Scorpio with Pluto coming up over it, or Mars in Taurus with Pluto opposing it. If you have been a very sexual person all your life, Pluto hitting your Mars may be a period where your sex drive goes very quiet, as if you now have to experience Mars in some other way. But if you haven't been sexual, if you have never really felt driven by passion, Pluto transits to Mars may signify the first time in your life you really do feel that drive or passion. Pluto can take away something if you have been doing it too much, or if you are too identified with it. If you have always been angry, Pluto squaring your

Mars may change you from being an angry person to someone who can control anger better or can let things go more easily. But if you have never been angry or never really been in touch with your anger, Pluto hitting your Mars could actually bring out the anger that has been down there all along.

Audience: In the cases where people's careers went under because they had been over-identified with their work, did they then go back to the same career later?

Howard: Usually not, or they went back to it with a very different attitude, because Pluto makes sure that you can't go back to things in the same way any more. They may go back to the same work, but they are coming from a different place, or they have changed their work in some way.

Audience: A friend of mine had her first child when Pluto went over her MC. Until then she had definitely been a career woman. She was thirty-eight and discovered, suddenly and unexpectedly, that she was pregnant, and her whole life has been transformed as a result.

Howard: It is interesting how, sometimes, you get a reflex where a transit throws you into the opposite house from the one it's going through. Pluto is around my MC now, and I have never spent so much time not working. Also, when Pluto was exactly on my MC recently, there was a rumour going around that I was dead. I loved it! My public image, with transiting Pluto on my MC, is that I am dead!

Audience: A sure sign of immortality!

Howard: Let me say a bit more about transits to the MC. What do you think happens if Uranus comes to your MC? Usually you get bored with what you are doing. With Uranus you usually have to be experimental and try the new, or the new is forced on you in some way. What happens when Neptune comes to your MC, in terms of your work? You can get confused about what you really want to do. I know some people who work at ITN Television. ITN is making a lot of people redundant right now, and I had two clients who work for ITN. They both have Neptune transiting around the MC now. They don't know whether they will still be in work or not. That uncertainty is typical of Neptune. Or you may decide that you want to go into creative work, or a field which is descriptive of Neptune, but usually there is confusion. I don't know if Neptune hitting the MC is a good time to choose to change work. I would wait for it to go past the MC, because you might go for something that really is a bubble. Later you will be clearer.

Audience: When Neptune hit my MC I realised I needed to let go of my career for my health.

Howard: With any outer planet hitting the MC, you might have to let go of something. Certainly for me, illness was the only way to stop me from over-working, even though for years I was getting the message, "Cut down on your work! Cut down on your work!" But I didn't listen to it. Let's see what you think about transiting Saturn hitting the MC. It's a funny one.

Audience: I have it now.

Howard: In one sense it can mean starting to really form a sense of what it is we want to commit ourselves to.

Audience: What's happened is that it has fallen on my progressed Sun in the 10th house opposition Neptune, and I am really confused about what to do. Do I carry on with what I am doing now?

Howard: What are you doing now?

Audience: I'm designing book jackets. But suddenly it doesn't satisfy me. I don't want to do it. I just go off to the pub. I take the phone off the hook.

Howard: That sounds like progressed Sun opposition Neptune! But it's a different thing with Saturn. I was talking earlier about my own Saturn return. It made me commit myself more, define myself more.
Audience: I am beginning to feel that. I know I have to make a decision, even if it doesn't happen right now. I am beginning to clarify what it is I really want to do. But it is going to be difficult.

Howard: That is often the feeling with Saturn. Liz says about Saturn that it can hit your MC or your Sun and you can get a definite sense of what you want to do, but you often have to wait to do anything about it. She says you are often suspended for a while until you can shift things on the material level. It is often frustrating because the idea has become clear, but you have to wait.

Audience: I know I want to change, but I am not ready to change yet. I need a few more years.

Howard: I have seen people come into their own with Saturn hitting the MC. Let me say this about Saturn. It is a bit of a cliché, but Saturn is exact and undeviating justice. It rewards you for what you have put in, and it makes you aware of your lack if you have been avoiding something. When it hits the MC, if you have really been working hard in a career, it can often reward you by giving you promotion and giving you more responsibility – if you want it. If you have been avoiding facing that area, or if there are certain skills you need to learn to further your work and you haven't been learning them, then when Saturn hits the MC you will feel the lack. You will feel as if you are being punished because you haven't done what you should have done and you have been cutting corners.

Watch Saturn, because it is not such a monster. If you have been working very hard at something, Saturn will reward you for it. Let's say Saturn is about to transit into your 6th house, and you are worried. "Oh no, Saturn is coming into my 6th. What about my health?" If you have been looking after your health pretty well, and have been taking care of yourself, Saturn will probably make you feel good about what you have done. "Oh, good, I am glad I have been working on it. Now I can really see the rewards." But if you have been eating badly or not taking care of your body, then when Saturn comes into the 6th, you won't get sick because Saturn's coming into the 6th. But you might get sick because of all the things you haven't done. Now Saturn is saying, "Yes, look at it. You have cut corners and now you have to pay." It is exact and undeviating justice. It gives you back exactly what you have put in. Jupiter going over the MC could bring new opportunities, but whether they actually result in anything or just pass by is another question.

Audience: I think there is also a problem with over-expansion.

Howard: Well, Jupiter tends to be manic. You could get very excited about some new possibility and overextend yourself, or you might really throw yourself into your work and ignore other things, which may or may not be a good thing. What if you are getting your progressed Sun coming over your MC? What do you think that says about work? I see the progressed Sun as a torch which shines on whatever it is touching, so when it hits your MC, you really could come into your own in terms of career. Or, if career hasn't been important, then you might really feel the need to shine.

Chart 2: Marianne

What drew me to this chart is that transiting Pluto is revving up to the MC. Also, the Uranus-Neptune conjunction in Capricorn is beginning to flirt with Marianne's Ascendant. One of the things I would look at right away, if she had come to me for a reading, would be career issues, because of Pluto coming up to the MC. I would also be thinking of the fact that Pluto rules her Scorpio MC, and it is in Leo in the 7th house. If the ruler of the MC is in the 7th, what might be necessary for Marianne to feel that her career is a vocation?

Audience: Working with other people.

Audience: What about Mars as the co-ruler of the MC?

Howard: I always go for Pluto first, but it's true that Mars is the co-ruler of Scorpio, and you could look at that too. It's in the 3rd house conjunct Mercury, which gives a sense of needing exchange. I have the same thing in my chart – a Scorpio MC with Pluto in the 7th, and my work does involve other people. One thing I have noticed about it – maybe you feel this way too, Marianne – is that, if you take the MC to be the mother and you have Scorpio there, there can be something about the mother's unlived passions or the mother's pain which is affecting you very strongly. If the mother was in pain or was frustrated, and you were somehow sensitive to that, even unconsciously, there could be some sort of career where you are sensitive to other people's pain, or you are trying to help people who are frustrated or having emotional problems. If the ruler of the MC is in Leo in the 7th, the mother's need for recognition, especially if she didn't get it, may somehow be a factor in your own psyche. Either you want recognition to please the mother, or you will live out what she didn't live out, or you are rebelling against her – you don't want to be what she's like at all.

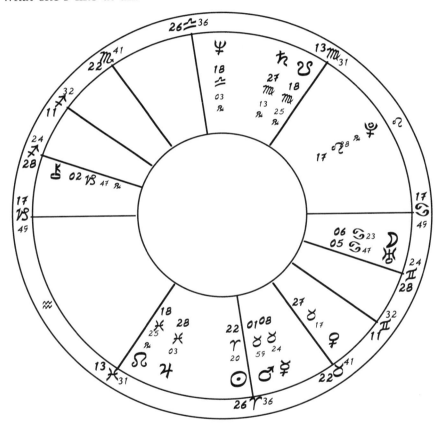

Marianne
13 April 1951, 2.00 am GMT, London
Placidus cusps

Marianne: My mother made it clear that the only reason she became a mother was because she accidentally got pregnant.

Howard: There is a Moon-Uranus conjunction in Cancer in your chart, suggesting that maybe mothering wasn't her natural thing.

Marianne: She enjoyed work, but obviously that wasn't an option once she got pregnant. She wasn't a career woman, but certainly I have always had every encouragement to do whatever I wanted. I wasn't being overtly pushed, but...

Howard: But the message was there. I have the same thing with my Scorpio MC and Pluto in Leo in the 7th. My mother wants to write a famous novel. That's actually what she really wants to do. She can hardly write a letter. When I finally got a book published, she was really happy, even though I was just an astrologer! She had trouble with my vocation – "My son the astrologer" wasn't so hot. But as soon as I wrote books it was better. Every time I say I am writing another book, my mother says, "When are you going to write a novel?" I think she would like to be Barbara Cartland. Finally I said, "I'll write a novel when you're dead!" She never asked me again. I also said, "I'll have to wait until you die because it is going to be very autobiographical and you'll be terribly upset." She is a Leo, and the ruler of my MC is in Leo. Her own need to shine and radiate and have some sort of public recognition wasn't fulfilled, but it was put onto her children.

Marianne: I didn't feel a lot of pushing in an obvious way. My mother never seemed to have any aims or goals. Maybe they were just unconscious.

Howard: The Moon-Uranus conjunction suggests a mother whose nature was probably quite Uranian. That is not the planet one associates with being happy just being a mother, even though it's in Cancer. If you have a Moon-Uranus aspect, you have to find some other way to use your maternal nature besides just the traditional way. You have to mother other adults, or have a career taking care of others. Mothering isn't just biological. This also applies to your chart, Karen. Usually we think of using the Cancerian or maternal instinct for a family. But if Cancer is on the MC, you need to use it publicly, or for the sake of society, not just for a child you may have. Tell me what kind of work you have been doing, Marianne, and what's been happening.

Marianne: For the last ten years I have been doing work which is involved with Eurobond Syndication.

Howard: Say that again?

Marianne: Eurobond Syndication.

Howard: I don't have any. Should I?

Marianne: If you watch the news when they talk about the financial markets, and you see rows of desks and everybody on the phone screaming, you can see the sort of environment I work in. Until the last year or so it suited me very well. It was an Aries thing, very outgoing, very fast. One of my ex-colleagues nicknamed us the midwives, which I thought was quite appropriate for the Moon-Uranus. Basically, four of us had brilliant ideas and we all used to make it happen. What's been happening is that the bull market has been going through a lot of turmoil. Many people are unemployed. Just before my Uranus-Uranus opposition, I walked into the office one morning to discover that I had a job but none of my colleagues did.

Howard: You still had a job?

Marianne: Yes. But everybody else had been fired. I thought the message might be that maybe I shouldn't be there either. What has been happening is that, by the time of my Uranus half-return, I started working part-time, spending more time on astrology. I have just completed a counselling course.

Howard: Yes, I was wondering about that.

Marianne: I have been feeling, at the moment – mainly because of having Uranus and Neptune transiting through my 12th house – that there is stuff simmering away.

Howard: Yes, it is simmering. It hasn't quite finished cooking yet.

Marianne: I am not actually doing anything with it yet.

Howard: Pluto will hang around 22° Scorpio for quite a while. Also, I would want to wait until Neptune cleared your Ascendant to really say something definite. How do you like the astrology and counselling side of things? Is that appealing to you? Do you think it is something you could do full-time?

Marianne: I am not sure. I think, probably because of the Sun in Aries, I actually have a major problem concentrating on anything for any length of time. I don't know whether I could stay in all day, every day, doing that kind of job, and I don't know whether it would pay enough.

Howard: Can I make a suggestion and be a little pushy here? This may not apply to you, so if it doesn't, discard it once you have thought about it. Strongly Uranian people may not always be suited to working either as counsellors or astrologers full-time, because there comes a time – especially if you're working ongoing as a counsellor – when Uranus, and in particular Moon-Uranus, gets tired of carrying someone every week, or carrying too many people.

Marianne: I have certainly found that. Doing the counselling course has proved it to me.

Howard: When I see something as powerful as an exact Moon-Uranus conjunction in the house of work, I think – even though this belies your Capricorn Ascendant, and even the Scorpio MC – that maybe you could carry a part-time caseload as an astrologer and counsellor, but not a full-time caseload. Then you could have something else that you are doing, something completely different. Did any of you know Pam Tyler? She was an American astrologer living here for a while. She spoke to the Faculty once about what it was like to be an astrologer, and she said, "Don't do it full time. Do it, but have some other thing you do which is completely different, so you are not always having to either carry other people or be open to their psyches." I get that feeling too, when I look at this Moon-Uranus.

Marianne: With Pluto approaching, I feel that the job I have been doing has been very enjoyable, but it has been very much motivated by trying to achieve. Now I am thinking of applying for a new job in the

---

same sphere, but this time I am thinking, "Let's earn as much as I can." I want to make money rather than being driven by ambition, so that I can attend seminars here.

Audience: Have you thought of financial astrology?

Howard: There are quite a few people doing some interesting things with financial astrology. Let me add a few other general things. I actually think, looking at your chart, that you should put off making a decision for a while, just to see what more happens, because the transits are not quite there yet.

Marianne: My decision is imminent.

Howard: I think the north Node in Pisces and the Scorpio MC ruled by a 7th house Pluto are indications of someone who could work as a counsellor or helper. Now this is me fantasising: Let's say that there are certain people in your field who would normally think astrologers are cranks, but because you seem solid and you seem reliable and you seem a good worker, they could think that maybe there might be something to astrology, because you have got into it. So you may be able to get people coming to you who would not normally go to an astrologer, because they believe in you as a person.

Marianne: I have found that to be true.

Howard: You see what I am saying. You don't look cranky.

Marianne: Most of my clients are from the financial world.

Howard: You could actually be someone who opens them up to things they might not necessarily be opened up to or look at. This is sometimes a role that certain people have. Two things interest me as well, if we keep going on the chart. One is that having the north Node in the 2nd house puts the south Node in the 8th. What do you think about the north Node in the 2nd? What do you think needs to be built in? What's good for Marianne?

Audience: Self-esteem.

Howard: Yes. And self-esteem can often be achieved through earning money in one's own right. By being able to earn money, you can get a sense of worth. It is also having your worth inside yourself. It is not relying on others' praise in order to feel you are worthy. That is a big lesson, if you can feel it from inside rather than needing other people to say you are great in order for you to feel okay. The north Node in the 2nd has to do with having your own sense of values, your own worth. When I see the north Node in the 2nd, even if you have a big inheritance and people want to give you money, it is what you earn yourself that really feels good.

It is the reverse if you have the north Node in the 8th house. These people should really learn to take from others, to receive. The lesson with the north Node in the 8th is to let yourself receive. In your case, Marianne, there is a little bit of that issue anyway, because you have Saturn in the 8th. It is very hard for some people to allow others to give to them and to help them when they have the north Node in the 8th, because they have the south Node in the 2nd and they are used to thinking, "What's okay is only what I get for myself, what I earn for myself." I spend a lot of time saying to people with the north Node in the 8th, "Listen, if you can get a government grant, or if your parents want to give it, take it. Or if you have a partner who has money, that's great. You have the north Node in the 8th, and you are meant to learn to be helped by other people's resources." But in your case it is the north Node in the 2nd. When I see Venus in the 4th, I want you to have a personal life too. You need private pleasures or things you are doing just because you enjoy it, not because you should be doing it.

Audience: Gardening.

Howard: Yes, that's good for Venus in Taurus in the 4th. The other thing I wanted to mention is a thing we talked about briefly already – the Jupiter-Saturn opposition. You see here that Marianne has Jupiter in 28° Pisces opposing Saturn in 27° Virgo. Isabel Hickey used to say that was two lifetimes in one. This is what she meant by it, although I don't think this quite applies to you: Jupiter opposition Saturn may have one very long phase where you are Jupiterian, where you are out for fun and adventure. It is as if you are really identified with the Jupiter side. Then something happens and you turn into a Saturn person, and you take on responsibility and you say, "I should settle down and be responsible."

It can also work the other way around. Maybe you have been Saturn for a long time – the good child, the good citizen, and the right kind of person according to society. Then one day you say, "I think I am going to let out my Jupiter side!" and you become a bit more abandoned and cut down on work and have more time for yourself and go on holiday more. With some people with Jupiter opposition Saturn, it is cyclic. You are very Saturn and hardworking, and then you need to just go away and be a bum for a while, and then you go back to Saturn again. Often it is hard for these people, because when you have two planets in aspect, it is hard to be one without the other. Let's say you have Jupiter opposing Saturn. You say, "I'm just going to go and sit on a beach and drink Campari and orange all day and not think about work." But if you have Saturn in aspect to Jupiter, you may actually start thinking, "Well, maybe I should bring a book along that I'll learn something from." You might feel a little guilty about totally relaxing. I don't know if you have that problem, Marianne.

Marianne: I always feel I ought to be doing something useful.

Howard: When you start to do Jupiter, Saturn comes in and says, "No." It does this even when they are in trine, which I have. But I also know that if I am getting very Saturn, and I have got a very busy schedule with work, and I have a lot of commitments and a lot of deadlines, I keep thinking, "Oh, if only I could just not have any responsibilities." But when I do have no responsibilities, I get depressed. If I am really allowed to live Jupiter fully, I start to feel guilty pretty quickly, or depressed, and I have to remind myself, "No, you don't have to feel guilty, you have earned this."

What I said earlier about Jupiter square Saturn can also apply to Jupiter opposing Saturn. In order to evolve, in order to expand, some hard work is required. You have to challenge yourself and do something which isn't necessarily easy for you to do, but the only way you'll evolve is through challenge and difficulty. I don't know if you have noticed it, but until 17 May this year there was a Jupiter-Saturn opposition in the heavens. It has been more or less active since October 1989. First it was in Cancer-Capricorn, and then it moved into Leo-Aquarius. It is over now, but for many, many people that I know, it was as if their growth in the last two years – Jupiter – has involved some real crises and real difficulty – Saturn. You couldn't have the growth without the difficulty. Do you see what I am saying? If someone has Jupiter opposition Saturn and opportunities come their way, it usually means there is going to be some hard work involved with it, or it is going to be quite challenging. It just doesn't come easily.

Marianne: I felt my friends would say, "Oh, you're lucky."

Howard: No, this chart works hard. It looks as if you want to do things well. That's all I have to say. It's not very helpful, but you can get some sort of sense from it. Things are still forming. Don't expect to know it all quite yet, or know exactly what you want to do.

Chart 3: Andy

Audience: My friend asked if we could look at his chart. He couldn't come today, but he wanted so much to hear this seminar because he has a lot of questions about vocation. Could you look at his chart? I will take notes for him.

Howard: He is forty-four now.

Audience: He's just going through Saturn opposition his Saturn. He lost the last few jobs he had through conflicts with authority. He wasn't made redundant only because of that, but that was one of the things that has come up. He is trying to get a company started, because he can't actually find any work right now.

Howard: So he is trying to start on his own? That's an interesting issue.

Audience: His wife is very much against it, and always has been. He may be trying to break up his relationship.

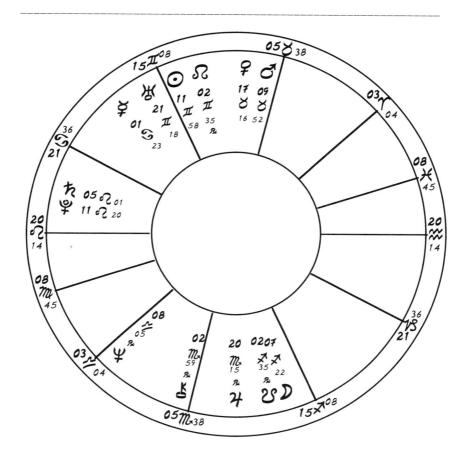

Andy
3 June 1947, 10.30 am, London
Placidus cusps

Howard: I'll tell you what hits me first. Transiting Pluto is going through the 4th house. This hits me even before the career issues hit me. I start thinking about transiting Pluto opposing Venus. That does affect the career, because Venus rules the MC. But it seems quite important to sort out some inner stuff first, and that is what I would say to Andy. Because of Pluto going over Jupiter, opposing Venus, and heading up towards the Moon, there can be so much discord or inner change going on that it might not be the very best time to try to take a lot on his shoulders in terms of a new career – unless he has someone who could help him with it. A lot of his psyche is meant now to be going inward and exploring his inner conflicts and getting his private life sorted out. If so much is wanting to go inwards, how much do you have left over for outer things?

Audience: I think that's happening in any case, in terms of his marriage breaking up. Saturn will be going over the Descendant later, and he is trying to sort out his marriage now. He has been living in a precarious marriage for many years. He has been semi-living at home, going home at weekends and pretending that everything is all right. All of a sudden it's blown up, together with his job, all at the same time. So he's got a situation which is quite difficult.

Howard: That would be described by Pluto moving through the 4th house, but it opposes the ruler of the MC. So it is both home and career. I don't know why, but I keep thinking that what seems more important is for him to get to know himself better, to work on his personality more. He might not appreciate that when you say it, and obviously he needs some sort of work to live. But it's as if he needs to go in for servicing. He needs repair and maintenance, and then he can come out and hit the road.

Do you see why I am saying that? It is because the transits through the 4th, 5th, and 6th houses pull you down to the private sphere of life, and not so much up to the public sphere, even if we consider transiting Jupiter. At present Jupiter is in the 12th house. Even though it is in the upper sector, the 12th is the most introverted house of the upper sector, apart from the 8th. This makes me start thinking that he needs to repair himself a bit, and go in for his 50,000-mile service, and then come out to deal with the career thing. That may not be feasible, if he really has to get his money act together.

Audience: I think he will have to get his money act together. But I think the area he has to address is the issue of passion in his life, because that's what he hasn't addressed. He's had a very active work life, which has allowed him to avoid the issue of passion in his marriage.

Howard: Yes, because he has possibly directed the Mars-Venus in Taurus into affairs, but not into the marriage.

Audience: I saw him for one chart reading. One of the issues I brought out was the issue of possessiveness. He said, "I've never been possessive in my life. I haven't got a possessive bone in my body!"

Howard: But Mars conjuncts Venus in Taurus square Pluto, which needs to possess so intensely. If he is not owning it, he is probably making his partners very jealous and possessive.

Audience: He did say, "I have got a very possessive wife."

Howard: Honestly, I think part of your work as an astrologer, besides offering Andy advice about career, is to try to help him become a little more sophisticated psychologically. That may even mean explaining very simply what projection is about. Give him some simple examples.

Audience: In fact we began on that. He is starting to think about it. The difficulty is that the whole issue of his parents and his relationship with his parents has never been considered before. Trying to bring up the issue of parents, when he has never thought of it before, and suggesting that it has anything to do with his present situation, seems incredibly difficult.

Howard: Well, that's great – you can be the guru! Do you know what I mean? You can start to get him munching on it.

Audience: His area of work is computers, and I feel that I haven't yet been able to connect him with the personal level of life.

Howard: It is a bit like what I said to Marianne. People may come to you thinking, "She's such a nice, solid, sensible woman," and they may listen to things coming from you that they wouldn't necessarily accept from other people.

Audience: I think that's true.

Howard: Often people who have Pluto in the 12th are terrified of looking at what's buried in there, because they are afraid they will be overwhelmed by their feelings. I think you have to respect that. Liz uses the image of a sea-wall which keeps what is in the unconscious from flooding, and you shouldn't break down that wall too quickly. You can take out one brick and let some of what's there seep through and catch it in a bucket and work with it. This is what I mean by giving bite-sized chunks. But I imagine Andy could become quite fascinated by his psyche, once he got into it, because that sometimes happens with Pluto in the 12th. They shut the door to it, but when they open it, they become obsessed with it. He'll come back with all sorts of revelations about his background and why he's the way he is. He'll see things even his astrologer doesn't see.

Audience: He had a dream which he wanted to bring for me to interpret. I said, "I'll see you for your chart, but you must go off and see a therapist if you want dream interpretations."

Howard: Yes, it could help if you could point him in that direction. Tell him it's going to ultimately help him with his career. Dangle that carrot. Ultimately it's going to help him with his 10th house Sun and his north Node in the 10th. Then he'll think, "This is a worthwhile investment, to look inside myself and pay money for it, because ultimately it is helping me with my career."

Audience: How does Chiron on the IC manifest?

Howard: What do you feel emotionally inside yourself, when you see Chiron in Scorpio sitting on someone's IC? What does it make you feel?

Audience: Wounded.

Howard: Yes, it must hurt. Chiron is where we have wounds, and to have it right at the IC in Scorpio, square Saturn in the 12th, must hurt a lot. It may be some sort of wound that his father had, maybe in relationship to women, because of the Moon in Scorpio in the 4th.

Audience: That's what I was trying to get at.

Howard: If you take the 4th house to be the father and the Moon in Scorpio is there, then there is some issue the father has about women which is causing pain, and that pain is affecting Andy because i t shows up in his chart. As a matter of fact, Chiron makes a T-square with Mars in the 10th and the Saturn-Pluto conjunction in the 12th. So the mother is involved too.

Audience: I think Liz talks about the 12th as the ancestral psyche. So this would be more than just his father's pain, it would go all the way back through past generations.

Howard: Yes, Liz would make a meal of this T-square. She would go into the whole ancestral past and the "family curse" because of the 12th/4th house influence. Andy has got a very busy 10th house, which means being out there in the world and achieving in terms of society. But there's an equally important inner life that needs to be dealt with, including the family past, and he has to live in two worlds. The chart really straddles both worlds.

Audience: We have just starting delving into the inner world, using astrology – something that he would say was odd.

Howard: It's a start.

Audience: Transiting Jupiter is right on Pluto. That could be very explosive.

Howard: Yes, Jupiter is on Pluto, and coming over the Ascendant. I'll tell you how I would work with him. I would appeal to the Leo Ascendant and say, "There is so much depth and richness in you, and so much potential for a person who could understand so much about themselves psychologically. You could be so good in the world, but you need to do this in order to get there." Do you see what I am doing here? Then maybe he'll think, "My God, by doing this I'll become better." Really, though, it is just a ploy to get him into it, because he is no greater or worse than anyone else in the world.

Audience: With the Sun in Gemini, he should be curious about his life.

Howard: Yes, but it hurts too much. There's too much pain down there. There's too much stuff that he doesn't want to look at, and probably his parents didn't want to look at it, and his grandparents didn't want to look at it. There is all this stuff around ambition, with Leo in the 12th, and the need to be important in the world.

Audience: I know he wants to, but he can't seem to achieve it. It might be a thought for him to eventually have his own company, rather than working for somebody else.

Howard: I'll tell you something more about what Charles Luntz says. He's quite funny about this. He has a chapter called, "Should you be an employer or an employee?" Here are his rules:

- Examine what is in cardinal, fixed, and mutable signs. For the greatest success on one's own, there should be a preponderance of planets on angles and in cardinal signs. That doesn't really apply here, so Andy loses out on Luntz' first rule.
- How many planets are in cardinal houses? That's not too bad in Andy's chart. The cardinal houses are the 1st, 4th, 7th and 10th. Lunz says that for a high executive position in the employ of others, but not calling for ultimate decisions, there should be a preponderance of planets in fixed signs. He is saying that the cardinal person should be the one starting their own business, but the fixed sign will be the best second-in-command.

Then Luntz says that as a general rule, all mutable signs are unsuited to being employers. They are likeable people who get along well with everyone, but they don't possess the drive necessary to get the work out of others. They are not fitted to assume great responsibilities, and are unequal to making important decisions. How's that for all you Geminis and Sagittarians?

Audience: Very true!

Howard: And Luntz says that the mutable signs are lacking organisational ability. In this chart, Leo makes up for that. But there is a lack of cardinal signs, even though we pick it up in the houses.

Audience: Is Andy biting off more than he can chew, or being over-promoted to a level above his calling or ability?

Howard: For the time being, I would say to him, "Sort out some of your private stuff and get to know yourself better, and that will help with your career. Then you can explore what you really want to do."

Chart 4: Gillie

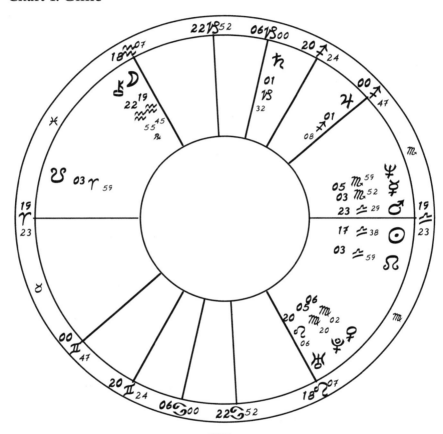

Gillie
11 October 1959, 5.25 pm, Glasgow
Placidus cusps

Let's look at Gillie's chart. I have another funny thing to tell you about Luntz' book. He has a chapter on the best time to go for an interview for a job. He says that what you want is a good transiting aspect to the ruler of the 6th house in your chart. If we're looking at

---

Gillie's chart, the Sun rules the 6th house, so we would be looking a t some good transit to the Sun. By the way, Jupiter is coming up to sextile the Sun.

Gillie: I have also got Neptune squaring it.

Howard: We'll deal with that in a minute. According to Luntz, one of the best aspects to have, at the time of the interview, is the transiting Moon in trine or sextile to the ruler of the 6th. That's a frequent aspect. In this case, you would want to schedule an interview (I'm not saying you're going to do this, but let's say you did) when the Moon was in Leo or Sagittarius, at around 17°, or when the Moon was in Aquarius or Gemini, at around 17°, because then the transiting Moon would be trine your Sun, which is the ruler of the 6th. It makes sense. Then he says – I love this – that if the appointment is a little earlier than when the Moon becomes exactly in good aspect to the ruler of the 6th, you should be well up on ways you can stall! You can talk about how nice the office is, and the upholstery on the chairs, until the Moon becomes exactly trine or sextile the ruler of the 6th. He suggests mentioning the weather and what's going on in the world, until the moment comes when the Moon makes its aspect. Then you should talk about the job itself. Who knows?!

We'll spend just a few minutes on Gillie, and then we'll have to tie it up. I haven't studied the chart yet, but what hits me first is how very busy and packed the 6th and 7th houses are. Remember, I said one of the significators for vocation was a packed house. Maybe the kind of work one does is described by that. When you get the ruler of an Aries Ascendant in the 7th house in Libra, and the Sun is on the cusp of the 7th, I start thinking about work which involves being with people, relating to people, maybe having to use one's personality in a way that deals with people and influences them.

Also, there is a lot of 6th house stuff, because the ruler of the Sun-sign is in the 6th and the Sun is also in the 6th, ruling the 6th but very near the 7th. The 6th house has to do with becoming very adept at something. To really feel good about yourself, if you have the Sun in the 6th house, I think there is a need to become an authority on something. You need to narrow down what your work is, so that you are a specialist in some field, rather than being more general. For instance, if someone with the Sun in the 6th wanted to be a nurse, I would say,

"Great, but find some branch of nursing to specialise in, because the more specialised you become, the happier you will be about your work." Or if you are a secretary, become a medical secretary or a legal secretary. The more technically proficient you can become, and the more you can carve a special niche for yourself, the better off you will be. There are other things in the chart which make me question this. I have just remembered something. Do you mind if I say it? I recognise the chart now. I once did your chart about eight or nine years ago, at a seminar on karma at the College of Psychic Studies. I said you had been a prostitute in a previous lifetime. I don't remember what I was looking at, at the time. Didn't I say something like that to you?

Gillie: Yes.

Howard: Let me try to get at what's happening in the chart. It's the end of the day and my brain is beginning to feel like tapioca pudding. When I see all that Libra – the Sun and Mars, the chart ruler – over there in the West, there really is a sense that you have a personality or a kind of grace that should be marketed or should be allowed to come out when you are working. People would like having you around, or you have some way of dealing with people that can be very charming. What are your issues?

Gillie: My issues are vocational.

Howard: Tell me all the different things you have tried, and what you've been interested in.

Gillie: I find it so difficult being in my body that it's difficult to plan a career.

Howard: I am glad you said that. With the Sun in the 6th, what do you think one of the major things to do in this lifetime is? To learn how to accept being in a body. But the Moon in Aquarius kicks and kicks.

Gillie: I can't commit myself to one thing.

Howard: I don't think it's just an issue about commitment. Commitment is something very specific. But keep talking.

Gillie: I always keep pushing myself into what I think I should be doing, but it never comes from my heart. I never quite feel I am a whole body involved with something, because I am not whole. Do you know what I mean? Bits of me go in for this and bits of me go in for that. I just end up rejecting all things.

Howard: Maybe it is an incarnation issue. Have you really fully incarnated? Remember, I was saying that some people have career problems because they have commitment problems. They don't like to lose possibilities and commit. These same people can have relationship problems as well, sometimes. It is a commitment issue, which is ultimately a kind of puer or puella issue about having to accept that life has to be lived within limits and one has to define oneself. That is so much a 6th house thing. The 6th house is the last of the personal houses, so it has to do with the pinnacle of defining yourself as a separate person. By defining oneself as a separate person one is saying, "These are my skills, these are my abilities, this is my niche." I have a feeling that the Moon in Aquarius just feels so trapped by it all. Do you see what I'm saying? That Moon in Aquarius in the 12th has a yearning to be everything, or to not be in a body. It is a yearning to be non-corporeal. The Moon is what we long for, it is what we are comfortable with, and it is really more comfortable being undefined when it is in the 12th house – being everything, being infinite.

Gillie: It's opposite Uranus.

Howard: I'm looking at that now, but I'm also looking at the whole of the rest of the chart. The north Node is in the 6th, and all those 6th house planets and the Sun in the 6th are saying, "Your job is to get into the body and start to form a real, solid sense of your uniqueness and your personality. Then find some sort of work which is a reflection of that." But you are still struggling.

Gillie: That kind of commitment feels like a death.

Howard: It is. It's a come-down. You know, this is just a suggestion, and I may be wrong. How I might approach this would be something like doing yoga, because it is a spiritual thing but it involves the body.

Gillie: I have done body work. I was a therapist doing body work.

Howard: You were a therapist doing body work for other people?

Gillie: Yes.

Howard: That's interesting isn't it?

Gillie: When Uranus went over my MC, I got bored and left it. Then I came back.

Howard: The Moon in Aquarius, conjunct Chiron and opposition Uranus, forms the delimiting opposition of a bowl chart. Everything is contained within the Moon-Chiron-Uranus, and the leading planet is Uranus. Remember, the leading planet often determines things, so Uranus shows restlessness and the need for change.

Gillie: I do that all the time.

Howard: You are really taken over by it, which is preventing you from doing anything solid with the 6th house. Sometimes you can have something like this Moon-Uranus, which prevents you from achieving in a more concrete way, because you don't have the commitment or the acceptance of authority to do it. Any way you can bring your energy right down into the body would help you start defining yourself better, because you wouldn't be out there unbounded. Then you would discover that you have good, honest Libran skills here, like the ability to get along with lots of different kinds of people, and to know how to make people feel good or relate to them in a way which makes them feel good. Just briefly, tell me all the different things you tried. You trained as a therapist? What kind of body therapy were you doing?

Gillie: Cranio-sacral. I've also worked with auras and energy work.

Howard: That's good 6th house stuff as well. One of the things I was thinking about was work to do with health and the body.

Gillie: I'm always drawn back to more subtle things, away from concrete things into more psychic work.

Howard: So is that a possible vocation?

Gillie: Yes.

Howard: I love this non-commitment to being in the body. Don't I know it! It took me thirty years to get into mine.

Gillie: I have raced cars, and done lots of different things.

Howard: Do you see how Uranus leads the chart? What else?

Gillie: I don't feel laid back about changing. To me it's actually very painful to change. Somehow I feel I should be staying with one thing.

Howard: You pose a tricky question here. Ideally I would say you should find one thing, with the Virgo stuff in the 6th – one thing that you could become an expert at. Not just a dilettante, but deeply an expert.

Gillie: I get bored easily.

Howard: Yes, here we go. This opposition says it all. I actually don't quite know what to say, because sometimes, if someone is very strongly Uranian and has a deep reaction as soon as something is manifest – they have done it for a while and it is known – maybe it is right to move on. Maybe you are the kind of person who just does that. But if you are not happy with that...

Gillie: Pluto is squaring the Moon right now.

Howard: Yes. Let's go back to Neptune square the Sun first. I am curious about Uranus and Neptune coming up to square the Sun from the 10th house. Career change seems to be around. Then we have Pluto in Scorpio starting to square the Moon and Chiron. To be honest, Gillie, I would need more time to do this justice, and we don't have any time left.

Gillie: It has been helpful, because I hadn't realised how strong you have to be to stick with something, to choose something and then go into it.

Howard: With Venus, the ruler of your Sun, in Virgo in the 6th house, you need to know something pretty deeply to really feel good about yourself. The problem is deciding on which something, and then sustaining the interest long enough. It is like saying, "Okay, Uranus, I feel you now, and you are making me restless. I want to move on, so I'll take some time off and do something different. But don't worry, Virgo and Saturn, I'll come back to what I was doing later." You can take breaks, but you can come back to something rather than leaving a wake of half-finished things behind you, which is a Uranian problem. As soon as something becomes corporeal or comes into form, it is not as ideal as what Uranus thought or imagined it would be. Uranian people have an image of the ideal job or the ideal relationship, and then when they get into the actual job, it is never the ideal, so they say, "I'd better get rid of this and look for something more ideal." So there are a lot of unfinished things left behind.

I feel there is talent here. If you really put your mind to something, you can do it very, very well. But you need to have some rein over that Uranus, without stifling it. I wonder, with Pluto coming up now to square the Moon-Chiron-Uranus, if there isn't someone you'll meet, because Pluto is moving through the 7th house. It isn't necessarily a lover – it might be a friend or even a therapist. It might be a good time to be in therapy with someone who can help you change the pattern you have with the Moon-Uranus opposition. It is up for change, that Moon-Uranus, with Pluto creeping up on it.

When you start getting transits to the delimiting opposition of a bowl, things really do change. When you get a square to the leading planet of the bowl, it wants to shake everything up and make it different from what it has been before. It is like throwing up iron filings and seeing how they land again, but ultimately I would like to see you land where you find something which reflects the north Node in the 6th – where you really explore something in a lot of depth and detail, and stay with it long enough to become very good at it, even if you have to take a lot of breaks in between.

All right, that's it. Thanks for coming, everyone.

Part Two: The Moon's Nodes

This seminar was given on 29 July, 1990 at Regents College, London as part of the Summer Term of the seminar programme of the Centre for Psychological Astrology.

Sun, Moon, and Earth

Some astrologers pay very little attention to the Moon's Nodes. They don't quite see how these non-existent points in space – I hope you all know they are not planets – can have much meaning. So they play it safe and stay away from them. But there are other astrologers who really put a lot of emphasis and importance on the Nodes, as keys to getting a bigger picture of a person's life purpose. All the planets have Nodes, but we are just talking about the Moon's Nodes today. Rudhyar called the Nodes "the path of destiny". You can't ignore that if it's in the chart. Other astrologers, such as Doreen Tyson, say the Nodes are pivots on which inner conflicts turn. I would put myself among the astrologers who pay a lot of attention to the Nodes. I think they are often the key to the chart. Also, in a very concise way, they symbolise some of the basic key dilemmas and issues and conflicts that a person will have to deal with in this life. I really do rate them highly, and hopefully today we will become more familiar with interpreting them and putting them into the context of the whole chart and a person's life.

You all know that astronomy is my favourite subject, and how brilliant I am at it! But I thought I should make some attempt here to explain the Nodes astronomically – although you are not allowed to ask any questions! To start with, just in case you haven't realised it, the earth moves around the Sun. The circle with the dot in it is the symbol for the Sun, as I hope you all know, and the big circle around it is the ecliptic. The ecliptic is the apparent path of the Sun around the Earth, or the orbit of the Earth around the Sun. The circle with the little cross in it is the symbol for the Earth.

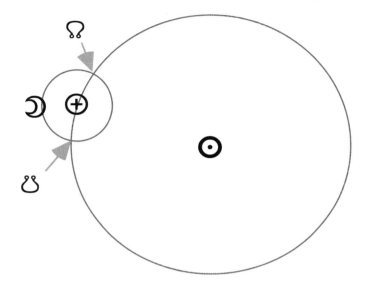

The Moon moves around the Earth. The Moon's Nodes are where the plane of the lunar orbit crosses the ecliptic. I want to emphasise this. The nodal axis occurs where the Moon crosses the apparent path of the Sun around the Earth. It's important because we are going to underline three symbols that the Nodes link together – the Moon, the Sun, and the Earth. Astronomically the nodal axis is based on the intersection of the Moon with the apparent orbit of the Sun around the Earth. What you get is this: The Moon crosses the ecliptic twice a month, once going from south to north, and that is called the ascending or north Node. And then it crosses again going from north to south, and that's the descending or south Node.

Nodes are points where you get an intersection. The Nodes always form an axis. The north Node is always 180° from from the south Node. I want to underline the fact that we are always going to consider the Nodes as an axis, as an opposition. That will become very important when we interpret the meaning of the Nodes. The north and south Nodes are not two separate things – they are one axis. I'll give you a little bit more astronomical information. We have two references to the Nodes in the ephemeris. First we have what are called the mean Nodes. "Mean" doesn't mean they're stingy. Then we have the true Nodes. Not all ephemerides list both. Some list one or the other. You should really be looking at the true Nodes, because they are based on more up-to-date computer technology. The mean Nodes are an approximation. Because they are an approximation calculated before they could compute the true Nodes exactly, the mean Nodes can sometimes be 2° or 3° different from the true Nodes. Essentially the Nodes move retrograde – they go backwards through the zodiac. However, if you look at the true Node in the ephemeris, it sometimes goes forward and then backwards. But it is essentially a retrograde motion. The mean Node is always shown as retrograde, but I encourage you to use the true Node. I think it is a more accurate placement.

The Nodes move backwards at the rate of 3' per day, and it takes nineteen months for them to move through a pair of signs. So if the north Node is in 0° Pisces, where is it going next? 29° Aquarius. Do you see that? If it is in 29° Aquarius, where is it going next? 28° Aquarius. Bear that in mind – otherwise you might get confused. It also means that the Nodes progress back, not forward. They always progress retrograde. When the north or south Node is near the early degrees of one sign, it is actually heading toward the previous sign. So something at 0° Pisces is almost like an Aquarian Node, whereas once it is at 29° Aquarius it is completely out of Pisces – it is going right back through Aquarius.

The Node takes nineteen months to go through a sign, and eighteen and a half years to go through the entire zodiac. A nodal return occurs every eighteen and a half years. I am going to talk more about that in a bit. Later in the day we are going to talk about transits and progressions involving the Nodes, and I want to look at the Node cycle itself. Do remember that the nodal cycle is every eighteen and a half years. So when you are eighteen and a half, when you are thirty-seven, when you are fifty-five and a half, and so on, you will have a nodal return. I would suggest you look in the ephemeris and think about when these nodal returns happened. Try to think about what was going on in your life when you were eighteen and a half, in relation to the fact that the Nodes were returning to their original place. The transiting north Node was conjuncting your north Node, and the transiting south Node was conjuncting your south Node. The north Node right now is in 7° Aquarius. If any of you were born with the north Node in 7° Aquarius, you are getting a nodal return. But that's all for later. We will also talk about nodal reversals. If any of you have the south Node at 7° Aquarius, you are getting a nodal reversal now. I think one of the best ways to learn about the Nodes, as with many things in astrology, is to study them in your own chart first.

There is another thing that is interesting. I was reading once in an article that nineteen years is the symbolic span of one generation. We can think about the Nodes in terms of generational things as well. Also, you can use the Nodes in mundane astrology, in the charts of countries, and often you can see important turning points or conflicts or dilemmas that the country faces when the Nodes are being accentuated in some way – or just through the natal nodal axis.

Another name for the north Node is the Dragon's Head, the *Caput Draconis* (which is Latin). The Hindus call it Rahu. The south Node is called the Dragon's Tail or *Cauda Draconis,* and the Hindus call it Ketu. Hindu astrology is pretty black and white about the Nodes. They say the north Node is good and favourable and positive and works like another Jupiter in your chart, and the south Node is a point of problems and difficulties and works like another Saturn. Now, I don't go along with that simplistic way of looking at it. I think it is quite a bit more complex. I'm going to base my interpretation of the Nodes on what I mentioned already – that they link together the solar principle, the lunar principle, and the principle of the Earth. The points are derived through the movements of those three bodies, and I actually think the Nodes are an attempt – I'll say it this way and then we will interpret it – to balance solar principles and lunar principles within the personality, within the body on the earth plane. In some ways, the Nodes indicate a struggle between the pull of the past and new qualities or traits or choices that need to be made. I'm going to link the south Node with lunar forces and Moon-like qualities, and the north Node with solar forces and Sun-like qualities.

Basic interpretations

The south Node and the lunar principle

In order to explain the south Node, I'm going to talk a little bit about the Moon and what I mean by the lunar principle. Wherever your south Node is by sign, this shows how the south Node energy is operating. The house of the south Node shows in what department of life that energy is going to be expressed. The same goes for the north

Node. I want to get into the south Node through talking about the urges in us which are regressive urges, urges of instinct and habit – doing what comes instinctively or automatically, or what some people call the line of least resistance. These are attributes that we would associate with the sign and house of the south Node. They show instinctive qualities or tendencies or ways of being or ways of meeting the world. There are going to be exceptions. I know all the questions you are going to ask already! What if the south Node conjuncts the Sun, and what if the north Node conjuncts the Moon?

Audience: Do you know all the answers?

Howard: We can make them up as we go along. I want to start simplistically now, with the south Node and the north Node, and then we will worry about what happens if you have got planets conjuncting the Nodes, or if you have got the north Node in Libra in the 1st house. That's a kind of reversal. What I am trying to emphasise is that all of us have, somewhere in us, a major split, a major pull in two directions. It's a major conflict between meeting certain situations in a very instinctive and automatic and habitual way, and choosing to be some other way in that situation, which may not be automatic but involves some sort of choice or decision.

I don't know if any of you have read *The Inner World of Choice* by Frances Wickes.[8] She describes moments in your life when you are on an edge, and you can go one way or another. You can fall into an old way of being and react in a natural, instinctive way, or you can see the situation and say, "No, I'm not going to come from that old place any more." This involves some choice. You say to yourself, "I'm going to come from a different place. I'm going to bring in something new." Then you have succeeded in acting rather than reacting, because the south Node is more reactive, according to the house and sign it is in. We do it because it is familiar – it somehow comes out more quickly or more naturally. But the north Node is more about acting rather than reacting. It is more about choice – seeing different ways and choosing the way which may not be the most instinctive way. It is more conscious. That's why I call the north Node solar – it comes from the

---

[8]Frances Wickes, *The Inner World of Choice*, Sigo Press, 1988.

_____

heart and head rather than the gut. This will become clearer. I'll be repeating this in a variety of ways.

Lunar goddesses

Myth is one way to understand what I mean about the south Node being like a lunar principle, and having to do with the pull of the past and with what's instinctive and habitual. I'm going to refer to lunar mythology to help elaborate on this. Some of you may have heard me do this in other contexts. I'm going to apply mythology to the Nodes. I want you to think about when the south Node happens in your life – when you are being lunar, when you just react in an instinctive and non-choosing way. Feelings take over, or a certain reaction takes over, and you start coming from an automatic, habitual place.

Now, when I think of Moon goddesses, one of the ones I like to talk about is Ishtar, who is Babylonian. I am going to be equating her with the south Node. You could take Isis as well. In fact, in certain Egyptian myths, one of the symbols for Isis is actually the same as the symbol for the south Node. It is an upside-down serpent, which is interesting, because Isis represents instinct and nature and rhythms. I am going to use Ishtar as an example of the lunar, south Node principle in us. She gives herself to whatever comes along, or to whatever she is feeling. You know how the story goes. Ishtar is married to Tammuz. They live together for six or seven months of the year in absolute bliss. She represents nature and the earth, and Tammuz is the life-giving spirit. He gives spirit to her, he makes her fecund and they are very happy together. It is spring and summer. Things bloom, things blossom, and she gives herself to joy.

Then something happens. When summer ends and winter comes along, sometimes she turns on him and has him killed. Sometimes he is just murdered. He goes into the underworld. Then, instead of giving herself to joy and ecstasy and bliss, she goes into pain and misery and despair and emptiness. I am trying to show you the cyclical feeling here. She grieves and mourns for him. This is winter. This is the barren time. The creative spirit isn't there. Then she goes down into the underworld, and usually she fights with her wicked sister to get him back. She does get him back, and for six or seven months they are really happy and blissful and they are getting on terribly well and everything is blooming. And then after a certain period she condemns him to death. Or they get into trouble and he dies and she gives herself to sadness and misery and pain. It is the cyclical nature of life which the Moon symbolises.

In terms of the south Node, what I am trying to illustrate is a kind of giving of yourself to joy. Then pain comes and you give yourself to pain, and then you give yourself to joy, and then you give yourself to pain. It is about going with whatever feelings are coming up for you, and just being with those feelings, rather than stopping and saying, "How should I feel? How should I be?" It is about being whatever you are feeling. It is purely emotional. It is as if you had ten planets in Cancer. It is whatever you happen to be feeling at the moment. If you feel one thing one day, you may feel something else the next day, and you just allow yourself to feel those things. Other people are driven completely crazy because they don't know what to expect. One day you are this and then the next day you are that.

Ishtar was also depicted as a prostitute. The Babylonians had icons of Ishtar which they put on their window sills, and she was called "the one who leans out". Their Moon Goddess was depicted as a prostitute leaning out of the window – just like in Amsterdam, in the red light district, where the the prostitutes are on display and lean out the window to attract whomever comes along. Ishtar will give herself to whomever comes along, to whatever comes up, to whatever is there. I want you to try to bear that in mind when you are assessing your south Node by sign and house, because it is a way of being that you automatically give yourself to or go into. It is something that has been conditioned into you early in this life or, if you believe in the theory of karma and reincarnation, it is a certain way of being that you have done a lot of before, so it is a style or way of being that is very familiar to you.

I will give you a quick example now, but we are going to go through all the nodal axes in a minute. Let's say you have the south Node in Libra. We are talking about the sign of the south Node as a way of being that comes instinctively to you. If you have the south Node in Libra, then what kind of things might come instinctively to you? What might you do automatically?

Audience: Compromise.

Howard: That's what I was thinking. One thing is compromise – wanting to blend or balance or keep the peace. I know that's a simplistic understanding of Libra, and there are a lot of Librans around who aren't just peacemakers – they are balancers. If you have the south Node in Aries, then what's your instinctive reaction to situations?

Audience: Energetic.

Howard: It's martial. It could be very egocentric, very selfish. That's what I mean about not stopping to think about how to be. The south Node is the way you automatically are, the way you give yourself to whatever comes up. That's why I am associating it with lunar qualities.

The south Node and karma

Now we must say more about this. You can think of times in your life when you just react in that automatic way. Let's talk a little bit first about this idea of the Nodes and past lives. There's a series of books by Martin Shulman called *Karmic Astrology*.[9] One of these books is on the Nodes. I reread it recently. I have really mixed feelings about this book, and I would only recommend it with a government health warning that it could be dangerous to your psyche. It is frustrating, because he makes some really good points, and then he gets a little bit too extreme. For example, if you have the south Node in Leo, you will be lonely for your whole life. He says awful, nasty things about my south Node. But sometimes he is right on. Then he gets carried away, and I wouldn't want you to take what he says as gospel or as absolute truth. I really do think it could drive you a little bit batty and disturb you.

Shulman says the south Node shows a sum total of themes that you have learned in previous lifetimes. It is not just from one lifetime, it is from a whole lot of past lifetimes. You have had certain ways of being that you have become very familiar with or very adept at, even certain skills and talents that you have developed a lot. The south

[9]Martin Shulman, *Karmic Astrology: The Moon's Nodes and Reincarnation,* Samuel Weiser, Inc., 1975.

Node then shows what you are bringing with you in your kit bag on this journey, in terms of what is very familiar to you. It's what you know already, what's been done before, what's been covered, what's been learned. There are exceptions, because ultimately we have to rework our south Node and clean it up in some way. If you want simple karmic astrology, the house of the south Node shows an area of life you have developed before. The sign describes qualities or a style of being that you are familiar with because you have had other lifetimes, previous incarnations, in which you have had practise to work on these things.

Shulman says that the south Node is the line of least resistance. It is not evolutionary to keep going over that ground again, to keep doing your south Node sign or your south Node house. I know there are exceptions. What if the south Node is conjunct the Sun? We'll get to that later. Shulman says the south Node shows where you are lagging. You are not picking up anything new if you stay too much in your south Node sign or house. The opposite point of the axis, the north Node, shows the growth that has to happen, the soul qualities that need to be built in now, the new things that you need to add to your kit bag. When you go on a journey you may acquire new things that need to be built in and developed. We should make some effort to develop the sign or the house of the north Node, as well as a planet conjunct the north Node. That's the clue the chart gives us about the qualities we need to develop this lifetime, in order to move forward in evolution or in terms of growth and development.

That's pretty simplistic, although many astrologers do read the chart in terms of karma and reincarnation. They believe the south Node shows the past, and it is confirmed when they do psychic regressions with people. These subjects are people who don't know their chart. If someone takes them back through some form of hypnosis or some other sort of regression technique, and they touch on previous lifetimes, a lot of karmic astrologers will confirm that the stories and issues that come up are a true reflection of the south Node.

I am not going to be talking about the Nodes only in terms of past lives. We are really talking about the Moon, and we are talking about lunar things, which are psychological. I want you to also think about the south Node as something which is instinctive from this life, but from earlier in this life – from childhood. I don't have to go all the way back into past lives to make sense of the south Node, but you can if you want. I think you can understand the south Node as something which is instinctive, or something which has been conditioned into us early on in some way. Or we are just born with a propensity toward doing that thing automatically. But you then start asking why you were born that way. It could be heredity, or it could be past lives that make you have those built-in qualities, because you are familiar with them.

Some of the things we bring over that are familiar, that we have already learned, and that have been conditioned into us from childhood, are good things. You don't want to throw them away – you need them. It is like learning that, if you touch the stove when it is on, you'll get burned. That's good conditioning, isn't it? You don't want to forget that. There may be certain qualities of the sign, and certain attributes related to the sphere of life represented by the house your south Node is in, which mean that you have inborn gifts. You have innate talents. You have certain abilities. That's why I don't go along with people who say you should avoid the south Node altogether, or who say you shouldn't do your south Node stuff because you have already done it before. Why not use gifts and talents and natural abilities? There's a clue to these things wherever your south Node is.

By the way, a book I would recommend most highly on the Nodes is Tracy Marks' *The Astrology of Self-Discovery*.[10] It isn't entirely about the Nodes – only a part of it is. In all the stuff I have read on the Nodes, her thirty-page section in this book makes the most sense to me. She has obviously immersed herself in it. This woman really lives her astrology. It makes me think she does nothing else in her life. The issue seems to be to get the best from your south Node, to reclaim and own and elevate the particular skills it gives you. If you have the south Node in Libra, then you have an innate ability in compromising, balancing, or diplomacy. It doesn't mean that you should never do this. It is just that if you do it too habitually – if you do it all the time in situations where it may be better for you to act differently or come from a more assertive or ego-centred place – then you will get into trouble. It is doing the south Node too much, or falling back on it all the time, or getting stuck in that sphere of life, that causes the problems. I'm going to give you some quick examples. If you

---

[10]Tracy Marks, *The Astrology of Self-Discovery*, CRCS Publications, 1985.

have the south Node in the 10th, what could you get too involved in that would keep you from growing in other ways?

Audience: Career.

Howard: Yes, you understand. And what have you probably done in a previous lifetime already, if we are talking about previous lives? You've probably climbed the mountain and got recognition, and it means that it is not so important in this lifetime to achieve recognition again, even though you may do. What's more important, if you have the south Node in the 10th? Where does it put the north Node? In the 4th house – personal life, domestic life, soul, inner work. The north Node in the 4th house is about your inner growth. It is not about how much recognition you get, with the south Node in the 10th, because you have done that before. Being successful is not as evolutionary for you as doing inner work or soul work or having a family or making your home nice. When I see the north Node in the 4th house, it's about the quality of your life, rather than the quantity.

The north Node and the solar principle

Now I'm going to shift to talking a little bit about the north Node. Let me use Isis and Osiris as an example for you. I was saying that Isis is the Egyptian Moon goddess. One of her symbols was actually an upside-down serpent. While Isis represents instinct and the cyclical side of nature, Osiris represents reason. He educated the people. He taught them mathematics and agriculture. We are already seeing here a solar principle represented by the north Node. Isis and Osiris give birth to Horus, who is the eagle-eyed one. Horus represents seeing and action together. I want to underline this. Horus is a combination of awareness and action. He represents broadened awareness, and then, on the basis of broadened awareness, you act. It is about seeing the whole picture, seeing the conflict and tension, seeing the choices, and then making a decision or an action based on your awareness.

Audience: It sounds a bit like Sagittarius.

Howard: Yes, Sagittarius has a feeling of broadened awareness and making a choice, although a lot of Sagittarians colour what they see by their subjectivity, so they are not really being that objective. But it's also along the lines of Zeus – a good Zeus or a good Apollo. Think of those two words – awareness and action – because we are going to come back to that when we talk about resolving the north and south Node polarity. I think it is a situation where we are pulled in different directions and we have to make some choice that is a more constructive or evolutionary choice about how to be. We have to do this even though it may not be the most instinctive way of being, or the most automatic way of being. When we talk about the north Node, we are talking about effort, making a little effort to build in that quality or develop ourselves in that area of life. We also are going to be talking about will. I want to define the will for you. I am making a comparison between instinct and choice, between being pre-programmed or stereotyped and using the will and making a responsible action where you are choosing rather than reacting. You will look at your life and you will see many times when you are standing on that see-saw, where you totter between the two. And you will see that if you go the instinctive way, the same old thing happens. If you make a new choice, you can start a whole lot of new things.

Solar gods

We were talking about the lunar goddesses who just go with whatever comes up, and give themselves to whomever comes along. Well, the solar gods are different. For instance, the myth of Gilgamesh is very interesting. He is also Babylonian. He is a solar hero-god, so I'm going to make him a north Node figure. He's got a task. He has got to get somewhere. He has an objective. He has made a decision about going a certain way. What happens is that, as he is going towards his objective, who comes along but Ishtar, the Moon goddess. She says, "Come with me." She tries to seduce him away from his choice, from what he consciously wants to achieve. Actually, he handles her quite well. He says, "Thank you very much, but I'm busy!"

I want to elaborate on this. This is a very simple theme. I am talking about being swayed by your instincts and your emotions in such a way that it takes you away from what you consciously want to become or to develop in yourself. I'm going to give you an example which I have mentioned before, years ago, in other contexts. She doesn't mind me talking about it. It is a story about Diana Whitmore. She runs the Psychosynthesis and Education Trust, which is one of the Psychosynthesis training institutes in England.

Originally, Diana was studying with Assagioli, who was the main developer of Psychosynthesis. This is an approach to psychological growth which takes the whole person into consideration. Assagioli was old and ill, and Diana was literally nursing him as he was dying. He said to her, "I'd like you to start teaching and lecturing about Psychosynthesis, because I think you have a good understanding of it." When you are with someone who is dying, they pass stuff on to you. Assagioli was really knighting her, in a way. When he said that to her, her reaction was absolute terror. She was terrified by the idea of having to take responsibility and stand up in front of a group and lecture. Her immediate reaction, her instinctive reaction – her south Node reaction – was "No!" It was to run away.

I want you to watch this kind of reaction in your own life. You can try to relate it to the house and sign of the south Node. Possibly it may be related to your Moon, and sometimes even to your Saturn, when you have an instinctive running away or an emotion of wanting to run and hide or do the opposite of what's put in front of you. Diana's instinctive reaction was one of absolute terror.

Audience: Do you know where her south Node is?

Howard: I feel funny about talking about her chart. I would have to chat to her about it. I had better not use the chart, because it is not really fair to her. I know she doesn't mind my telling the story, and I thought it was a good example of an instinctive reaction. But when you start going into the chart, it is a little different.

Audience: What would the north Node do in that situation?

Howard: The north Node can choose. Once she got over the terror, Diana said, "I would like to carry on Assagioli's work." What she did was interesting, because she didn't deny that she was terrified of being in front of people. She visualised the part of her that was scared and vulnerable and very insecure about her ability to do it well. She imagined this part of herself as a kind of little furry animal, and before she went up to give a public lecture, she put the furry animal under her arm and she talked to it. She said, "Don't worry, I know you are there, but I am not going to let you take me over. I have you but I am not you." She acknowledged it, but then she chose to go out there and confront the task of teaching and lecturing.

I am trying to use this as an example of an instinctive reaction. Had Diana just reacted from fear, she would never have gone out there. That's like being taken over by your south Node. You are automatically reacting. Diana had to make some effort, without denying that her frightened reaction was there. I believe that, if she had said, "Oh, great, I'm going to lecture, I'm not afraid, I'll be fine," she might have gone out there and opened her mouth and all the fear would have jumped out at her. It is better to acknowledge it is there and to include it, but to come from a different place. When you are doing that, you are getting more heroic and solar, because you are not being seduced by the lunar goddess.

I am not putting down the lunar side. I think there are times when we need to spend more time with our feelings, and to accept them. We always need to accept our feelings and make space for them. But we don't have to always come from them. I'm not just talking about feelings. If you have the north Node in a water sign, then it is actually feelings you need to develop, so it may mean not coming from your habitual thinking so much, and choosing to allow your feelings more exposure. The point is that it is not just doing the automatic response. It is acknowledging that the instinctive response is there, and then coming from the north Node by sign and house as a choice.

Will and choice

The tension or conflict suggested by the nodal axis actually helps us to develop the will, and to make choices. Here are some definitions of the will. The will is "the mental agency that transforms awareness into action". I think that says it very clearly – it is something that takes awareness and then puts it into action. There is a Japanese saying: "To know and not to act is not to know at all." In the play, *Waiting for Godot*,[11] there is an interesting bit where someone says, "What shall we do?" The other person says, "Let's go!" and then the stage instruction is, "Nobody moves." Familiar?

Another meaning of the will is "the bridge between desire and action". These are things for you to meditate on in order to understand the will. I'm relating all of this to the north Node area of life. Someone said, "Memory is the mental organ of the past. Will is the mental organ of the future." Any time we need to make choices, or to come from or develop the north Node sign or house, we are creating new possibilities. The will is the seat of volition. I like this phrase: "the responsible mover within". We are talking about a little bit of effort, the consciousness to choose to go in a certain direction. Will is an act occurring between insight and action. There is something between insight and action which is experienced as effort or determination. It is not instinctive. It is not what you do habitually.

Here's one more definition: "The will is that part of the psychic structure which has the capacity to make and implement choices." Human beings have a very evolved cerebral cortex, which is the part of the brain which makes choices. This is different from what is called the reptilian brain, which is the more instinctive, stereotyped part of the brain. You can remove the cerebral cortex and certain functions will keep going. The cerebral cortex is not necessary to the survival of basic bodily functions. But the development of the cerebral cortex means we have the ability to see different situations and then make a decision about how to be. That is how we differ from the animals, because animals tend to be more pre-programmed, more instinctive.

I was reading once about how dogs mate, and there are something like seventeen different steps they have to go through before they get to the Big It. And if they are interrupted, they have to start all over again, and it is only at certain times of the year. That is what I mean by stereotyped and pre-programmed. That is coming from the reptilian brain, the animal brain, the seat of the instincts. But the will is the seat of volition, and human beings have a more developed cerebral cortex, so we can choose to mate in different ways, and we don't have to go through the same stereotyped steps. It can even be at different times of the year! I would associate the north Node with

[11]Samuel Beckett, *Waiting for Godot*, Grove Press, 1987.

that area of the brain – the cerebral cortex – and the south Node more with the reptilian or instinctive brain.

Let's get more definite. Tracy Marks gives certain guidelines in working with the Nodes. Step one, she says, is to rework your south Node way of being. That doesn't mean throwing away the south Node. But you need to try to develop the sign and the area of life represented by the house of the south Node, in as constructive and useful a way as possible, because it is inborn talent and innate tendencies. We rework our south node, we elevate it, we try to come from what Martin Shulman would call a higher place in terms of our south Node. That will become clearer when we look at the axis. The second step, Tracy Marks says, is to awaken your north Node. You rework your south Node, you awaken your north Node. The third step is to integrate the axis, to express both Nodes in a harmonious relationship – not to do just one or the other, but to harmonise and balance the axis. The signs are how we express the nodal energies, and the houses are where we express them.

Tracy Marks talks a lot about what she calls the nodal ruler, which is the planet that rules the sign that your north or south Node is in. If your north Node is in Aries, then the nodal ruler of the north Node is Mars. If your south Node is in Libra, then the nodal ruler of the south Node is Venus. She would say that, if you want to learn more about how your Nodes are operating, you should look at the ruler of each of the Nodes, and where that ruler is placed by house and aspect. I have found this to be true. If you have the north Node in Libra in the 5th house, that is probably an indication that you need to develop more self-expression and creative work, because the 5th is the house of self-expression. The north Node is where you need to develop things, and Libra and the 5th house mean you need to express yourself in a creative or harmonious way. If Venus, the ruler of the north Node's sign, is in the 10th house, then you might be able to make a career of it. If Venus is in the 11th house, it may come out more through groups. If Venus is in the 12th, it may come out more through hospitals or institutions, or more privately. You can do this with the south Node also. To get a sense of where your south Node energies may be displaced, look at the planet which rules the sign which your south Node is in, and what house it is in. It gives you more information.

The nodal axis by signs and houses

This is pretty basic astrology, but we might as well go through the different axes. My idea is to cover the various polarities through which the Nodes manifest. This afternoon I want to look at things like aspects to the Nodes, and transits and progressions involving the Nodes, and synastry involving the Nodes. You will probably have noticed, if you have done synastry, that there are often very important nodal connections with partners, and with parents and children and very important close friends. We'll look at that later.

Aries/Libra and the 1st and 7th houses

We will start with looking at the north Node in Aries and the south node in Libra. This can also describe the north Node in the 1st house and the south Node in the 7th. I am just trying to save time by doing this. Then we'll have to compare it to the opposite, with the south Node in Aries or the south Node in the 1st house, opposed to the north Node in Libra or the north Node in the 7th. All right, you're all going to work now. Just take the signs – north Node in Aries, south Node in Libra. What have you done before? What comes instinctively?

Audience: Cooperation.

Howard: What needs to be developed more?

Audience: Will.

Howard: Assertion – standing up for yourself, being able to be more independent, more autonomous. That doesn't mean you should lose or deny whatever abilities you have of cooperation and being understanding. There are times when you may instinctively come from a compromising place, and you need to assert yourself more. It might be scary – it might be a little frightening. It is more unfamiliar to stand up for yourself or to make others adjust to you than it is to be the one to adjust. The same thing applies to the north Node in the 1st house. It is about developing your ego, forming an identity, rather than being whatever other people want you to be. Now let's look at the south Node in Aries, or the south Node in the 1st. What have you done too much of? Being your own boss, not learning about relationship, being too impetuous and not reflective enough. Libra is an air sign. What do you need to build in, with the north Node in Libra or the north Node in the 7th?

Audience: Compromise. Thought for other people.

Howard: Yes. More objectivity – seeing the relationship rather than just what you want. I think this is pretty clear. What we are really trying to do here is somehow combine the best of both ends of the opposition. You work your south Node in Aries so that you keep your leadership qualities. You try to avoid losing Aries, but you build in Libra so you can be more objective and able to compromise. Do we really need to say more about that pair? This is a way of starting to interpret the axis, and then you can elaborate and get more detail. Obviously you have to look at the whole chart to assess it fully.

Taurus/Scorpio and the 2nd and 8th houses

Now we come to the north Node in Taurus and the south Node in Scorpio, or the north Node in the 2nd house and the south Node in the 8th. What we want to do is to look at some of the issues that come up with this axis. If you have the south node in Scorpio, what might be your instinctive way of responding to situations?

Audience: Secretly.

Howard: One may be controlling, or secretive.

Audience: Intensity.

Howard: With the south Node in Scorpio, your instinctive reaction is to be Scorpionic, which may mean being really intense and making a drama out of a crisis. It's like having a fight with a partner and saying, "I'm going to kill you or I'm going to kill myself. I'm going to leave, it's finished forever." It's very dramatic and sweeping and sometimes very destructive, and you may tend to see a crisis in anything, always looking for where there is danger. That's the instinctive response. Martin Shulman would say that in past lives you had a lot of crises, and that's what you're always expecting more of. Or you were very intense and very passionate and that's your instinctive way of being – very dramatic and emotional about things. That's the south Node in Scorpio, and to some degree the south Node in the 8th.

Along this axis there are also lots of sexuality issues, and a lot of issues about holding on and letting go. But let's stay with the thing of creating a crisis and being very intense and passionate. Everything is like a major trauma, and you can explode very quickly. If that is the south Node in Scorpio, what do you need to build in if you have the north Node in Taurus? Instead of going around saying, "Oh my God! It's the end of the world!" all the time, you need more earth. You need to say, "All right. I'll just hold on. I won't destroy everything. I won't go into a frenzy. I'll make dinner."

Audience: So you need to learn to be ordinary and steady and preserving.

Howard: Yes. You need to say, "Well, this is what life is like. Sometimes people do that. I'll just carry on and not make a big deal about it." It is being more down-to-earth, more practical.

Audience: And it's also about learning containment.

Howard: Yes, and enduring, rather than having to destroy something or tear it down or challenge it. It is a little bit different if we take the houses in this case. If you have the south Node in the 8th, what might you have done in the past in terms of money and resources?

Audience: Shared them.

Howard: That's possible. I would think first of relying too much on other people's resources. The south Node in the 8th is about needing other people in order to establish your own value system or your own self-esteem. The south Node in the 8th means you instinctively look to other people to value you in order to feel you are valuable, or you need other people's money in order to survive. There may have been a certain amount of sharing in the past – you are right. But if you have the north Node in the 2nd, what's the growth point now? What is it that you need to make more effort to do? You need to develop your own income, even if you have an inheritance. Some people with the south Node in the 8th are born into an inheritance. They are born into money, as if a past tendency is still continuing and other people's resources help you out. Even if that is the case, the north Node in Taurus or in the 2nd house has to do with finding more worth and value by becoming self-sufficient, and by having your own source of income, and by developing resources and values which would make you feel more solid. The north Node in the 2nd has really achieved something when you can say, "I know my worth, I know my value because of what I have developed. I don't need other people to prove my worth or tell me that I am valued. I can find it from within myself." That, I think, is the essential thing.

Now, with the south Node in the 2nd or the south Node in Taurus, what have you done too much of?

Audience: Hoarding.

Howard: Yes, maybe hanging on to too many things for yourself, and not sharing. Or you have been too self-sufficient, with the south Node in Taurus or the south Node in the 2nd. It's like saying, "I can't take from others. I shouldn't be receiving money from the government or my family or my partner. I've got to be standing on my own." If you have the south Node in the 2nd or in Taurus and you have the north Node in the 8th or in Scorpio, it is an indication that it is good for you to receive, to take payment. I have seen charts where people have the north Node in the 8th and they have been uptight about parents or a partner wanting to pay for their college education. I would say, "You have the north Node in the 8th, and you are meant to learn to consider other people's values. Other people's resources will help you along if you have a true purpose or goal you want to achieve." I see nods in the group. I am happy for people to come in with little echoes.

Let me see if I have any other keywords for this axis. One pair of keywords might be stability versus intensity. Another might be accumulation versus sharing, or accumulation versus elimination. There is another one – self-indulgence versus self-denial. This comes up along the axis. In fact both signs can be prone to it. I call it appetite/indulgence versus appetite/mastery, because when we are talking about Taurus/Scorpio we are talking about basic creature comfort needs. Sometimes when you have this axis highlighted, you get people who go from being too indulgent in their senses, whether it is food or sexuality, to saying, "No, I must control it, I must have power over these things." They go from overeating to undereating, or from promiscuity to celibacy. You get that issue along the Taurus/Scorpio axis, and some sort of integration, some sort of balance, is needed. But remember that we are talking about the north Node as the area which we should work to develop more.

Let's elaborate a little. If your instinctive response is to create crises, to be dramatic and intense, then actually choosing to hold things, to be more contained, not to make a big deal, can be very difficult. Everything in you is wanting to flip, wanting to create a fight, wanting to challenge what's happening, and it can be quite a step to say, "All right, I'll just sit on that for a bit," without becoming repressed. You have to acknowledge that your instinctive response is to want to go berserk about something someone is doing. But to come from the north Node in Taurus is to stay more calm and cool, and just ride it. But with the reverse (the north Node in Scorpio), your instinctive response may be too pacific – "All right, I'll accept it, I won't cause any problems." What do you need to develop if you have the north Node in Scorpio?

Audience: Depth. Passion.

Howard: Yes. And also, challenge and risk. You might need to create possible disruption and say, "Look, I'm not going to put up with this." You actually have to chose to be more intense or confrontative or challenging of something, rather than being too placid. Those of you with the north Node in the 2nd house, please find a way of being more self-sufficient or earning money in your own right. You've just got to have your own money. You'll feel better if you have skills and talents that are your own and can't be taken away from you, and when you feel your self-esteem from within yourself rather than imported by having other people say you're worthwhile. Those of you with the north Node in the 8th, you need to learn more sharing, more intimacy. If I see someone with the north Node in the 7th or the north Node in the 8th, I am always inclined to push them into relationships. I want you to get in there and to have things brought up and to learn through being involved. I don't think you are meant to be celibate for all time if you have the north Node in the 8th or the north Node in the 7th. Your growth comes from those areas which have to do with intimacy and opening to others. When I think of the 8th house in terms of intimacy, I think about the importance of being with someone, and being able to expose what is inside you and share more of what's going on without attacking it. Obviously you want a balance between the two. You don't always want to be plodding and placid, but you don't always want to be creating a crisis at the slightest little discomfort. If someone says something that offends you, sometimes you need to just ride it rather than create a conflagration.

Audience: Can you be clearer about the distinction between the north Node and the Sun, and the south Node and the Moon?

Howard: When I talk about the north Node as a solar principle and the south Node as a lunar principle, I am using those things symbolically, to help us understand that the north Node is like a solar force. The Sun is what you use consciously and radiate and develop as an individual. Whatever sign your Sun is in, in order to become who you are and to really radiate who you are, you need to develop that sign. It takes a certain amount of will or effort to develop the sign the Sun is in. I think it is quite similar with the north Node, so in a sense it is almost like another Sun or solar principle, because you have to make an effort. You often have to battle with forces within yourself to become the sign that your north Node is in, or develop the house which your north Node is in, just as it may be a struggle to fully develop the house your Sun is in.

I am using this symbolically as a way of explaining the quality of the Nodes. The nodal axis is almost like another Sun-Moon midpoint. When transits or progressions hit your Sun-Moon midpoint, there may be the same kind of pivotal dilemma, just as when your north and south Nodes are being blown up. There is a choice or a blending between reactive lunar forces and active choosing forces. Astronomically the Nodes combine the Sun, the Moon, and the Earth.

Audience: You have said they are similar. In what way would you regard them as different?

Howard: It is hard to answer that. Very often, what I find is that the nodal axis supports the Sun and Moon issues. It is like a repetition of a theme, although sometimes you'll get something that is a little contrary. The nodal axis shows a key conflict in your life that you often have to resolve on the practical level, out there in the world, whereas the Sun and Moon have more to do with character, with who you are inside.

Gemini/Sagittarius and the 3rd and 9th houses

This brings us to the next nodal axis, which is the north Node in Gemini and the south Node in Sagittarius, or the north Node in the 3rd and the south Node in the 9th. I have to admit that of all the oppositions, the Gemini/Sagittarius one seems the least opposite, because of all the mutability that they share. I think that, when you get the south Node in Sagittarius or the south Node in the 9th, there can be a natural inclination towards philosophy or towards higher understanding. But the challenge is to apply it in your everyday life, to apply it when you are walking to the corner shop to buy milk and orange juice, to bring it into the everyday. If you are doing too much philosophising or theorising or abstraction, and there aren't enough details and facts to support it, or you are not taking it and using it in an everyday practical way, you are not fulfilling the need of the North Node. It needs to be used in a more immediate way. The other thing is that there is a tendency toward escapism and running away. Now, this won't apply across the board, but if you have the south Node in Sagittarius or the south Node in the 9th, when things get difficult, what might be your instinctive response?

Audience: Travel.

Howard: Yes. Get on a plane, or go all abstract about it, and look at it from a really big, philosophical, objective place. But if the north Node is in Gemini or in the 3rd, what is it saying? It is saying that you shouldn't always run away. What you need might be right here in the immediate environment. It is not always somewhere else. We are talking about "the grass is greener" syndrome.

Audience: So don't get on a plane, get on a bus!

Howard: I have the south Node in the 9th, and it has been hard for me to travel because of my arthritic condition. I want to escape into signs and symbols and hope that they will beam me up onto another planet! That is the south Node in the 9th.

Audience: There is a strong moral issue with this axis, because Gemini and the Mercury principle are amoral.

Howard: I agree. That's why I am talking about taking philosophy and sifting it and applying it – making it practical and material. When you get the reverse, with the south Node in Gemini, there is a tendency to diversify too much, to take five different courses in different subjects and to know a little bit about a lot of different things. With the north Node in Sagittarius, you need to go a lot further with something, rather than just dabbling in everything. We are talking about issues to do with finding something you like and going further with it, rather than scattering yourself in a Gemini way and knowing just a little bit about too many things.

 With the south Node in Gemini, you can get too analytical. What is "too analytical"? It is too much left brain, and you need to open up and find ways to accept the right brain, the more holistic and synthetic way of thinking. But with the south Node in Sagittarius, your thinking can be too general and not specific enough, and you need to develop the logical side more. With this polarity you are getting analytical thinking versus intuitive thinking. I am putting the analytical with Gemini and the intuitive with Sagittarius. With the north Node in Sagittarius, or with the north Node in the 9th, maybe you need to develop more faith – that bit of you which can be inspired and not tear things to pieces or criticise them or devalue them or debunk your inspiration or pull apart anything which enthuses you. You need to let yourself go with your faith, rather than taking everything apart. If someone has the north Node in the 9th, you might encourage them to broaden their horizons. But if someone has the south Node in the 9th, every time something gets hard, they run away. Then you say, "Wait a minute, you are not fulfilling your north Node, which is about staying somewhere and seeing what happens if you stay with the immediate."

Audience: Sagittarius has a reputation for being a dabbler as well.

Howard: Yes, that's true. That's why I say this axis is a bit funny. But I think that, ultimately, Gemini is more all over the place than Sagittarius, in terms of being too diversified and too dabbling and too swayed by every little passing thing. Sagittarius is more goal-oriented. If you are very Sagittarian, you are so occupied with getting to your goal that you can miss other things along the way. But if you are very Geminian, you are so distracted by everything that comes along that you never get to your goal. Somehow you need to keep your goal in mind, but not miss things along the way. If I am travelling to get somewhere, I may not be enjoying all the little things along the way to getting there. That's Sagittarius.

Cancer/Capricorn and the 4th and 10th houses

Cancer and Capricorn are clear because they are quite different from each other. We can look at the north Node in Cancer opposed to the south Node in Capricorn, or the north Node in the 4th opposed to the south Node in the 10th. If you have the south Node in Capricorn, or the south Node in the 10th, what might you have already done in previous lives? What is built-in and instinctive?

Audience: Career. Being in a position of authority of some kind.

Howard: Yes. It is almost like being the parent – being strong, capable, responsible, in charge, and not showing your weakness.

Audience: Being like father.

Howard: Being organised, structured, and not getting swayed by moods and feelings.

Audience: Not being emotional.

Howard: You have probably worked hard to achieve a certain amount of success and prestige before. With the south Node in Capricorn or the south Node in the 10th, what do you need to learn about?

Audience: The feeling nature.

Howard: You need to open up to the emotions and let the child in you come out. You need to show that bit which is more vulnerable and sensitive. Also, I think sometimes it's important not to be so structured. Let yourself be swayed by your feelings. It is almost the reverse of what I was saying at the beginning. With the north Node we were talking about not going with the instinctive, but with the north Node in Cancer, you need to allow what your feelings are bringing up in you, and where your moods want to take you. If you have the south Node in Capricorn, you have probably had times when you wanted to stay in bed, but you had to get up to go to work. It may be, with the north Node in Cancer, that you need to sometimes say, "No, I'm going to stay in bed because that's what I feel like doing, and I'll work later. I'll make up for it later." That might be better than cutting off from feelings in order to be disciplined or dutiful or responsible or adult or as you think people want you to be.

With the Cancer/Capricorn axis we are talking flowing and allowing of our moods and feelings, versus censoring and filtering and saying, "I can't have that because this is what I'm doing." There are also home and career issues. If you have to blend the two, it is asking that career remains important, but not at the expense of the home and not at the expense of the private and personal.

Audience: You might work from home.

Howard: That's it. What we are getting at is some sort of compromise. Now, if you have the south Node in Cancer or the south Node in the 4th – let's take the south Node in the 4th – what could be habitual and instinctive?

Audience: Staying home.

Howard: Hiding away. You are into your inner world – you are in therapy eight days a week and you are obsessed with your own subjective and personal stuff. If you have the north Node in Capricorn or in the 10th, then what do you need to be doing? You know the answer – getting out into the collective in some way, for others rather than just for yourself. You need to be establishing yourself through some sort of authority or work in the world.

Audience: It's also about accepting authority.

Howard: Yes, or working within society rather than just being at home within the context of your family or your private life. Also, you may need more discipline, more getting up out of bed even if you don't feel like it. You need more filtering and structuring, to develop your desire to rise, to achieve in a concrete way that is recognised by other people. I think, if you have got the north Node in Capricorn, that you are a closet conventional person who actually needs some recognition from society. That might be so even though other parts of you may be the rebel, and even if you say to yourself, "I don't need those conventional accolades or acknowledgements." You may discover, when things start to hit that north Node, that you actually do need your father's approval. I am using father in a symbolic way. There is another issue with the south Node in Capricorn. You could be too judgmental, too critical. What do you need to develop more of?

Audience: Tolerance. Sensitivity.

Leo/Aquarius and the 5th and 11th houses

Howard: All right. Let's move on. If you have the north Node in Leo, what do you need to develop more of?

Audience: Self-expression. Creativity.

Howard: Yes, self-expression – creating from inside yourself, rather than just being what the group demands or what you think others want you to be. It is about learning how to be more spontaneous, how to play, how to have fun. That fits with the north Node in Leo or the north Node in the 5th. If someone has the north Node in the 5th, if they are deciding whether to be a parent or not, I would probably go more towards parenting, because the north Node in the 5th suggests growth through children. If that is not a possibility, there are other ways you can live 5th house energy. You see how you can use the north Node in terms of advising or counselling someone, because you can be pretty unabashed about pushing someone into that area. It's okay to do that.

Audience: I would like to know more about what the north Node in the 5th means when you see someone with an issue about children. I was doing a chart for someone who kept trying to have a child but couldn't seem to do it. She wanted to keep on trying. She said, "What about children?" Her north Node is in the 5th house. She had been married for ten years. She said, "Am I the right age for having children? Do you think I will ever have a child?" I said that all I could suggest was that creativity was an issue that she has got to be conscious of. Do you think that's the sort of thing you could say about people with the north Node in the 5th?

Howard: I think you have done the right thing in seeing the issue of children as a creativity issue. Then you could talk about any blockages she has around creativity, which could help psychologically. But if there is a physical thing which means she just can't have children, then I would look at other ways to use the 5th house. With the north Node in the 5th, what would you encourage a person to do?

Audience: Be themselves.

Howard: Allow out more of what's inside. Maybe encourage them to take courses in art. Get them to go to the theatre. Get them to do 5th house things. Also, the north Node in Leo says that you are allowed to be somewhat selfish and to exercise your power. There's a group of people – I think they were born between the second half of 1943 and the first half of 1944 – who have the north Node in Leo conjunct Jupiter and Pluto. I remember seeing a person who had this combination. I think the Sun was there as well. The Sun, the north Node, Jupiter, and Pluto were all in Leo in the 1st house. It made me think, seeing all that Leo stuff with the south Node in Aquarius, that this person really had permission to be a tyrant. They had permission to really assert their will and have authority and power. If they are going to make a mistake or err, they should err on the side of being the bully, because of the north Node conjunct the Sun conjunct Jupiter and Pluto in Leo in the 1st house.

Audience: Howard, why do you say that it is a bullying energy?

Howard: Maybe I am a little bit on the side of the bully in this case. The south Node in Aquarius in the 7th wants instinctively to be part of the group, to always be what others want. This person needed to build in more assertiveness, to say, "Look, this is what I want. Now do it," instead of always saying, "What do all the rest of you want? What do you think I should want?"

Audience: It is about being a star.

Howard: Good. That brings up another issue. When we reverse it, and find the south Node in Leo and the north Node in Aquarius, Martin Shulman would say that you have been the *prima ballerina* in a previous lifetime. You have been the one who has been on stage and lauded for who you were. Now you have to put energy not just into promoting yourself, but also – with the north Node in Aquarius – into promoting the aims of a group or society, or promoting ideals which will affect others and not just give you recognition.

I have seen a number of cases like this. I am thinking of a woman who has the south Node in Leo in the 10th and the north Node in Aquarius in the 4th. At a very young age she desperately wanted to be a dancer, and she was training with the Royal Ballet. Then she got lots of trouble with her knees. Do you see the south Node in Leo in the 10th in this? Her desire to be a star, when she tried to go too much in that direction, was denied her, and it pushed her into the north Node in Aquarius. She actually became an astrologer and was concerned with giving knowledge and advice to other people – that is the north Node in Aquarius. I have seen other cases with the south Node in Leo or the south Node in the 5th where the person is frustrated in their personal creative ambitions and winds up using their talent not just to promote themselves or to be the star, but to help others.

If you have the south Node in the 11th or the south Node in Aquarius, what have you done too much of? You've been what the group wanted you to be. You blended in with the ideals or the belief system of the group that you are part of. And what do you need to do more of?

Audience: Individualise.

Howard: Yes, even if it means being a bit disruptive or challenging. But if you have the north Node in Aquarius, you need to learn to be part of a group, part of society, rather than just having it your way. You are also getting a head versus heart issue here, with Leo being the heart and Aquarius being more objective and detached. I would encourage people with the north Node in Leo to open up the feelings and the heart, rather than always being cool and objective and reasonable. The south Node in Leo can be too dramatic, too emotional. It is a bit like Scorpio that way, and needs to develop a little more objectivity – seeing the bigger picture and seeing things from the other person's point of view, rather than taking everything so personally. The south Node in Leo needs to learn not to take things so personally. You grow when you don't take things personally, when you see them from another perspective. If someone rejects you, you can take it personally, or you can see why it had to be in terms of the bigger picture.

Virgo/Pisces and the 6th and 12th houses

Virgo and Pisces are also very clear. If you have the south Node in Pisces, what's the thing that you did too much of in a previous lifetime? What is the line of least resistance?

Audience: Sacrifice.

Howard: Yes, blending and merging. The south Node in Pisces or in the 12th may be too open, too easily influenced. It might not having enough definition or boundaries for keeping things out. It's just too open. If you have the north Node in Virgo or in the 6th, what do you need to develop more of?

Audience: Discrimination.

Howard: The ability to say, "No, that's not my problem." If the south Node is in Pisces, you have a lot of imagination, but what do you need to do with it, with the north Node in Virgo?

Audience: Apply it.

Howard: You need to learn technique. Technique is the liberation of the imagination. You need to develop technique, to work hard to develop actual skills to give the imagination form. With the south Node in the 12th, what's easy for you? To retreat, to be alone, to hide – privacy, a dream state. And with the north Node in the 6th? I think you need to be contributing in some way by having skills which are formal, which are concrete or practical. Health issues come up here.

Audience: Work in hospitals.

Howard: That would be a good balance.

Audience: You could say the issue with both signs is service. What is the difference between the Piscean side and the Virgoan side of service?

Howard: Well, Pisces tends to lose itself through service. "I'll forget about myself and just do what other people need." But Virgo tends to identify itself by being of service. If you are a Virgo you say, "I'll find my identity by helping you." If you're Pisces you say, "I'll forget about myself by helping you." You can lose yourself through service or get a sense of who you are through service. Virgo will tend to get more of a sense of identity through being a server, whereas Pisces might just be what others need them to be, and therefore lose themselves. Let me say more here. With this axis you have issues about seeing the part or seeing the whole. I don't know how to put it another way, but it's the difference between the details and the bigger picture.

Audience: It's a bit like the Gemini/Sagittarius axis.

Howard: You do get that across the mutable signs, with Pisces being more like Sagittarius and Virgo being more like Gemini. Jupiter rules both Pisces and Sagittarius, and Mercury rules both Virgo and Gemini.

You get right brain and left brain issues here. If you have the south Node in Virgo, what qualities might come instinctively to you? What might you do too much of?

Audience: Discrimination.

Howard: Maybe you're too analytical, too critical. The tendency is to be very judgemental. With the north Node in Pisces or the north Node in the 12th, what do you need to develop? You need more acceptance, more tolerance, more understanding and empathy.

Audience: Is this an issue of order and chaos as well?

Howard: Absolutely. It is a bit like Cancer and Capricorn, with Cancer being like Pisces and Capricorn like Virgo. It's an issue between being structured and being all over the place in a watery way. The north Node in Pisces may need to learn to be less disciplined. Tracy Marks gives a good example of this in her book.

Audience: It's her own axis, isn't it?

Howard: Yes. She has the south Node in Virgo in the 9th house and the north Node in Pisces in the 3rd. She tells a story about when she had to give a seminar on the Nodes. She was working in a very south Node in Virgo way, wanting to get every word she was going to say in the seminar figured out. She had a handout she wanted to work on early in the day, so that it would be ready for the seminar. She also wanted to go to the local shop to buy some beverages for lunch. All this was the Virgo south Node. She woke up really early on the morning of the seminar because she had all these things she had to get together and put in order – the handout, the beverages. As the morning began she felt a bit rushed, because she had to finish the handout which she wanted to give to people. But she had to go to the shop to get the beverages. So she got the beverages and was coming back from the shop, and suddenly she heard the meowing of a cat up a tree. This is what she says in her book. She was suddenly caught on the pivot of that axis. She was thinking, "I've got to get home and do what I need to do and get everything ready – south Node in Virgo – but there is

something right here, something immediate which needs help."
There's the north Node in Pisces.

Audience: A cat is a small animal. The 6th house is about small
animals.

Howard: It's funny, but yes, it is a small animal. She made a choice to
do her north Node in Pisces in the 3rd. She called the fire brigade and
got them to rescue the cat, and therefore didn't get her handout
finished. She had to make a choice between order and forethought –
Virgo and the 9th house – and compassion and immediacy – Pisces and
the 3rd house. She chose to do what was right in front of her. Then, of
course, she said that the handout wasn't really necessary after all.

Audience: What a perfect story.

Howard: Yes, I think it is also, with the north Node in Pisces
accepting humanness and not having to be perfect. You get this a little
bit with Gemini/Sagittarius, too. If you give a lecture, the Pisces or
the Sagittarius tendency is to trust that you'll know what to say at the
time and be able to feel what the group needs to hear. But Gemini and
Virgo say, "I've got to figure out everything I'm going to say, and have
it all written down." Tracy Marks, with the south Node in Virgo and
the north Node in Pisces, prepares it all in advance, and then she
doesn't read her notes. She just does it, which is maybe a way to
balance the axis. Otherwise you are just reading your notes in a Virgo
way, and you are not letting enough inspiration come in.

Audience: Do you think that is about learning to trust the cosmos?

Howard: Yes, that's the north Node in Pisces. You don't have to be in
control – something bigger than you will come and help you.

Audience: It's like the difference between religious practise and faith.

Howard: Yes. It doesn't have to be all worked out and put in place by
you alone.

Audience: Which would you put more accent on? The sign or the house? My south Node is in the 3rd house in Pisces.

Howard: That's the opposite of Tracy Marks – she has the north Node in the 3rd in Pisces. I would go for the house of the north Node first, and then the sign. If you have the north Node in Virgo in the 9th, I would go much more for opening up your intuition and then analysing things. You could blend the two in that way, rather than being too gullible.

Audience: Are you saying that as a general principle you should go for the house first and then the sign, or only in this specific instance?

Howard: I'm going to change that a little bit. I spoke too quickly. I would go for the Virgo north Node first, and learn to be less influenced by what someone else says. You just did it. You didn't take what I said without questioning it. You challenged it. You wanted more definition. That was a good example. I was testing you!

Audience: I have the north Node in Virgo as well, but it conjuncts Neptune, and you get real problems with that.

Howard: We'll do the planetary aspects to the Nodes next.

Natal aspects to the Nodes

Conjunctions

I am going to give you guidelines for the aspects, and our first topic is planets conjunct the south Node in your natal chart. I would allow about a 5° orb, because I have seen that work. Now, what I said earlier about the south Node applies to a planet conjuncting it. Whatever that planet represents is also a carryover from the past – it is something that is inbred and instinctive. There is a natural pull towards the energy symbolised by that planet. It can come automatically and compulsively, and we may live from it too much.

For instance, I remember doing a chart for a woman with the south Node in Virgo conjunct Saturn, and she seemed to be pervaded by fear. Everything seemed a challenge, everything seemed frightening, everything seemed difficult. She lived in a very tight structure. You see not only the south Node in Virgo, but also the south Node conjunct Saturn, as if she had done a lot of Saturn in the past. She was still too much with Saturn and obviously needed to develop her north Node in Pisces more. If you have the south Node conjunct Neptune, it is as if you have been a Neptunian in some other lifetime, or maybe you are bringing over issues to do with lack of discrimination or not enough boundaries, or issues to do with alcoholism or addictions.

Some of you were on the "Subpersonalities" seminar I gave recently, and we talked about how a subpersonality can be a kind of psychological satellite inside us that we tend to come from. It almost takes us over sometimes. You may get a subpersonality building up around a planet conjunct the south Node, and it can be almost compulsive. For example, the south Node conjunct Jupiter can give a tendency to go overboard, innately and instinctively.

Audience: What if you are projecting the planet that is conjunct your south Node? I mean, what if you are running away from it?

Howard: The guideline would be that it is in us, so we need to own it and rework it. Then we need to be careful not to overdo it. But you must take it back first, before you can rework it. You must reclaim it. Are you talking about Pluto with the south Node?

Audience: No, Saturn.

Howard: If you have the south Node conjunct Saturn, it should be innate in you, and if you are not very Saturnian, then there is something awry. There is something not right. That's why both Tracy Marks and Martin Shulman always talk about reworking your south Node, and making sure you are using it.

Audience: Should that come quite easily, then?

Howard: It's meant to, but there may be other things in the chart which conflict with it. I would take this as a kind of lesson – we should make the most of what our south Node has to offer. The danger, of course, is overdoing it, but if you are underdoing it, then it's not kosher. You're not playing by the rules.

Audience: I found that I started off with all the negative characteristics of the north Node. I had to develop the south Node in order to come back to the north Node and develop its more positive characteristics.

Howard: That's a possibility too. Sometimes, if you are not doing your north Node properly, you'll get trouble through the north Node itself. Let's stay with Virgo. If you have the south Node in Virgo and the north Node in Pisces, and if you are being too methodical and too disciplined, you may get trouble through your north Node. You could slip into alcohol too much as a way of relaxing, or go a little potty every once in a while – the Pisces side of the axis. If you are not doing your north Node enough, or if you are not paying attention to it, you may get trouble through your north Node energy.

Audience: Howard, I sometimes think planets on the south Node are an indication that there is some work we have to do with that planet before we can make the link with the north Node.

Howard: It is as if you are not done with it. You have been involved with it before and you need to go over it again. You didn't clear it and you aren't at peace with it in some way. It still needs attention, and you are bringing it back to have to look at it. It has been there before and it is still there. It is like repeating a grade at school.

Audience: It is worth remembering that the Saturn conjunction with the south Node in Virgo also opposes the north Node in Pisces. In a sense it is making the north Node more problematic.

Howard: Usually, if you get a planet conjunct the south Node, it pulls you more towards the south Node. I can see, with Saturn there, why you might want to avoid it. But somewhere there are inbuilt qualities of conservatism, caution, and discipline. Tracy Marks says that planets conjunct the south Node should be brought into consciousness and then reassessed. She says that at some point we may have to let go of the grip of that planet. So if you have the south Node conjunct

Mercury, if your tendency is to be too analytical or to go into your head too much, and that's what's been built in, you may need to learn to let go of intellectualising or verbalising or being analytical about things. I can only give you these general guidelines, but you get the picture. You are bringing the planet over from the past. It needs to be reworked. It may be a compulsive subpersonality. Now, you tell me. What happens if a planet conjuncts the north Node?

Audience: Here is a trusty ally in your life's mission!

Howard: It's true. It's very important to develop what that planet represents by focusing on it, by building it in. Then there is a sense of soul growth and evolution and movement and progress.

Audience: Even if it is the ruler of your south Node?

Howard: Then you start getting the need to integrate the axis better.

Balancing the axis

As soon as you get the ruler of the north Node conjunct the south Node, or vice versa, we come to the issue of trying to get a balance. It heightens the need to have a balance between the two principles and to make room in your life for both sides. I know this gets confusing, because you can have something like the north Node conjunct the Moon. Then we are a little confused, because the Moon has to do with the pull of the past and what's instinctive, yet it may mean that there are instinctive things that are really worth furthering and developing. It also means parenting or nurturing. Anything to do with emotions, if the north Node is conjunct the Moon, is important to develop.

If you get the south Node conjunct the Sun, that's a little bit of an anomaly. I tend to think you have done that Sun-sign before, but you are here to do it better on another level. You know how we talk about every sign having different levels. You may have the south Node conjunct the Sun in Pisces. You have done one level of Pisces before, and you have come back to redo Pisces, but more constructively, because the Sun is there. You must develop the qualities of your Sun-sign, although we are wanting to not overdo the south Node sign. If they are in the same sign, it is a little confusing, but I think it is possible to interpret it.

Audience: Would you take a slightly larger orb for the Sun conjunct the Node?

Howard: Maybe 6° or 7°. I would be a little conservative, because the Node isn't a planet, it is just a point.

Audience: I was just thinking about out-of-sign conjunctions. What if you have the Node in Cancer conjunct the Sun in Leo?

Howard: Out-of-sign aspects are a little weaker. You are not getting the full impact. That's my feeling, although I would still read it as a conjunction. But it doesn't have the same effect as when it is in the same sign.

Audience: What about the nodal rulers in the same house or sign?

Howard: Again, you have to work more on balancing the opposite principles represented by the nodal axis. It puts more of an emphasis on integration.

Audience: So the same thing would apply, for instance, with the north Node in the 1st house in Libra.

Howard: People with Libra rising often get everything backwards. You know what I mean – you get a reversal of sign and house. Let's think for a minute. The north Node is in Libra in the 1st. How would you interpret that?

Audience: You have to learn to assert yourself through relationship.

Howard: Yes. It is about learning how to assert yourself, but in a Libran way.

Audience: Through compromise.

Howard: Or with style, diplomacy, grace, and beauty. That would put the south Node in Aries in the 7th. There is an instinctive tendency either to let partners push you around too much, or to have all the power in the partnership. What if you have the north Node in Aquarius in the 5th? Where can you express your creativity?

Audience: In groups. In group art. In a dance troupe or in the theatre.

Howard: Or maybe in something like community theatre, where you are using your creativity – the north Node in the 5th – but it has got an Aquarian slant. You are promoting an ideal or principle or belief. Actually, if you let your intuition play around, you can synthesise these things without too much difficulty. What if you have the north Node in Cancer in the 10th? You need a career which involves something to do with the Cancer function.

Audience: You become a carer. But you would have to have responsibility with the job. You would have to run the hospital.

Audience: I know someone who has that – the north Node in Cancer in the 10th – and he has always been after status. The way that he is starting to get it in his life is through his nurturing. He "discovered" somebody, and through nurturing that person's career he is becoming famous himself.

Howard: I think I know the same person. Where you have something like the north Node in Leo in the 11th, you might find yourself by helping others, by promoting others. So it would be a very good position for an artist's agent or impresario. The north Node in Leo in the 11th seems like a contradiction, but need it be?

Audience: You can lead a group.

Howard: Yes, you can find your power and self-expression in a group.

Audience: If you have got something like that, does it mean that the whole business of integrating the two ends is much more important than, say, where there is something clear like Saturn conjunct the north Node?

Howard: Yes. When you start getting things mixed up like that, then we come back to what I was saying before. The integrating and balancing of the polarity seems to be what you are meant to learn about. It is as if you have gone to one extreme with one principle in one lifetime and the other extreme with the other principle in another lifetime, and now you have to have them both without overdoing either. But I would always favour the north Node sign or house.

Audience: The astrological rule is that if something is stated two or three times, it is really important.

Howard: It usually is. The Nodes don't stand alone. Usually the whole chart confirms or reiterates their themes.

Audience: In a way I would like to get away from the reincarnation idea, because otherwise you are saying that the south Node is the baddie and you have got to go to the north Node.

Howard: I am trying to be careful not to fall into that trap, although there are some cases where someone really does stay too much in the south Node and really needs to be pushed into the north Node. I don't want to give the impression the south Node is bad. Integration seems to be the key in all cases. I remember a chart client who has always stayed in my mind. It is a woman with the south Node in Capricorn in the 1st house, and the south Node conjuncts her Moon. If you come in with the south node in Capricorn in the 1st, what does that say? Can you give me some keywords or ideas?

Audience: She would have instinctive ease in handling authority.

Audience: She would want power.

Audience: Maybe she would be too tied up with controlling things, with controlling the environment.

Howard: Do you know what happened to her? She was born to a Catholic mother out of wedlock, and her mother actually hid her birth from everyone. She really kept it a secret. I thought it was interesting, because if we do too much of the south Node we are in trouble – and she was almost denied it right from the beginning. She didn't have the right to exist, she didn't have any recognition, she wasn't acknowledged. She was kept hidden. In some cases, the south Node is something we are deprived of. We can't go that way, we aren't allowed, because there is such a need to develop the other principle.

Audience: She was denied a mother, in a way. Her mother couldn't be a real mother. Is that the Moon conjunct the south Node?

Audience: What you are describing is also very Saturnian. She was rejected from birth, wasn't she?

Howard: Yes, right at the beginning. That's the 1st house. She was denied the Moon, and also denied Capricorn authority, and the traditional family, the family society says we should have. It's as if she didn't have permission to have that Moon in Capricorn, or maybe she has to live it in another way. But with planets conjunct the north Node, we are always here to develop that principle. It is a real clue to development. We have permission. If you have the north Node conjunct Venus, tell me what needs to be developed.

Audience: Love.

Howard: Yes. Union, love, creativity.

Audience: Harmony.

Howard: And values. What about the north Node conjunct Saturn? What needs to be developed? What do you have permission for?

Audience: Discipline. Authority.

Howard: What does the north Node conjunct Uranus give you permission to do?

Audience: Be crazy!

Audience: Go around electrocuting everybody.

Howard: It gives you permission to be original, inventive, electrifying.

Audience: Can you say again what the north Node conjunct Saturn means?

Howard: The north Node conjunct Saturn means it is favourable to develop Saturnian qualities, which we have already discussed.

Trines and sextiles

With planets trine or sextile the north or south Node, you know that if a planet is trine one end of the nodal axis it is going to be sextile the other. I would only allow a 3° orb. The idea is that a planet trine or sextile either end can aid the integration of the axis – it can aid the integration of the polarity. Now, I can't go into examples. I don't have any in my head, but you can check out your own chart. Some writers do warn that when you get a planet trining the south Node, it may pull you into the south Node more. It may actually overwork the south Node. But I don't know if that's true.

Squares

What I do keep an eye on is a planet square the nodal axis. That can be quite tough, quite a challenge.

Audience: What orb?

Howard: With a square, 3° or 4°. But I am always most interested in exact squares or exact aspects. For example, if you have Jupiter square your nodal axis, there can be a tendency to overdo the south Node because of Jupiter, and then swing and overdo the north Node. Or if you have Saturn square the nodal axis, it can make the resolution of the axis a lot more pressing, but also a lot harder to do. There is really a very severe test in terms of the resolution of the polarity. If you don't resolve it, you really suffer, and if you do resolve it you are very much rewarded. But you feel it as a tough challenge. It is almost like "Last

Chance Saloon" when you have Saturn square the Nodes. You really feel the effects if you mess it up.

Audience: And Pluto?

Howard: I think it's the same with Pluto. With Pluto square the Nodes it makes balancing the polarity very pressing – it's a life-death struggle to do it. You are really put through it in order to resolve that axis. Some people may have a nodal contradiction between the house and the sign, and it is not difficult for them to make room in their life for both ends – there's no problem. Someone may have the south Node in Libra in the 5th and the north Node in Aries in the 11th, and they set up a sports centre for children. You can see how you are bringing in the Libra and the north Node in Aries as well. Other people may have real difficulty getting that nodal axis into any kind of balance or making room in their life for both, and the people who have the difficulty will often have squares from planets to the nodal axis. But the funny thing is that the square makes resolution all the more pressing.

Audience: I have what you call a contradiction, and I find resolution very difficult. I have the north Node in Cancer in the 10th and the south Node in Capricorn in the 4th.

Howard: So the effort to make a home life and the effort to make a career are always causing conflict.

Audience: I suppose I get some help from the Moon in Pisces, which is trine the north Node and sextile the south.

Howard: That's what you should go to for help in resolving it. The fear is, "I have to give up one in order to get the other," and I don't know if that's the truth.

Audience: What about Uranus square the Nodes?

Howard: I think there could be a lot of tension in resolving the polarity – going to one extreme and then the other. I wish I could give more exact answers. What I am trying to do is just alert you to these

configurations, and then leave you to your own devices. You'll know
when you really understand it. I'm going to talk about my chart, like
Tracy Marks does. I have the south Node in 15° Scorpio, and Pluto has
been on it while I have had this crisis with arthritis.[12] It certainly
has thrown me into the north Node in Taurus, because it is really
forcing me to be in the body. Saturn is at 15° Leo in my chart, so you see
how the transit of Pluto has brought out the T-square that Saturn
creates with the Nodes. If you have a T-square created by a planet to
the Nodes, watch out for a transit or progression which comes into that
degree of the modality, whether it's cardinal, fixed, or mutable.

Audience: I was going to ask you about the missing leg of the T-cross. Is
it very active?

Howard: In my case Saturn in Leo squares the Scorpio and Taurus
Nodes, and Aquarius is the missing leg. It's in the 1st house. I would
say that bringing Aquarian energy in, or being with people who have
planets around that degree of Aquarius, may be very helpful as well as
challenging in terms of enabling me to get through the difficulty. One
of my very closest friends has the Sun in Aquarius, and when I was
really ill he was chauffeuring me around and helping in very
immediate ways. It was that literal – I needed that Aquarian energy.
I needed someone to be a friend, because I was not able to get around.

   If you get a T-square formed by a planet square the Nodes, look
to the empty leg. Do you understand that principle? It is possible to get
grand crosses if you have the nodal opposition running up against
another opposition which squares both ends of the axis. It just makes it
more pressing. As I say, it is a life-death issue. It is a much greater
challenge. When you mess up you really feel it more, and when you get
it right you really feel it more.

Audience: With an opposition, I think you would have to be doubly
sure that you weren't projecting it onto other people.

---

[12]Editor's note: for some time before his death, Howard suffered from a
condition known as ankylosing spondylosis, a fusing of the vertebrae which is
thought to be hereditary and which, although not fatal, can result in increasing
immobility and pain.

Howard: Yes. Always, with oppositions, we have to ultimately stand in the middle and realise that we have both ends.

Audience: If you have got a lot of planets around the south Node, how do you advise someone to get to their north Node energy? I have the Sun, Mercury, and Venus all with my south Node in Cancer.

Howard: It is more difficult. If you have Venus conjunct Mercury conjunct the Sun conjunct the south Node in Cancer, the only answer I can give is that you have to develop your Cancerian side, but not at the expense of the north Node in Capricorn. You have to have your boundaries and your structure, but if you start becoming too Capricornian, then you are losing your Cancer side.

Audience: What about quincunxes to the Nodes?

Howard: I haven't made any kind of study of it. I tend to stick to looking for the conjunctions and squares, and maybe the trines and sextiles. But that doesn't mean other aspects aren't important. I would make the orb exact, though. If it was an exact quincunx, it would operate more like a square.

The Nodes and the angles

Audience: What about when the Nodes aspect the angles? There is no energy, is there, in either the Nodes or the angles. How does that work?

Howard: Tracy Marks talks about that. She has it in her own chart. She has the nodal opposition squaring her Ascendant/Descendant axis. She talks about how it has made it very difficult for her to project herself, although I haven't seen that problem! Can I first turn it around a little bit? Let's talk about being born with the north Node conjunct the Ascendant and the south Node conjunct the Descendant.

Audience: I plead guilty. I've got that.

Howard: All right, let's bring you in. The Ascendant is what's appearing in the world as you are appearing. As you are emerging out of the darkness of your mother's womb, there is a particular thing coming to life. When the north Node is on the Ascendant, it is coming into life as you are being born – it is appearing. The Ascendant is such an important point to develop in order to form our individuality. It makes it extra-important to find constructive and clear ways to give expression to the sign that the north Node and Ascendant are in. So what's yours?

Audience: Well, just to make things difficult, it's an out-of-sign conjunction. I have a Scorpio Ascendant and a Sagittarius north Node, with both of them conjunct Saturn.

Howard: Does anyone want to venture an interpretation for that?

Audience: It is as if you have to find meaning in every crisis you go through.

Howard: It is called "To Hell with Love!" You have to go down into the pit and love it and find meaning there. You have to bring a torch with you. Ultimately that would be the challenge – to go down without fear, and with a Sagittarian light.

Audience: And have the faith to go down there, too.

Audience: Even if you don't have the faith, you get dragged down there anyway!

Howard: And then you have to develop the faith.

Audience: I'm a double Sagittarian, with the north Node conjunct the Sun conjunct the Ascendant. I have heard it called a "double whammy".

Howard: It just adds to the importance of developing the Sagittarian capacity to find meaning in things, and to explore different philosophies.

Audience: I have a question, but it isn't about the angles. I can understand the north Node more clearly in my chart than the south Node. The south Node is in the 2nd house conjunct Mercury.

Howard: I would say the south Node conjunct Mercury in the 2nd is about thinking too much for yourself, and maybe too practically. Maybe you need to be more open to what other people say, or to what they feel underneath. Do you try to do that?

Audience: I think so. But I am not sure, since the south Node and Mercury are in Virgo, if I upset people sometimes with what I say. I can be very critical. Maybe I need to learn to be more open, more Piscean in how I say things.

Howard: What I am picking up is how important it is to be travelling along the axis, learning something and then sharing it, picking up something and sharing it, discovering something and sharing it. Someone tells you something and you take it back, digest it, and bring it out in your own way. Some people don't have much trouble with their nodal axis, especially when the Nodes are in Sagittarius and Gemini. That may not be such a difficult axis. Sometimes Virgo and Pisces aren't so difficult either. But if the south Node conjuncts the Descendant, what's that telling us about the people we have relationships with?

Audience: It all dates back to the past. We have been with them before.

Howard: They may encourage us in our south Node tendencies, or we have known them before and we are repeating it. It is almost as if we have to meet the same people we knew before, but we meet them as a new person. We aren't the same way we were before, because the north Node is conjunct the Ascendant, so we have to meet them as a new individual, but they are the same people and some of the same conflicts come up that were there before.

What about the south Node conjunct the Ascendant and the north Node conjunct the Descendant? That's a little bit of a reversal, isn't it? I think you are really here to learn about how to live with other people. The tendency with the south Node conjunct the

Ascendant might have been that you were too uncivilised before, too self-centred. It depends on the sign, but maybe there was too much self.

Audience: I have the north Node in Aries on the Descendant, and the south Node in Libra on the Ascendant. I also have my Sun in the 7th house.

Howard: This is one of those that gets a little complicated. We talked about it recently, didn't we? Can I tell the story to the group? I was desperate to get into the toilet, and there was an "engaged" sign, and so I was waiting and waiting. You were there waiting with me, and you finally went to knock on the door for me, to tell the person inside to hurry up.

Audience: I wouldn't have done it for myself.

Howard: Maybe that's the south Node in Libra on the Ascendant – you can only assert yourself for someone else. The north Node in Aries on the Descendant might mean you need to learn to do it for yourself as well as for others, because you have the Sun in Aries as well. What this does emphasise is the Aries/Libra axis of assertion versus cooperation, and getting a healthy balance between the two – how to be assertive without being too much of a tyrant, and how to be cooperative without being a doormat. You will probably get in trouble with other people if you go to one end or the other too much. It is like instant karma.

Audience: I also have the south Node conjunct the Ascendant in Libra, but it conjuncts Mars. And the north Node is in Aries on the Descendant, and I don't want to know anything about relationships.

Howard: When I see the north Node in the 7th, I would say that, if you have the possibility of forming a relationship, get into it, because the north Node there says you need the experiences, even if they are difficult. I have to say that. I trust interpretations to follow the north Node, even when the person objects. I would be firm about it, wherever your north Node is.

Audience: Howard, I also have got one of these Aries/Libra nodal contradictions. I have got Aries rising. Mars conjuncts the north Node in Leo, and the Moon is in Libra in the 7th.

Howard: Mars conjunct the north Node in Leo is a strong indication of taking power, making others adjust to you, and being the centre of things.

Audience: And the Moon in Libra?

Howard: Work on doing your Mars conjunct the north Node in Leo, but not to such a degree that you are out of balance. The Moon in Libra in the 7th, if it is not too badly aspected, means that you have an innate ability to be balanced in relationship, and that could help to develop your north Node in Leo.

Audience: The Moon actually squares the nodal axis. It's an out-of-sign square.

Howard: I would think that it would be one of those situations, if we take it in terms of past lives, where you might have gone to both extremes, of being too assertive and also too compromising. Now you have to learn to be assertive, but...

Audience: ...Without roaring.

Howard: Yes.

Audience: Could it also have something to do with the time factor? You can't live your north Node at the age of twenty, for example. Maybe you come to the north Node in mid-life. That's my experience.

Howard: One would hope, as you get older, that you will have built in the north Node and balanced the opposition. But I must admit that I have seen people forced into their north Node at quite a young age. For example, with the north Node in the 1st house, you might be forced into independence at a very young age. It's as if you can't get to your south Node in the 7th. You can't get other people to take care of you. You are pushed into it.

Audience: But maybe you do it from your own experience?

Howard: Yes. I think each case would be different. What you say makes sense, but I have seen other cases. Tracy Marks and I both have the north Node in the 3rd, and it's funny, because I had real speech problems. I was about seven before I learned how to talk. I might have talked, but no one understood me! The 3rd house is communication, and with the north Node there, by the age of four I was having to have speech therapy. It was as if I was being forced into the north Node in my 3rd house very, very early.

Audience: You're using it right now.

Howard: I never stopped! The same issue came up with writing. With the north Node in the 3rd, it was a tremendous effort to sit down and write. Yet the rewards you get from making that effort are great. The north Node in the 3rd may have difficulty with communication and writing, but if you can keep at it, the rewards are profound.

The Nodes and the Part of Fortune

Audience: Could you tell me about the south Node conjunct the Part of Fortune?

Howard: Liz and I were talking about the Part of Fortune the other day. There are so many Parts. There is even a Part of Illustrious Acquaintances.

Audience: You just made that up!

Howard: No, Erin talks about her Part of Illustrious Acquaintances all the time. Anyway, to answer your question, I would rather see the north Node conjunct the Part of Fortune than the south Node.

Audience: I have it the other way.

Howard: Do any of you work with the Part of Fortune? The Part of Fortune is the Sun plus the Ascendant minus the Moon. That's how you figure it out. But what do you find?

Audience: It's a way of connecting the Sun-Moon relationship to the houses, to the material world. It's the same distance from the Ascendant to the Part of Fortune as it is from the Sun to the Moon.

Audience: I have found that it comes up in the synastry of my family. I've been doing a lot of work on family charts lately, and there were things I just couldn't find a way to explain. I put the Part of Fortune in my parents' charts, and all of a sudden the missing links popped up to some of my brothers, and with couples as well.

Howard: I have seen relationships where one person's Venus is on another person's Part of Fortune.

Audience: In my family charts I found contacts like the MC or Saturn of one person to the Part of Fortune of another.

Howard: The Part of Fortune is meant to be a favourable point, as you know. I would generally encourage the person to develop that area, almost like the north Node. Let me give you a positive interpretation that you can gloat over. If the south Node is conjunct the Part of Fortune, it may mean that you have done something right in a past life, and now you have brought good luck back with you, so when you are in dire straits, something lucky happens.

Audience: I like the south Node with my Part of Fortune.

Howard: Well, I've given you one positive way of interpreting it.

Audience: I've got Venus conjunct it as well.

Howard: That's why you like it. But if you got lazy and were just relying on luck or other people to do everything for you and rescue you, then you may run into some difficulty.

Transits and progressions involving the nodal axis

Let's move on. I want to talk about transits and progressions to the Nodes. But I do enjoy it when you come in with your examples.

Transiting conjunctions to the Nodes

First let's talk about transiting conjunctions to the south Node. I have found that it reawakens the south Node issues when any planets, especially Saturn and the outer planets, transit your south Node. Those of you with the south Node in Scorpio will have Pluto coming over the south Node, or it has already done so. I think it is bound to bring up crises and a lot of emotional issues. When a transiting planet conjuncts the south Node, the sign and the qualities of that sign become extra-important as your next stage of growth. You have to combat it, or develop it, or face it. Does anyone here have the south Node in Capricorn? Uranus and Neptune would be around there now.

Audience: Yes, Uranus just finished going over my south Node.

Howard: Did you notice anything when Uranus hit? Can you say a bit about it? I'm curious. Did it bring up work issues or achievement issues?

Audience: It brought up a lot around work and relationships.

Audience: I also have the south Node in Capricorn, and Jupiter and Chiron are going over the north Node in the 8th house. Uranus and Neptune are going over the south Node in the 2nd. I had to stop working in this country, because I'm an illegal alien. But because of a bad housing situation, with everyone projecting their Pluto onto me – which was kind of interesting, since I suppose I'm a good hook – I had to start working again. So now, of course, I have to keep looking over my shoulder wondering just how long it will take the Home Office to catch up with me. But it's very interesting, because I have always been very self-sufficient.

Howard: What degree is your north Node?

Audience: 13° Cancer.

Howard: Neptune's on the south Node in the 2nd right now. Do you see the kind of deceit and secretiveness around it? May I make a suggestion?

Audience: Go for it.

Howard: It seems as if you might get away with it if you do it from your north Node in Cancer place – "I am here to learn so that I can help people as an astrologer."

Audience: One would hope. I've been very reliant on friends because I was booted out of housing, which is why I had to get a job, and then I didn't have a place to stay for a week and a half.

Howard: You are not self-sufficient any more, are you?

Audience: God, no! I have been relying on everybody, and have been really tearful and pitiful and needy.

Howard: You're being pushed into your north Node, which is where you may have to be.

Audience: Absolutely. It made me face up to the fact that I have got to get in touch with all that sticky emotional garbage, and learn to rely on folks.

Howard: I have the south Node in Scorpio in the 9th, and that's the house of higher education. When I started my Master's degree I was a complete failure, and hardly went to any classes. Then Uranus went over my south Node about seven years later, and I went back to college and finished the Master's degree. Uranus went over the 9th house south Node. It was a much better experience and I really enjoyed it. When things go over your south Node, there is a chance to redo something and maybe get it right the second time. In your case it is a little more complicated, because you are getting transits to the Cancer north Node as well.

What I am trying to say is that transits over your south Node will throw you back into an old, familiar area, and it may be a chance to rework your south Node in a different way from how you have done i t before. I believe in looking at fast transits over the Nodes, too, like the day the Sun goes over the south Node. See what happens on the day Venus goes over it.

Audience: It seems to me that a transit over one Node will also activate the other. It is the axis which is activated. You have to think of both.

Howard: I agree with you. It is an axis – the two poles feed each other. What if you have a transit conjuncting your north Node? Let's say Uranus hits the north Node. I think it is going to awaken it. It's a real opportunity. I did a chart recently for a woman with the north Node in Capricorn in the 1st house, and transiting Uranus was coming over it. For the first time in her life she was finally standing up to her husband. She had the south Node in Cancer in the 7th, and her husband wanted to do something that she didn't want to do. With Uranus conjuncting her north Node in Capricorn, she finally stood up to him. She said she drew a boundary, instead of just being her south Node in Cancer in the 7th and going along with him. It's funny – the issue was that he wanted to travel and she didn't. It was during the Uranus-Jupiter opposition. Uranus was on her north Node in Capricorn in the 1st and Jupiter was on her south Node in Cancer in the 7th. Now, what if Neptune comes over your north Node?

Audience: You might lose your sense of direction.

Howard: I think it can cause some sort of crisis which may then help you get more into your north Node. It could be an inspiration to get into your north Node, or it could be a crisis through which you then discover your north Node. I want to give that as a general principle. When an outer planet hits the north Node it may bring a crisis, because you are being confronted with something that you have to build in or develop, which you may not want or which may not come naturally.

Audience: Maybe you shouldn't be developing it, then.

Howard: I would say the opposite, although with Neptune you could be off beam for a while about how you develop it. I think the time has come to confront it rather than run away from it, because there is a difficult transit over it. Is it all right for me to say that? I would also watch transits which square your nodal axis. I am trying to tell you things to look out for and to keep an eye on. Also, the best thing you can do after today's seminar is to go back over your life with an ephemeris and check to see when you had transits conjunct or square the Nodes, especially the outer planets. Really think about what happened during that period of your life. You are going to get more understanding about it than I can give you today. I did this myself, in preparation for the seminar.

Audience: Last autumn, Howard, transiting Pluto was squaring the transiting nodal axis in Aquarius/Leo.

Howard: Yes, that was in the heavens. Pluto in Scorpio was square the Aquarius/Leo nodal axis, and there was a change of power and big shifts in the world. That's a good point – transiting planets lined up with the transiting Nodes mean things happen collectively as well.

The transiting Nodes

Now we come to the transiting Nodes themselves. Here are just a few guidelines. Remember that they move backwards, and spend nineteen months in a sign. There are a few things that I would watch for. First of all, watch for when the transiting Nodes change houses in your chart. You will get something like the transiting north Node moving from the 7th to the 6th. When the north Node transits into a new house, there's further growth and development and new experience to be gained through that area of life. When the south node transits into a new house you may get experiences that are unresolved from the past meeting up with you again. Ghosts and issues reappear that you need to work through or meet again. What I am advising, if you haven't done it already, is to work with your own chart on this. You can start where the Nodes are right now. The north Node is at 7° Aquarius and the south node is at 7° Leo. See what houses these are affecting, and if they are hitting any planets.

Audience: What orb are you using for the transits, Howard?

Howard: I would make it pretty close, even in terms of conjunctions or squares – maybe 2°. I know I keep talking about myself. But it's actually useful information. When I started to have trouble with my spine, with my movement, the transiting south Node in Leo came up to conjunct my Mars-Saturn conjunction, and I had the operation when the transiting south Node was on my Pluto. Mars, which is to do with physical energy, met limits, which is Saturn, through something that was physical. That's also Saturn. It's made me very alert to the transiting Nodes.

   Now, when the transiting south Node hits a planet, it brings up karma with that planet. It brings up all the issues which that planet represents. If the transiting south Node hits Mars, anywhere you have been misusing your power or assertion will become an issue. The transiting south Node conjunct Pluto may bring up some very deep emotions and complexes that you have to work through. What about the transiting south Node conjunct Venus? What might that bring up?

Audience: Relationships. An old girlfriend turns up.

Howard: Yes. Or some relationship pattern that's very familiar reappears. I would still say it's an opportunity to access talents and abilities that are ingrained but that you haven't integrated yet. I would give it that positive interpretation. When the transiting north Node conjuncts a planet, it will awaken that energy, and ask that you bring the energy into your life in as constructive a new way as possible. Is anyone going through it at the moment? What do you have?

Audience: I have got Venus conjunct the north Node in Scorpio in my birth chart. It is part of a T-square, and Pluto is coming up to conjunct Venus and the Node in the 12th house.

Howard: That sounds complicated. Let's break it down. I was talking about the transiting Nodes, but you are talking about transiting Pluto over the Nodes. But that's pretty interesting anyway. Transiting Pluto is coming to conjunct your north Node and Venus. Is there any relationship around?

Audience: It's very complicated and difficult. Because the conjunction is in Scorpio in the 12th, I think I have to learn to be alone. Before, I went haywire in relationship.

Howard: When transiting Pluto hits a north Node-Venus conjunction, it is also about accepting parts of one's own self. It is about valuing yourself in a new way. Maybe it would be a good time to change your hairdo. That's not to say you need to! But you know what I mean. It would be a good time to transform your appearance in some way.

Audience: My children say I should dye my hair.

Howard: That would be interesting.

Audience: It could be about more than just the body – not just hair, or clothes, but the way the soul is shown to other people.

Howard: I was thinking that there are inter-personal relationships, but there are intra-personal ones as well. That's what I meant by valuing yourself.

Audience: I have got the south Node going through the 8th house right now. I have already looked at Pluto transiting square my natal Pluto in the 8th. I hadn't actually looked at the south Node conjuncting it.

Howard: I would sit down and make some interpretations based on that.

Audience: Howard, presumably you have also got Pluto square Pluto as well as the transiting south Node going over it.

Howard: I don't want to go into all the details about it, but yes. Often that is the case – it seems the cosmos gangs up on you. Sometimes I think, "Who planned it that the transiting south Node would be going over Mars-Saturn-Pluto at the same time that Pluto is squaring it?" And Pluto is going over my south Node. What I've been hiding from or not dealing with, or karma from the past, is making itself very apparent.

Audience: But Pluto square Pluto often brings a new life, doesn't it?

Howard: One hopes! It's hard. I said it in *The Gods of Change*, and that was before it happened to me. Now I know. Transiting Pluto square Pluto is one of the most challenging transits you can get.

Audience: Would you see new life coming, with Pluto aspecting the north Node? Or do you think the fact it is square the south Node means that the way you use the south Node is transformed?

Howard: Both. It is not only the south Node getting transformed. It is also about being thrown into the north Node as a way of development. That's why I want to go to Wiltshire and be beamed up. North Node in Aquarius, come and get me!

Audience: You were asking about the transiting north Node. I've got the transiting north Node conjunct my Chiron. One of the things I want to do in the spiritual group I'm involved with is to learn spiritual healing.

Howard: And I would say go for it, although obviously without losing your balance, and making sure you maintain a healthy ego. If the transiting north Node is conjunct Chiron, it is saying that it is evolutionary now to be involved with anything that Chiron represents – such as healing.

Audience: The same week I would be doing the course, transiting Jupiter would be opposition natal Chiron, conjunct the transiting south Node and conjunct my MC. So it's reinforced.

Howard: But it is asking, if the transiting Leo south Node is being effective, that when you are doing the healing, you are doing it for others, not to show the world what a great healer you are. You see how the south Node in Leo could contaminate that. The ego could grab it.

Audience: I have my south Node in Leo in the 5th house in exact conjunction to Pluto. I have a feeling that it has taken me this long to sort out my own power issues before I could even consider doing my Chiron conjunct Ascendant.

Howard: I agree. That's an important one, because when ego starts creeping in you are either going to burn out or get frustrated or not do it very well.

Audience: I think there is a problem with this ego thing. Something I am worried about is the "great spiritual healer" nonsense that would contaminate everything, but on the other hand, you can't keep deferring trying to do it because you're worried about the off-chance that you're going to bring in ego.

Howard: I would just keep an eye on it.

Audience: I'm very conscious of it.

Howard: It may be partly motivating you, and that's not so bad. It's when you start to get a little inflated that you can get in trouble.

Audience: I was just realising that the north Node is starting to transit my MC. My natal north Node is in conjunction with Chiron in the 4th house, and a whole issue is coming up about whether I am going to change my career and actually move into astrology. I've cut my book jacket designing down to three hours a day, so I can just concentrate on astrology.

Howard: It is interesting how it is an Aquarian north Node over an Aquarian MC, which is associated with astrology.

Audience: It sounds like the transiting north Node is opposition the natal north Node.

Audience: Yes, I've got that coming up. It's a little while off.

Howard: We're going to come to the whole issue of the nodal cycle in a minute.

Audience: The issue is being brought up in the group because it is a 10th house issue!

Audience: I started my designing work with the transiting north Node going over my Ascendant. I am finishing the work now under a progressed Venus-Mercury conjunction with my natal Ascendant, and the transiting north Node is at my MC.

Howard: That's interesting. Starting it when the north Node was conjunct your Ascendant was like a birth. Then it would have gone backwards into the 12th. Now it has reached the MC and you are coming up to a nodal opposition – the transiting north Node is moving to oppose the natal north Node.

Transiting to natal Nodes: the nodal cycle

Now we are going to talk about aspects between the transiting Nodes and the natal Nodes. The nodal return is every eighteen and a half years. You get one when you are eighteen and a half, thirty-seven, fifty-five and three-quarters, and seventy-four and a half. Then the next one would be...Oh, God! I can't do the addition! Ninety-three and one-fifth?

Audience: Ninety-three. My Grandma's having a nodal return right now.

Howard: Thank you. Anyway, every eighteen and a half years you're going to get the transiting north Node conjunct your natal natal north Node. That is a nodal return. You'll attract into your life experiences which really highlight the nodal axis, and which will present you with choices regarding the reworking of your south Node and the further development of your north Node and the integration of the axis. It is the same old story. When the transiting north Node conjuncts your natal north Node, what pulls you forward conjuncts what pulls you forward. And when the transiting south Node conjuncts the natal south Node, the pull of the past pulls on the past. So with the nodal return, the pull of the past confronts the pull of the future. The issues become very marked.

Now we come to the nodal reversal. This is when the transiting north Node conjuncts the natal south Node, and the transiting south Node conjuncts the natal north Node. Are you ready? This happens at nine and one-quarter years, twenty-seven and three-quarters, forty-six and a half, and sixty-five. After that you can do your own addition. What could the transiting north Node conjunct your south Node mean?

Audience: You are very open for integration.

Howard: You always come back to the same theme, which is whatever theme the natal Nodes are about. If the transiting north Node is conjuncting your south Node, then there is a chance to reclaim some of the south Node abilities and perhaps update them or balance them with the opposite principle. And if the transiting south Node conjuncts your north Node, then what comes most naturally to you at that time will be the new thing you need to build in. You can choose to do that. When we talk about the one that happens at twenty-seven and three-quarters, we are getting near the time of the Saturn return.

Audience: And the progressed lunar return.

Audience: When I had the transiting north Node conjuncting my south Node, I applied for this course, in that same month. My south Node is in Aquarius.

Howard: That fits very well, doesn't it?

Progressed planets to the natal Nodes

Audience: Could you say something about progressed planets hitting the natal Nodes? It seems to me that would be really important, because it doesn't happen very often.

Howard: It is really important. The progressed Sun hitting your north Node is the most important. Even the progressed Moon hitting your north or south Node is important. The progressed Sun is always like a torch which shines on you. If you have the north Node in Cancer, and then you get the progressed Sun conjuncting that north Node, there are going to be many opportunities to open up your feelings or your nurturing abilities in new ways.

If you have the north Node in Capricorn and the progressed Sun comes along to make an aspect to it – any aspect, but particularly a conjunction – you are going to have lots of opportunities to progress in a Capricorn way, or to develop in terms of work, or to develop greater discipline or commitment. I think, with the north Node in Capricorn, there is the need to commit yourself to something. Have any of you had the progressed Sun conjuncting the north Node? Do you remember it? Do look if that happens. It won't happen to everyone. You have to have the Sun heading toward the Node from birth. If you are an Aries and you have the north Node in Taurus, you will get it. I would also consider the progressed Sun conjuncting the south Node as really important. What might that do?

Audience: It might give you an opportunity to see more clearly what it is that is trying to pull you back. It throws light on the past.

Howard: It will bring up old issues which are still not resolved. But it will also bring up talents and resources that are there in you but which need to be brought out further – talents which you already have, not necessarily new ones which need to be developed.

Audience: I have the progressed Moon conjunct my north Node in Leo, and I have been taking stock of what I am doing with my creative work. I keep feeling I need to go in a new direction.

Howard: That's a good example. I like transits and progressions to the north Node, in terms of making new discoveries and breakthroughs. Even if there is a crisis which precipitates it, you are more likely to get through the crisis if the transits or progressions to the north Node are encouraging a new awareness to come at that moment. It is a time of opening up to something new that will be a breakthrough for you.

Audience: Could it could be a call from outside, a meeting with someone who opens you up? I think sometimes transits to the Nodes come out through relationships.

Howard: Yes. You may meet someone who is a teacher or a mirror, or you may meet a situation which is a mirror. But you wouldn't get it outside unless it was ready to come up inside.

Audience: Progressions of the Nodes themselves presumably will also have an effect.

Howard: Yes. But I haven't worked with that at all.

Audience: They move very slowly.

Howard: They only move 3' minutes a day on average, so you are not going to get a whole lot of movement if you are doing nodal secondary progressions.

The Nodes in synastry

Planets on the south Node

Now I'll talk a bit about the Nodes in synastry, and then briefly look at a chart of someone here. Then I have an exercise for you around the themes of the Nodes. Let me give you the guidelines for synastry. Let's say another person's planet conjuncts your south Node. That's the first thing I want to look at. Let's say you have the south Node in 15° Scorpio and you meet someone with the Sun at 15° Scorpio or Venus at 15° Scorpio. If someone's Sun shines on your south Node, what is the interaction going to bring out in you? It may bring out your innate abilities. That's the nicest way of looking at it. It will reinforce your south Node tendencies.

Audience: Will a relationship like that make you complacent?

Howard: It depends on the sign. Let's say I have the south Node at 15° Scorpio and I have a tendency to create crises or be overly dramatic. If I meet someone with the Sun at 15° Scorpio, they'll probably encourage me. They'll egg me on to make a crisis, rather than helping me to calm down and be more practical. If I am in a relationship and thinking about breaking it all up, if I meet a friend with the Sun at 15° Scorpio and I ask their advice, they'll probably say, "Yes, you should break it up." Do you see what I'm saying? Where the other person is coming from resonates with my south Node in Scorpio. So it depends on the sign. I agree, very often there will be a feeling of ease. Very often, when someone's planets conjunct your south Node, there is great familiarity. Let's start with someone's Sun, Moon, Venus, Mercury, or Mars conjunct your south Node. The way they assert themselves, or what they believe in, or where they are coming from, is very familiar to you.

Audience: What orb would you allow?

Howard: I would give it up to 5° degrees.

Audience: I think that anybody with that sign emphasis, even if there isn't really a conjunction, would bring out your south Node.

Howard: Yes, I agree. That's why I was hesitating about giving an orb. Sometimes someone who is just strongly Scorpio can have that effect if you have the south Node in Scorpio. But it is more powerful if it's a conjunction. Let's think about it. If someone's Mercury is conjunct your south Node, you will instinctively relate to the way they think. If someone's Venus conjuncts your south Node, there is a very good chance that you are familiar with them in terms of relationship in the past. If someone's Mars conjuncts your south Node, there is probably a tendency to understand their assertion, their forcefulness, or maybe you have had battles before. If someone's Moon is conjunct your south Node, then you are going to be very familiar with how they feel and how they respond. Now, when we get to Saturn, it's a little different.

Audience: What about Jupiter?

Howard: Jupiter will egg the south Node on as well. They are a bit similar. Jupiter is where you are expansive, and the south Node is what comes naturally. The other person will be expansive in a way which is instinctive to you, so they will encourage you. I don't think it is a bad thing to have the south Node encouraged, because it makes you review it and examine it and see what you may need to call back into your life. The danger, when someone's planets conjunct your south

Node, is that you stay stuck in your south Node. They just keep reinforcing it. That might not be so good for you. What I have noticed, especially with the Sun or Ascendant conjunct the south Node in another person, is that the relationship often starts out very strong and promising, but it runs into difficulties after a while. It may let you down or disappoint you, because the other person is putting you back into your south Node energy too much, and you need to have a conflict.

Saturn is different. The south Node comes habitually, but Saturn is what is a bit blocked and hard to express. So you have ease or a tendency to go instinctively into areas where the Saturn person has trouble. The Saturn person may learn from the south Node person, because the south Node person has greater facility with that point in the zodiac where the Saturn person has restriction.

Audience: Might not the Saturn person encourage you to consider more seriously things that you have taken for granted?

Howard: Absolutely. That's a very good interpretation. The Saturn person makes you focus on yourself more. Good – you've got a sense of it. Someone's planets on your south Node give a familiarity which can be a very strong attraction, but you need to make sure that it is not reinforcing your south Node principle too much at the expense of the opposite principle.

Audience: I've seen a lot of south Node contacts in family charts.

Howard: It is one that often shows up in families. I would say that there is a tendency to bring out south Node issues – and maybe you have known each other before. Very often the children you attract, or the parents you attract, are people you've known before. That's why there will often be a lot of south Node connections.

Planets on the north Node

Now, let's say that someone's Sun is on your north Node. What would that do?

Audience: Encourage you to do well.

Howard: I would encourage a relationship with that person. You can learn from that person, even if it seems a bit difficult. It's because they are introducing something or tuning you in to something that has yet to be developed in yourself, that you are not that familiar with.

Audience: What about someone's Moon on your north Node?

Howard: What comes instinctively to the Moon person, you are going to need to make an effort or a choice to develop. They can help you with that, because you see them do it instinctively and it is an example for you.

Audience: A friend of mine has got the Moon conjunct the Sun, and they are both conjunct my north Node. She is a clairvoyant and has offered to help me with astrology by sending me clients. She gets a lot of clients who want astrological charts.

Howard: That's a good example, isn't it? Who she is will further your development. I've seen examples of north Node and Mercury synastry, where the Mercury person has helped the north Node person discover their talents and abilities and strengths. What I am saying is that someone's planet on your north Node is a very favourable indicator for relationships.

Audience: How about Pluto?

Howard: It's true even with the difficult planets. It is likely that someone with Pluto on your north Node will take you down into the underworld. They will put you through things that are hard, yet out of it you will hopefully emerge having strengthened your north Node energy and the house it is in. And that can't be a bad thing. Have you had that happen?

Audience: No, I'm the one with the Pluto.

Howard: Then you're putting the other person through it! They may not meet the challenge.

Audience: What kind of experience would I get from that? How would it reflect back on me? What would their north Node do to me?

Howard: Make you much more aware of your Pluto qualities, especially if you haven't been in touch with them. I always feel it is a two-way street, and it is not only for the person whose energy is shining on your north Node. It is not just the north Node which gets something out of it, but somehow what the north Node reflects back is going to strengthen that planet's principle in the other person.

Audience: In terms of the planet that is shining?

Howard: Exactly. I would read it as a two-way street. It is beneficial for both. It is not just one giving to another.

Audience: What about composite nodes? How do you read the Nodes in a composite chart?

Howard: I don't use them, but Liz does, and she gives lots of significance to them, and also to the transits and progressions to the composite Nodes. She'll be doing something on the composite chart in the next term.

Audience: What about someone's Saturn on your north Node?

Howard: It is similar to Pluto. Someone's Saturn will force you to examine your north Node. They may criticise you or they may judge you or they may teach you more about your north Node. One of the main points I want to emphasise is how often nodal contacts come up in synastry. Look at your important relationships. There is almost always going to be some north Node or south Node contact with the other person's planets or Ascendant. It's very common.

Audience: I have my north Node in Aquarius. I have had only four years of my life where I have not been living with an Aquarian. They keep on coming.

Howard: I'm quite happy with that combination. If you have your north Node in Taurus, it is good to be with a Taurean. If you have the north Node in Gemini, it is good to be with a Gemini. It doesn't have to be the Sun-sign of the other person. Someone can bring out the energy of your north Node through anything important in their chart. You can also get another person's planets trine or sextile your nodal axis, and that should help to further the integration of the axis within yourself. But you can get another person's planets squaring your nodal axis as well. These are things to look out for.

Planets in square to the Nodes

Audience: How would the square affect the synastry?

Howard: It's not easy, especially with someone's Saturn squaring your Nodes. It isn't even easy with someone's Sun squaring your Nodes. They are going to present you with situations which highlight the conflicting pull of the axis. It's going to be either a breakthrough or a breakdown – which then hopefully could lead to a breakthrough. We don't have the time – and I don't have the energy – to go into all the different synastry combinations. I just wanted to alert you to these things. Sometimes these are not things that we necessarily notice. Some of us don't pay that much attention to the Nodes, and I am hoping that this seminar will encourage you to pay more attention – because you are going to get more meat for interpreting through paying attention to them.

Nodes aspecting Nodes

You may meet someone with whom you have a reversed nodal connection. If you have the north Node in 3° Gemini you may meet someone with the south Node in 3° Gemini. There is going to be an age gap of nine years and three months between you, or twenty-seven years and nine months, which could be a parental link. Or there might be a gap of forty-six years, which could be a parent or a grandparent, or a gap of sixty-four and a half years, which could also be a grandparent. If my south Node is on your north Node, then what comes instinctively to me is what you need to develop, and the same applies the other way. If my south Node is on your north Node, then obviously my north Node will be on your south Node.

Audience: That sounds very productive.

Howard: I think it *is* very productive. Even when there is a big age gap, both people are learning from each other. An older person can learn a lot from a younger person, as well as a younger from an older.

Audience: It could be that the houses are reversed but the signs are the same. I'm thinking of an example of someone with the north Node in Gemini in the 1st and the other person with the north Node in Gemini in the 7th.

Howard: I was talking specifically about signs.

Audience: So it wouldn't work in quite the same way with reversed houses?

Howard: If I have the south Node in the 3rd and you have the north Node there, you could probably learn from my instinctive abilities.

Audience: Because you would have the same approach due to the same sign polarity?

Howard: The same house polarity, even if they are in different signs. But it's not so strong.

Audience: Wouldn't there be some conflict with someone's south Node on your north Node?

Howard: Sometimes that happens. What comes easily to you is what comes with difficulty to another person because they have to work at it, and what comes easily to them is what comes with difficulty to you. There can be envy in both people. But hopefully you can get beyond that and see that you have something to teach each other. Those are all the general guidelines. Let's take five or ten minutes to look at a chart from the group. It's interesting in terms of the Nodes. Laura, can I let you speak for yourself, with Mercury conjunct your south Node? Explain to us how you understand it. Do listen, everyone, because Laura has a lot of insight into her chart.

An example chart: Laura

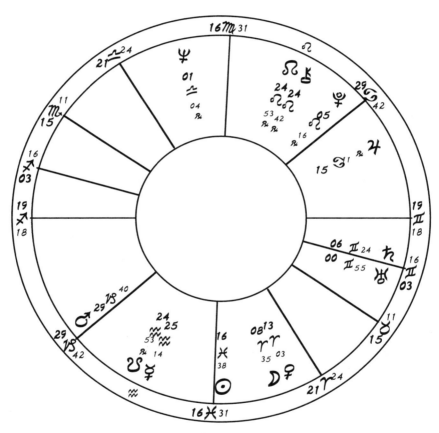

Laura
8 March 1943, 3.20 am BST, Brighton
Placidus cusps

Laura: What really always comes over to me is that, as you rightly put it, the Nodes are the key to one's life, and for me that's communication problems. At first it doesn't look as if I've got a problem because of the Sun-Jupiter trine from the 3rd to the 7th, but in fact I have always had a problem communicating, especially with men, and with my father. I even used to dream about phones – I would try ringing and couldn't get through to him. I'm always dreaming about travel, too. Another thing is that there was always a thing about the group. As a child I was very lonely, but as I grew older I wanted to join groups, which I finally did at thirty-seven – a spiritual group. I always thought that I shouldn't just serve my individuality, and I thought I ought to be a real groupie.

Howard: So when the transiting south Node came back to conjunct your south Node in Aquarius, you joined a group.

Laura: Yes. And rather than thinking that I should shine as an individual, I thought that was being very egotistic. I should shut up and stay in the group and blend into the background.

Howard: It brought out the polarity with the north Node in Leo.

Laura: I kept trying to subdue my desire to shine in my own way and interrupt people and bring out this Leo thing. I kept thinking, "It's wrong." When I came to see you, you said to me, "No, you've got to be an individual and be disruptive." It was very releasing.

Howard: I created a Frankenstein's monster.

Laura: In fact I can now dare to speak up and feel all right about it. The odd thing is, I no longer feel the need to do that. I can't explain what that means, exactly, but having recognised the need to be an individual and have an original voice and say my bit, it has dissolved something, and I can shut up now.

Howard: Let's talk about that. The north Node is conjunct Chiron in Leo in the 8th. It's a close conjunction – it's in the same degree. If you are born with the north Node conjunct Chiron, what is that telling you?

Audience: You can heal yourself by going into your north Node.

Howard: That's one part of it. It is where you have wounds. What else is it telling you? What do you need to develop?

Audience: Your healing ability for others.

Howard: But in Laura's case it is healing from a Leo place, and not from an Aquarian place. Can I come in here? I think, with Mercury conjunct the south Node in Aquarius, there may be an automatic assumption that if you could just tell someone the truth or enlighten them with your mind, they'll get better. But it's not just to do with your mind – you have to do it with your heart and your feelings.

Laura: Exactly. That was the problem. I was always coming from a cerebral place, and being split off from my feelings. So people wouldn't listen, because of course I was just talking from somewhere else. It wasn't really felt.

Howard: I know a little bit about Laura. May I reveal things?

Laura: Yes.

Howard: How can we do this quickly? I think it has to do with two things in Laura's life. One is about father issues. What happened was that your father had a mental breakdown. Now, how old were you?

Laura: About ten.

Howard: You can see that in the chart if you take the 4th house to be father. Mars rules the 4th because Aries is at the IC, and there is a Mars-Pluto opposition. That's one indication of it. What I deduced from that was that you grew up thinking, "If I can just know things, if I can understand things, then I don't have to go crazy." Was it something like that?

Laura: Yes, I had a great fear of chaos and insanity.

Howard: So knowledge became a way of having control or power, or a way of avoiding insanity. That is borne out by the south Node conjunct Mercury. It is about wanting to go back to understand and create order.

Audience: And with Mercury in her 2nd house, it would be her most valued possession.

Laura: That's true. Writing, books, all things to do with knowledge, are valued possessions.

Howard: The other thing is that Laura's mother is Greek and didn't know English very well, and Laura had to speak for her.

Laura: That's true.

Howard: You immediately got a way of winning love through your Mercury, and Mercury was also a way of having control over things. I think this is repeated by the Uranus-Saturn conjunction in Gemini on the cusp of the 6th. It is a lot about the mind, especially with the Sun in the 3rd. But then we shift to the north Node in Leo conjunct Chiron. This is what you communicate from the heart, or what you can share from difficult things you have been through. Leo is what you have learned from your personal experience, rather than what you have read in books.

Laura: That's something that I have recently learned – there's really no point in imitating other people's ability to communicate. I always thought that everyone else could do it better than I could. I always felt that someone else had written it better. But that feeling has suddenly gone. There is an ability to synthesise things and put them out in my own way. That's been the real breakthrough.

Howard: You'll be more effective that way. You have that nice Jupiter trine to your Sun helping you. I don't know if I was clear before – too much living in the head, or thinking that ideas and knowledge will give you the answer, isn't going to get you that far, because it is the south Node. But what you have gone through in terms of your personal experience, and speaking from your own centre, will really get you there.

Audience: The north Node is in the 8th house as well – something to do with being transformed by the darker side of life. You can't really do that if you're up in your head.

Howard: Yes. The ruler of the south Node is Uranus and it is in Gemini, so you are getting a repeating theme – you have the south Node conjunct Mercury and the ruler of the south Node in Gemini. You are getting a repeat statement about knowledge being used a certain way in the past, but you can't continue to use it that way now.

Laura: It also has to do with owning my own sort of creativity, instead of feeling that others are better.

Howard: Saturn conjuncts the ruler of the south Node. It's judgemental. It's interesting to me that the north Node is ruled by the Sun in the 3rd house, in Pisces and trine Jupiter in Cancer. It is what comes from your heart, from your feelings.

Audience: There's also Neptune in the 9th.

Howard: I have mixed feelings about Neptune in the 9th. I think it gives Laura a very good channel to spiritual things, but I also think it supports the idea that if she could just find the answers, everything would be all right. It makes philosophy and religion the gates to heaven. Wherever Neptune is, that's where we are looking for that lost paradise, where we are hopeful that we will be redeemed. Transiting Pluto is moving into Laura's 11th house now. Are you still involved with the group?

Laura: Well, yes. I took this whole thing of being individual to the point where I felt like leaving the group, but strangely, that feeling dissolved. Having made a stand and said what I had to say, it seemed to alter everything.

Howard: That's the north Node. You stood up with your Leo.

Laura: It just dissolved everything, and then the anger went, and it didn't seem as if I needed to leave the group.

Audience: Do you think the same issue could come up again in about two years, when Pluto forms a square to the Nodes?

Howard: Yes. I am curious to see what happens when Pluto squares your Nodes.

Laura: Well, it doesn't worry me now. Before, I felt that if I left the group I would die. Now I can just take it or leave it.

Audience: Do you think self-confidence has come with Uranus and Neptune moving through the 1st house?

Howard: Yes, definitely.

Laura: I also remember what you said about children and love affairs with the north Node in Leo. That certainly helped me to develop the north Node and be more confident.

Audience: I wouldn't have thought that being a member of a group was as important to Laura as her sense of spirituality.

Laura: But I do feel a need for the group.

Howard: I think the group has been a path towards finding yourself. It is a case where the south Node has been doing the leading, but it has led you to the north Node.

A guided imagery exercise

Now I'd like to do a short exercise with you, as a way of ending. Before we start the exercise, you have to do a little thinking for a few minutes. I want you to think of a quality belonging to your north Node, by sign or house, that would be worthwhile for you to develop. For example, if you have the north Node in Taurus, you might want more stability, or want to be more in touch with your body. If you have the north Node in Sagittarius, you might need to travel or have more faith. I am asking you to think of a quality which could be helpful in realising yourself more fully. Try to use the north Node as your guideline. Do you need to be more assertive, to be more balanced? Do you need to be more feeling? Do you need to be more disciplined? Just pick out one quality, because we are going to do an exercise to help develop that quality. This is a north Node exercise. All right, has everyone found a quality? Are you all absolutely focused?

Now, close your eyes and take a number of deep breaths, and just relax. Let your shoulders drop. Let your feet relax, and your legs relax. Wherever you are holding on, just let go. I would like you to imagine yourself as already having the quality that you would like to develop. You have it in a very high degree of purity, a very high degree of intensity. Just see yourself with that quality already there. What do you look like with that quality? What's in your face? How do you walk? How do you stand? You are seeing yourself with that quality. Now I would like you to merge with that image. Just walk right into that image, just merge with it and feel that quality as part of yourself. Feel your body pervaded by it, and most important, feel that quality penetrating every one of your cells. Every one of the cells in your body possesses that quality. You are letting this quality fill your whole body and flood though your veins. Now I want you to imagine a situation in your everyday life, your current life, where you are expressing this quality. Feel this quality which is in all your cells now and flowing through you, and see yourself in some situation in your everyday life where you are coming from this place that you have chosen to develop. Then choose another situation in which you can express this quality that you would like to have. Really feel with your whole body that you are pervaded by and emanating that quality. See the situation in lots of detail. Now take another half a minute, and gradually take time to come out and open your eyes.

You can see what we are trying to do here. Developing the north Node often takes some choice and some will. If the time is right, you can really help it along by doing a meditation like this – where you imagine every cell in your body permeated with that quality. If you take a minute to do this every day or every few days, it is as if you are alerting yourself to that quality, and it helps to build it in. If you can imagine yourself with it, walking with it and radiating it, you are going to do a lot toward manifesting it, because our cells contain all sorts of possibilities and we are just alerting them to what we want to happen. Hopefully, what you want to become is aligned to your north Node and is ready to be developed.

All right. I want to thank you and Tracy Marks and Martin Shulman. So, thank you all.

Part Three: The Astrology of the Helper

This seminar was given on 15 December, 1991 at Regents College, London as part of the Autumn Term of the seminar programme of the Centre for Psychological Astrology.

Putting Neptune under Saturn's microscope

Two years ago I gave a lecture at the Faculty of Astrological Studies Diploma Awards Ceremony – that was in October 1989 – and I called the lecture, "Help me, I'm a Helper!" When the Faculty asked me to do that lecture in October 1989, they probably asked me about seven or eight months in advance. I had to think of a title for the lecture, and I looked in the ephemeris to see what would be happening around the time I would be lecturing. It was the final transit of Saturn conjuncting Neptune in the heavens. If you think back to 1989 and what kind of year it was, you will remember that while the Saturn-Neptune aspect was going on, walls were crumbling everywhere. Then I thought about this occasion where people were getting their Faculty Certificates and Diplomas, and they were about to embark on doing astrology, some of them professionally, some of them just to know more about it.

I thought about Saturn-Neptune, and Neptune is the planet I most associate with service. There are other things in a birth chart which have to do with service, but I associate Neptune with the desire to rescue, to heal, to save, to help others. And transiting Saturn was on it. This inspired an idea in me that maybe I could do a lecture that looked at the motives or reasons for helping. Why do we help? I wanted to put Neptune's urge to help under the microscope of Saturn and examine all the different reasons and motives that might go into our urge to rescue and care for people, to help people, to be there for others when they are in need. I was doing a Saturn number on Neptune, which simply means examining Neptune more thoroughly. Then I gave this talk a few times and decided to expand it into a one-day seminar, and I devised some exercises for you to do around this theme. It will be more of a workshop in the afternoon, because you will be looking into yourselves to get clear about some of the motives that might go into the urge to be an astrologer.

Some of you may be working in fields like alternative medicine, or you may be nurses or doctors. Are there any doctors here? As an astrologer you are a professional helper – you put yourself in a position to give guidance. But even if you are not a professional helper, you may be the kind of person who always seems to be going out of their way to do things for people, or you may always attract people who need help. People who are in crisis invariably end up sitting next to you in the bus or standing behind you in a queue, or they just sniff something in you and gravitate towards you – they know you are someone who will be caring and will do what you can.

Namaste

That's really what I am going to be doing today – asking you, and myself, "Why do we do it? What motivates us to help other people?" I want to start by talking a little bit more about Neptune, which to me is associated with the idea of feeling other people's pain, caring for others, wanting to make things better for other people. There is a Sanskrit word, *namaste*. It is a kind of spiritual greeting, a spiritual hello or goodbye, which you will find in various traditions. Someone will say, "*Namaste!*" to you. What it means, loosely translated, is, "I honour that place in you which means that, when you are in that place and I am in the corresponding place in me, there is only one of us." I will repeat that, as you might not have got it at first. "I honour that place in you which means that, when you are in that place and I am in the corresponding place in me, we feel our unity with one another." It is a way of saluting the divine in all of us.

You know my views on this. I think that the deepest level of the psyche is unboundedness – the infinite, where everything is interconnected. There is no such thing as a separate thing in the universe. Everything is related, everything is affecting everything else. You might know the work going on in particle physics – read Fritjof Kapra's book, *The Tao of Physics*.[13] Or read any of the scientists who are writing about the relationship between mystical thinking – what is known as the perennial philosophy, a term used by

---

[13]Fritjof Kapra, *The Tao of Physics*, Shambhala Publications, 1991.

Huxley – and modern scientific discovery. You will see that the mystics and the scientists are saying a lot of similar things. When they developed equipment that was good enough to find the subatomic particles that make us up, they realised that these particles couldn't be located in time and space. They were like a wave. They were everywhere. These are the things that make us up. Whitehead called it the "seamless coat of the universe". Independent parts have no real status in the universe when seen from the viewpoint of mysticism or particle physics. Some new people have just come in. What happened to you? Did you get lost?

Audience: Yes.

Howard: I was just talking about Neptune, which must be strong in all your charts if you got lost. You might remember that, at the Neptune seminar, I put a quote on the board by a German Dominican monk called Henry Suso. He said, "All creatures are the same life, the same essence, the same power and the same one, and nothing less." You might have had experiences – sometimes we call them peak experiences or transcendental experiences – where you actually felt your connectedness, your oneness, instead of seeing the differences between you and the world and other people. You might have actually felt that you shared a common humanity – you felt that unity with everything.

Then there is the humanistic psychologist, Carl Rogers. This is from his book, *On Becoming a Person*.[14] Carl Rogers said that the more deeply you look into yourself, the more you discover the whole human race. I really firmly believe that. The more you look at what is inside you and discover what is going on there, the more you discover universal things that all of us have and are going through. It means getting to that level which is beyond the physical, and even beyond the psychological – it is a deeper level. To me, these kinds of statements, these kinds of things, really reflect the essence of Neptune. I didn't have time earlier to write this quote on the board. It is a quote by Einstein, who was a Pisces. Let me read it to you.

A human being is part of the whole, called by us universe, a part limited in time and space. He experiences himself as thoughts and feelings, as

---

[14]Carl Rogers, *On Becoming a Person,* Houghton Miflin, 1995.

something separated from the rest, a kind of optical delusion of consciousness.

What Einstein is saying is that our sense of separateness is a delusion – what the Hindus would call *maya* – and our path must be to free ourselves from this prison by widening our circle of compassion to embrace all living creatures and the whole of nature in its beauty. This is a scientist saying something which is really a very mystical idea.

Neptune and unity

Neptune is that bit of us which doesn't want to be separate, that bit of us which wants to transcend our sense of separate self and merge with something greater beyond ourselves. When I say, "Neptune is that bit of us which doesn't want to be separate," I am just generalising it and giving it a name. You can do that with different planets. Pluto is that bit of you which wants to die and be reborn. Mars is that bit of you which wants to assert your autonomy and individuality. A lot of you have heard me talk about this before. Alan Watts spoke of the "skin-encapsulated ego", the "me in here versus you out there" reality. This is really what is inculcated into us as we grow up. Our parents teach us to see ourselves as separate. Also, our language does it as well. We have pronoun, noun, and verb structures – "I throw the ball!" I do something to the ball, rather than being the ball at the same time that I throw it.

Now, I am harping on this because I want to begin by acknowledging that place in you and me which is universal and unbounded. That place is where we share with one another and the rest of existence. I believe that this place where we feel our connectedness to everything is actually the original source of all our empathy and compassion for other people. Somewhere we know we are one. On some level we feel it – the sense of unity that we have with the rest of life is probably the true source of the desire to heal and look after others. One way of looking at it is this: If I feel my oneness with you, then if you are suffering, I am suffering as well. I am in pain too. This is on the level of the heart. If I open my heart and see you suffering, and I am aware of our common humanity, then I will feel pain as well.

There may be another part of us which is witnessing that suffering and saying, "Maybe what is happening is right. There is a need for that experience. There is a bigger reason for it in terms of some larger unfoldment of humanity, of the collective, of the planet. It is not wrong that it is happening." But from the level of the heart you are still going to suffer if someone else is suffering. If that sense of the unity of life is a living reality in you, and not just an intellectual concept that you read somewhere and thought sounded true – if it is something that you really feel, that you have really glimpsed – then if anybody is in pain, if people are starving in Africa, if they are in trouble anywhere, we feel it. We share it on some level. I think that in its purest form, helping or performing service for others is a way of tasting the unity of life, a way of enlivening our sense of oneness.

Somewhere deep inside us, we intuit, or we remember, or we know, that our deepest level is unbounded. Now, you have also heard me say that we don't always live on that level. I call it the Neptunian level because there are no boundaries, there is no separateness. The skin is our most common boundary – what is inside the skin is me and what's outside the skin is not me. Neptune transcends the skin boundary, so what's outside the skin is also me.

I am stealing this bit from Ram Dass, who is a New Age philosopher and mystic. He said that life is a bit like television. You can view it on different channels, just as you can watch the news and then change the channel to watch sport or a soap opera. Each channel gives you a different perspective or a different angle on life. You might call Channel One the Oneness and Universality Channel – that place where we see what we share rather than how we are different, and where we feel our unity with all life. We are not always on Channel One. Well, maybe you are, but my set doesn't get it all the time. Then there is Channel Two, which I would call the Separateness and Individuality Channel, where we are aware of our differentness. That is what we see – "I'm a man, you're a woman. I've got one kind of body, you've got another. I have my nose, you have your nose. I have my thoughts, you have your thoughts." That's also true about life, on another level. It depends on what perspective you tune in to. I think that, if you were permanently tuned to Channel One, you probably wouldn't even be here in the body, and certainly not on the seminar today. There is something they call a Bodhisatva, which means an enlightened person. Bodhisatvas are permanently tuned to Channel

One. This idea of feeling your universality and the oneness of life is the idea of being enlightened. According to certain traditions, there are people who are enlightened but who actually chose to come back to do service for others and help the world in some way. That is what is meant by a Bodhisatva. Are there are any Bodhisatvas in the audience?

The motives of the helper

What I want to do is, as I said, a kind of Saturn number on this, and look more closely at serving – which in its purest form comes from this place where we feel our unity. But it gets mixed up with other things. There are more personal motivations. We can often have hidden agendas around why we serve. I am not putting down the fact that there may be personal motives, or that the ego is getting something out of it. But I think we should try to become aware, as much as possible, of what some of our hidden agendas are. If we have a hidden agenda, or we are getting some perk, or we are building up our ego, or we are helping others to get love or to get power over people, or we are helping because we feel we are a bad person and we had better do good things to make up for it, then it becomes very important to know what's going on.

With a hidden agenda the role of being a helper can become almost more important than anything else, because if we are not helping, then we are not satisfying that particular perk. We put a lot more investment into helping other people get better, because if they don't get better then we are not helping, and then we are not getting what our egos wanted to get from it. Having a lot of investment in trying to make someone better means you will get angry and upset if they don't, and you will push too hard. Then you end up with burn-out, or other things which we will be talking about later.

I think it is pretty clear that, if you are the kind of person who likes to be strong for others, or who wants to care for or heal or soothe other people, a lot of it will stem from that place of *namaste* where you sense your unity. But it is also going to be mixed up with some personal and very egocentric motives. I don't think anything is 100% altruistic. There will be something you will be getting from it which your ego is grabbing. This is what I want to investigate – possible sources of the more personal motives for helping.

Hidden agendas

What I am going to do – and we are going to relate this to the chart later – is start by making a list of different hidden agendas, different personal motivations. We will talk about each one on the list. Some of these may click with you – they may apply. Others you may not resonate with, or you may think don't apply to you. I am asking you to listen to the different types of hidden agendas that we will be discussing and looking at, and even if you don't think a particular one applies to you, or you can't connect to it, I would let it slosh around on the unconscious level for a while. Just keep it in your mind, and you may discover a week later, or a month later, or even a year later, that you get this "Aha!" kind of feeling – yes, it does apply, even though you didn't think so immediately. A lot of the motives on the list are from very early in life. Some of our more personal agendas for helping come from a preverbal stage. We don't really readily remember things which are preverbal, which are on the level of the unconscious and which come from a time when we are only a year or two old.

Mother and caretaking

To begin looking at some of the hidden motives, I have to do something which I do in almost every single lecture or seminar I give. You could all probably do it for me. I'm going to go back to mother, my favourite topic. A lot of our personal motivation for helping will stem from mother, because that is our first caretaking experience. What gets set up between you and mother is already a picture of what caring and caretaking are like. That makes an impression on us which will influence any time later in life when we care for other people. Those later times will resonate to some degree with what the original caretaking was like, because early things cut very deeply. We form impressions about life, about ourselves, and about what the world is like, based on what passes between mother and ourselves when we are children. This may stay with us until adulthood, and it can get involved with issues to do with caretaking or helping others.

Now, I know that you know my rap on this – human beings are born unfinished. More than any other species of animal, we have to stay with the mother or a caretaker for a very long time. Liz was recently giving me a comparison on this very topic. She said that a baby crocodile is born with a full set of teeth that it can bite with. When a crocodile comes out of its egg it already has teeth, it has a fairly coordinated body that can move and walk, and it has an innate aggressive instinct which means it can fight off predators and go for food. But what are we like when we are born? We are toothless, we are totally uncoordinated. I can't think of that quote from Shakespeare which talks about our puking and spewing.

Audience: It's actually mewling and puking. Do you want the whole quote?

Howard: Yes, let's hear it.

Audience: It's from *As You Like It*.

> All the world's a stage,
> And all the men and women merely players:
> They have their exits and their entrances;
> And one man in his time plays many parts,
> His acts being seven ages. At first the infant,
> Mewling and puking in the nurse's arms.

Howard: Funnily enough, it's also the reverse. In our total dependency in early childhood we are almost omnipotent, because we get everyone to do things for us. We can't feed ourselves, so if there isn't anyone there to look after us, we are going to die. This is absolutely true – we are all born helpless. We are all born potential victims. I want you to note that, because it means that somewhere buried in us is a sense of being a helpless person. Somewhere deep inside there is a memory or an imprint of the time when we were totally helpless, mewling and puking. Now, because of this, we have an incredible physiological and psychological need for caretaking. The face of mother, or a mother-substitute – whoever does it – is our first mirror. If she is smiling and looking lovingly at us, then we feel we are lovable. If she is scowling or she is angry or she is seething, then we think we are bad. We don't feel right. Her body is our first information system. If she is happy, then the world is a good, safe place. If she is not happy, the world is a dangerous place, because if she is not happy, if she is not well, she may die, and then we are going to be abandoned and we will die.

I can't emphasise this enough. One thing I am fairly sure of is that mother is the whole world to us in the beginning. You may not remember that, but you never forget it! What passes between mother and ourselves does contribute or reflect or give flesh to what we expect will pass between ourselves and the world later on. Ericson talked about basic trust versus mistrust, which we learn about in our first two years of life. If mother is a good enough mother (she doesn't have to be perfect), we develop a basic trust in life. But if she is not there in the way we need, then we can develop a certain mistrust. We don't feel life is on our side, and that starts a whole series of troubles later on, because if you don't believe that life is on your side, if you don't have trust, then it is going to affect all your relationships and how you deal with the world. It is like the base of a pyramid, which affects everything built on the top later.

The separation of the ego

So there we are with mother. When I am talking about mother, I always think about the Moon. When we are talking about what passed between you and mother, you can also think about whatever house you assign to the mother, whether that is the 4th or the 10th, depending on how you see it. According to the latest psychological thought in terms of bringing up a child, it seems that it is most advantageous for a newborn child if mother does all she can to adjust, accommodate, and centre herself around the child for the first year of life. This wasn't always advised. Back in the 1950's we had Dr. Benjamin Spock in America, and earlier, Truby King had quite a different philosophy or approach to how you were supposed to mother or handle the "neonate", the newborn child. Their approach was, "Make the child adjust to you. Make the child feed on a schedule, rather than giving food when the child wants to be fed. Don't go and pick the child up if he or she is screaming."

A lot of us who were brought up in the 1950's might have had parents who followed this kind of advice. The reason why this more recent idea has come along – that it is better or more advantageous for the mother to adjust herself to the child – is that we need time to adjust to being a separate entity. In the womb we think we are mother, and mother is the whole world, so we think we are the whole world. When we have our physical birth, we take on a body – being born means taking on a body, and it heralds our heroic journey to develop an independent and autonomous self. But it doesn't happen right away. It takes four to seven months before we have a total psychological birth and we actually realise our separateness from mother. Before that we think she is an extension of us – we are merged with the Great Mother. At around six months we begin to see that mother is not us.

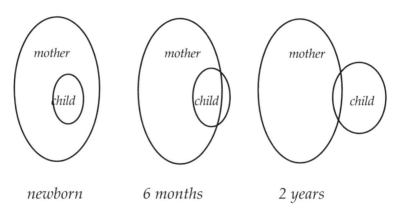

newborn   6 months   2 years

The big egg represents mother. Right at the beginning, our whole sense of identity is enmeshed, it is contained – who we are is contained within her. It is a strange thing. When we are hungry now, we know that the food comes from outside. But we have to get into the infant's way of seeing the world. To the infant, the source of the hunger, which is obviously something from within, and the source of relief, the milk given from without, actually seem to come from the same place. It is all from within the baby. So the baby thinks he or she is everything. The baby cannot differentiate the fact that there is a source from inside, an anxiety due to hunger, and a relief which comes from outside. It's a ouroboric sense that we are everything. By about six months we start getting that little egg out of the big egg, so we have the beginning of an "I" which is separate from mother, no longer enmeshed in her. It can take two or three years to realise our separateness from mother, and perhaps some people never do it. What we are really doing is moving out of the Moon and toward the Sun when we do that. We are moving toward an ego.

It is quite interesting, because what transit do we all get at around six months old, when we first start to realise that we are separate from mother? Think about what transit we all have. We have transiting Sun opposite our natal Sun. I think that is a very apt description of this differentiation stage, because you have two egos – the baby's and the mother's. The Sun represents the "I". The first time you have an opposition is the first time you have an "I" opposing mother. I mean ego as a sense of yourself as a separate entity. You are ego-less at birth. You don't have an ego because you are not aware of yourself being separate. But once you get out, you can start relating to mother, and she becomes a specific and circumstantial mother, a mother with a name rather than just the Great Mother who is everything.

Now, the idea is that you really can't get enough love in the first year of life – there is never too much. There is no child in the first year of life that can be loved too much. To feel the sense that others are there to help us, others are centring around us, others love us so much, gives us self-love. It really makes us feel like someone special. It gives us a sense that we are lovable. I always believe that self-love is the most important love. Without it, it is tricky feeling that other people can love you. When you are looking at relationship things in the chart, the tendency, naturally, is to go to Venus or the 7th house to get a sense of what someone is like or what they will need in relationship. But I would look at the Moon as a relationship significator, because the placement of the Moon and the aspects to the Moon describe what passed between you and mother, what you met through mother. Mother is the first big romance in your life.

It may be hard to believe, but at that stage when we start to separate out, to differentiate at around six months, we tend to get a little scared. You see, when we thought mother was everything, if we needed something, she knew it. If we were hungry, she knew it. But when we become separate, we are not always sure she will be able to read us correctly. Ken Wilbur once said, "Where there is other, there is fear." As soon as you get separateness, you are into fear, you are into the possibility of death, you are into time. It is a very Saturnian thing. What happens is that you move from a Neptunian and lunar state, where you felt merged, into a more Saturnian state of being a separate person. And therefore you get afraid. You get fear around separateness. This is what is called separation anxiety, but ultimately you need to go through it in order to find out who you are in your own right. You need to separate in order to get to your Sun, which is your individuality.

There is a point I am trying to get to here. The person you could read on this is a Swiss psychoanalyst called Alice Miller. Liz will have talked about her quite a bit. Alice Miller writes about these issues in her first book, which is called *The Drama of the Gifted Child*.[15] She says that sometimes, rather than mother adjusting to us and being there as we need her, the reverse happens. We find ourselves in this tiny neonate state, actually having to adjust ourselves to mother, to be what she needs, to comply with her needs, rather than the other way around. There are various reasons why this may happen. Mother is ill, or she is ailing, or she just has a very shaky identity and she is not a very strong person. Or she has a lot of instability, or she didn't have good mothering herself and she doesn't have a certain psychological maturity. And then we start to worry about her.

If she doesn't seem happy, or if she seems frustrated in some way, we start to think, "What can I do to make her better? What can I do to help her? What will happen if I don't help her and she doesn't get better? She might die, or she might go away, and if she dies or goes away, that means abandonment, and I'll die." I hope you're following my thread here. If we don't have a mother who is able to centre herself adequately around our needs, or who seems miserable or frustrated for some reason, we have these antennae that we develop. "If I am this way, it makes her happy, and she needs me to be this way in order for her to be all right." We develop what some people call an "as if" self, a false self.

This means only letting out those bits of ourselves which we know mother likes, and not letting out the bits which we feel she doesn't like in us, or which make us feel that we are doing something shameful or dirty. Ideally, as children, we need to feel that we are

---

[15] Alice Miller, *The Drama of the Gifted Child*, Basic Books, 1994.

loved for all of ourselves, for everything in ourselves. But invariably there will be times when we do certain things that might not be pleasant in the mother's mind, when we mess ourselves or whatever. Then we can get a sense that some of me is okay but some of me is bad. Some of me is shameful.

The reason I am talking about this is because I firmly believe the inner child of the past is still alive in us right now. No matter how mature and clever and sophisticated we become, we all have an inner child in us. What I am trying to talk about is some of the issues that the inner child may be carrying around. Whatever the inner child in you feels is felt very intensely, because as a child our life depends on our mother. As babies we can't think, "Oh, mother is frustrated, so she can't look after me. Maybe it's because I was a bad mother in a previous lifetime." We can't be rational about it. As a child we don't have the equipment to be rational about it. If mother doesn't come when we need her, first of all we think, "What's wrong with me? I must be bad!" That's called introjecting the bad mother – you identify with the bad mother. You are not equipped to understand it from a cerebral place. Later on you can look back and say, "Well, she didn't have very good mothering," or "This or that was going on in her life." But as a child that kind of thinking just isn't possible. You don't have that part of the brain developed until you are a bit older.

Moon-Saturn and Moon-Neptune: mothering mother

Mother being happy, mother being well, is equated with our survival. I tend to see problems with Moon-Neptune and Moon-Saturn aspects, especially the tricky ones – squares, oppositions, inconjuncts, any of the hard angles – but even sometimes with trines and sextiles, and usually always with conjunctions. Moon-Saturn and Moon-Neptune are the two aspects which often describe an experience of having to learn to be what mother needed, rather than mother adjusting to us. In a sense we almost became the mother to our own mother.

I find it interesting. I know a number of people who have that aspect of Moon-Saturn or Moon-Neptune, especially Moon-Neptune, who have ended up late in life having to be a mother to their mother. It happens so much – people with Moon-Neptune end up having to look after their own mother later on. I think there might have been some of this going on in the first year of life, where we had to adjust to her, we had to adapt to her. We figured out what she liked and we tried to become it in order to keep her alive. We wanted to make her happy and well because our survival depended on it. What I am saying is that all this could become part of your personal mythology, part of your deeper assumptions about life. It may be that, if you had to help mother, if you had to be the one who looked after her, if you had to be whatever would make her better, that sets up a pattern later in life. The inner child in you has a compulsion or need to help people who are suffering, to help people who are in pain. The inner child in you is still equating that person or that situation which needs help with the mother that you needed to save back in childhood.

Let me slow down a bit. As a child it is a very appropriate defence mechanism to try to make mother happy, because we need to survive. But the problem with a lot of these appropriate defence mechanisms is that they become obsolete, and we still use them. As adults we don't need other people to survive, but the child in us may still believe that and may still be trying to please people or help people. We want them to like us, we want to keep them well, because the child in us is thinking that if we don't, if they die, it is like mother dying, and then we'll die, we'll be abandoned.

Audience: I was thinking about survival issues, and all the Kleinian stuff about children's destructiveness and envy, which would surely be Pluto issues.

Howard: Yes, I think you get it with Moon-Pluto as well, although I don't know how often the Moon-Pluto person turns out to be a helper later in life like Moon-Neptune does. For some reason they deal with it a little differently. The Moon-Pluto type and the Moon-Saturn type may become very cautious and reserved and wary of everything. But Moon-Neptune tends to think, "If I don't help, if I don't try to make it better, then I might die," because Moon-Neptune is still equating helping other people with the mother.

What is Neptune? Neptune has a lot to do with having to make sacrifices and having to give something up. If you have a Moon-Neptune aspect, it means that, right from birth, you are having to make sacrifices or adjustments around mother. So you don't get the kind of mothering you need. You end up having to adjust to her, as I was saying. Then what happens? This is the odd thing – a lot of people turn things around and try to be the ideal mother they didn't have – but for other people instead of themselves. It is an unconscious thing. You may not grasp it right away when you think about it. We try to become for others what we are really looking for ourselves – the ideal mother or carer whom we didn't have. One personal motive for caretaking or helping may be that we are unconsciously trying to be the ideal parent that we didn't get.

Audience: It doesn't always work.

Howard: No, it doesn't, because there is an investment in it. As soon as you get an investment in something, a hidden agenda, you are going to get in the way of it in some way, or people will sniff something not right about it.

Audience: There seems to be a choice between being the ideal mother and being very vulnerable, perhaps even abandoned.

Howard: You can do it both ways with Neptune. You could be the victim or you could be the saviour. It can go either way. In a way, even if you are being a saviour, you are coming from a victimised place, a place which thinks, "I've got to do this for others because no one is going to do it for me."

Moon-Saturn does that as well. It develops a false autonomy, a false strength on the surface. It says, "I'm not vulnerable." The reason it does that is usually because Moon-Saturn has such frustration trying to get its needs fulfilled in childhood that the person more or less decides that it is better to stop admitting they need things. "I'll be the strong one, I'll be the one who is self-reliant." That is not true autonomy. True autonomy develops when you have been loved enough, and then something natural in you says, "Well, it is time for me to separate and start to become more autonomous." But if you are thrown into autonomy too soon, if you are thrown into having to recognise your separateness too soon, there is a desperation about it. "I have got to be strong and I have got to be self-reliant, because if I am not, I'm going to die. No one is going to be strong for me out there." There is a hidden victim under Moon-Saturn's autonomy. It is a premature autonomy that has evolved out of having not had enough love. It is more desperate than natural autonomy.

Sun-Neptune: mothering the father

Sun-Neptune aspects may have to do with a time when we are a little older. They may have to do with wanting to make Daddy better. Obviously there are many different ways this aspect may apply. But there is a possibility that, if you have Sun-Neptune and you choose later in life to be in a helping profession, or if you are someone who does a lot of helping, there is a part of you which is actually trying to make Daddy feel better. And that can then be projected onto other people. If you had a father who was dying of cancer, and then you grow up to be a doctor, there may be a connection between the child who is wanting to make Daddy better and the decision to be a doctor later on.

I am not condemning this. I am not putting it down at all. But I think you should be aware of it. If there is a very personal motivation when we are helping other people, like trying to make Daddy better, and if it stems from childhood, it is going to be very intense. You are not going to be very cool about it, because if you don't make other people better, if you are equating it with childhood issues, then you are going to die, or you are not going to get the love you need. Then you will try harder to make other people feel better, and you won't set your boundaries. You'll let them ring you in the middle of the night. You'll go out of your way too much for them, because you have got to make them feel better. Inside you you are thinking, "I've got to get mother or father to survive." So you become uncool about it. This is when you start getting problems.

Burn-out is a real thing that carers experience. I think the seeds of future burn-out are related to where you are coming from when you are performing an act of service. The more you are performing it from the place of a sense of true unity, the less burn-out you get. The more there are personal motives, the more invested you are, the more burnt out you get. But we all have personal motives. I am just trying to make you aware of this.

Audience: At what age does Sun-Neptune start operating?

Howard: I think it is a little later, in terms of when Daddy becomes more obvious – if he's around. I would put it at around one year old. What happens at about six to nine months is that we start separating from mother, and usually then we start to notice father more, because he is something other than mother. In fact, a father around is quite helpful, because he can be an attractive outsider to whom we are drawn and who can help us break our intense symbiosis with mother. That happens any time from nine months on. But if father doesn't seem well, we may try to keep him happy and try to make sure he survives. I'm just giving you guidelines on this. We could interpret Sun-Neptune aspects in many different ways, but in terms of our topic today, that's one way of thinking about it.

I'm going to give you a break now. I brought some biscuits. I want you all to survive. I have a Moon-Neptune aspect.

Moon-Chiron: healing the mother's wounds

I was reminded during the break that this issue of trying to save mother and equating it with saving others can also apply to Moon-Chiron as well as Moon-Saturn and Moon-Neptune. Moon-Chiron means you will be very sensitive to your mother's pain. That's one way it can manifest. It can manifest in other ways, too. With Chiron you may have a mother who is a healer, but you will be sensitive to her pain more than someone who doesn't have a Moon-Chiron aspect. Whatever planet aspects the Moon, when we are around mother we experience that planet. We feel that planet around her. If you feel Chiron, you may be feeling her wounds.

Neptune: serve or suffer

I have told you in other seminars about Isabel Hickey, whom I studied with in Boston. She was my teacher in the late 1960s and early 1970s. She died quite a number of years ago, but I always feel her around somewhere. She was very powerful. She had the Sun in Leo with Scorpio rising and Uranus in Sagittarius in the 1st house, and with that rising Uranus she would fight everything she didn't like. She wasn't only one of New England's leading astrologers – she was also a spiritual teacher. One of the things that she used to say to people who came to her for a reading and who had a strong 12th house or a prominent Neptune – Neptune rising, Neptune conjunct an angle, Sun-Neptune, Moon-Neptune – was, "Serve or suffer." Then you would pay her $30.

It sticks in your mind when a person who has a lot of authority says, "Serve or suffer." She looked at it karmically. Right now I am looking at Neptunian types from a Neptune point of view, but I have got a Pluto approach to it as well. Isabelle Hickey said that if you have a strong Neptune in this life, it could mean that in some previous lives you took more than you gave, and now you have a very giving Neptunian energy strong in your chart because you have to redress the imbalance. You may have to give more than you receive, wherever Neptune is in your chart and whatever planet it is touching, in order to make up for being too selfish in a past life. That's how Isabelle Hickey would describe it. I think there is some reality in this. From what I have seen, doing charts for people with a prominent Neptune or a packed 12th house, they often find themselves in a position where they have to give more than they get in return, or they are put in a position where they have to give up their own will in order to adjust to the needs of others around them. Neptune is very anti-ego.

Maharishi Mahesh Yogi used to talk about this slightly differently. He wasn't speaking as an astrologer when he talked about it, but he used to say that it is possible that people can have incarnations on other planes besides the earth plane. He used to call these other planes of existence, where you were alive but not in the human system, the Devic realms. He said that when you were in that realm, when you had lifetimes in that realm, everything was infused with golden light, and everything was perfect and beautiful and there was no separation and no confrontation. He used to say that you didn't have to close your eyes in order to transcend. The idea when you meditate is that you close your eyes to go inside. He said you could just have your eyes open and you would be transcending because of the beauty around you, the light around you. These Devic realms are obviously a really nice place to be, but there comes a certain point when you need to incarnate in the earth plane again.

I began to wonder if certain people, who come into this life with a signature in their chart of Pisces or a strong Neptune or a strong 12th house, are remembering the Devic realms. They come into this plane and find this earth rather harsh, and they think, "What's going on here, with all this fragmentation and pain? This isn't my place. I need something much more beautiful, where there is unity and wholeness, not this suffering and pain." Some Neptunian people may not even want to be here. They may just want to get out or escape, because they don't feel this is their home.

But other Neptunian types might think, "What can I do to bring my ideas of unity, beauty, truth, and justice to this world? What can I do to make this place more like that other place I remember?" You may get a motivation to serve or help coming from the memory of something more ideal, more beautiful. You are trying to make this world a bit more like the Devic realm. I find it interesting, because so often I see people with a strong 12th house or Pisces or Neptune prominent who have to work with the most damaged people around. They are the ones who end up working in institutions, looking after the mentally ill and the physically handicapped. It is almost an extreme reaction, because they have a memory of someplace much more beautiful. They try to turn their backs on human incarnation because they don't like the pain, and then finally they have to deal with it, and they do it in an extreme way. Maybe they have avoided looking at the pain during lifetimes in the Devic realm. Then they end up having to deal with some of the people who are the most damaged, the most suffering in our society, partly to make up for the fact that they have avoided it before.

For some people there seems to be a period of time when they have to do that kind of extreme work. Then they can go on to do the same work in ways which aren't so extreme. They go from working in institutions, working with the handicapped, to working as an astrologer with people who are a little less damaged or have less pain. You can see the move from the institutional worker to the alternative healer or astrologer. Let's think of this in terms of karma and reincarnation. If you get someone coming for a reading, and they have strong Pisces or a strong Neptune or a strong 12th house, this is something you might discuss with them. Obviously you have to be careful when you are talking about karma in a chart, because how can you be absolutely sure? You can present it as a kind of metaphor, an analogy, to people who resonate with that way of looking at it.

Pluto: making reparation

Let's move on to another motive for helping. This one is slightly different. It picks up on what someone mentioned earlier, which is that there may be some Plutonic reasons which are influencing our motivations for serving. I have many different ways to approach this. But the general idea is that some of us may choose the path of being a helper or server in order to assuage some deep guilt or sense of badness we feel about ourselves. It is as if making things or people better is a way of atoning for certain sins we think we have committed, or compensating for something that has left us feeling that we are bad and have made bad things happen. There is an urge to make reparation.

You know the idea that you can be redeemed if you serve, that you can repent for some kind of sin through service. For instance, in my case I can wake up some mornings and for some reason I can be in a very foul mood. Mostly I moan about all the work I have taken on, or the fact that I have a deadline on a book that is difficult, or I have to write a lecture. I have about an hour or an hour and a half where I am stuck in the birth canal. I moan, and if you call me up between 9.00 and 10.00 in the morning I won't be very nice to you if you get me in that phase.

I haven't been doing charts recently, but when I was doing them, sometimes I would be in this mood when the client was due to arrive. I would think, "Oh my God! How am I going to do the chart? I'm not in the right place." Then the 11.00 appointment would come, and there was something about having to put myself aside and forget about myself in order to focus on the client. Whatever happened – you become a channel, or you open up to something – when the reading was done, in almost every case I ended up feeling much better for having done it. It is as if opening yourself up has transformed you a bit. It is a spiritual thing. You actually get help, even though you are meant to be the helper. There are cases where you can pick up gunge from people as well, and then you have to do a little aura cleaning, or have a bath and pour cold water over yourself. But if you put yourself aside and do something for someone else, then something inside you transforms.

Let me continue a bit with this idea of serving being motivated by imagined sins. Again, I want to go back to childhood with this one. I want to go back to a very early, preconscious time – although sometimes it can be a little later – when there were issues which may have left us with a sense of being bad. Therefore there is an impulse to try to redeem our badness and make up for it by being a helper. This relates to the womb again. In the womb we think we are everything. The universe is ourselves. We feel as if everything is connected to us, everything is related to us.

Then we are born and we are no longer the universe. We have bodies, we have boundaries, but something in us still thinks that whatever happens around us relates back to us. This goes on even after six months. If mother dies or gets killed or leaves the family, there is a tendency to relate everything that happens back to you, as if this has something to do with you. It most likely doesn't have anything to do with you. Things are usually much more complicated. But because you have so recently moved away from the sense of being related and connected to everything, you still think that whatever happens out there must be related to you. If something bad happens, you have to find out what it means, because it's your fault. And it's your fault because you're bad.

I'm not against finding meaning in things. I think it is important. There was a Psychosynthesis conference many years ago in Zürich. Those of you who are familiar with Psychosynthesis will know that there is a lot of effort put into getting access to the higher self through imagination and intuition – talking to your Wise Man or Wise Woman, going up mountains and finding the Wise Person inside you. That is not all there is to it, but it is a very solar thing – you are going up into the light, the higher chakras, the higher mind, the higher feelings. You are not going back into the belly. This course in Zürich had been going on for two or three days, and they had been doing a lot of going up mountains to talk to the Wise Person. Some people always find their Wise Person hidden in a cave. Everyone was being very spiritual. At the end, what happened was that a mad dog, a rabid dog, appeared at the place where the course was being held. I'm not sure whether it bit anyone or not, but they then spent the rest of the conference discussing why they had attracted a rabid dog. They came up with all sorts of things, such as, "We are getting too much into the light, and we have to attract something else to remind us of the other side of life." They had to find meaning in it. Jung said that meaning makes many things bearable.

As small children we tend to believe that anything that happens is related back to ourselves. This idea is very poignant, and it's often quite sad to see a child picking up blame when it is not true. In the movie, *Kramer vs Kramer*, when the mother leaves, the little boy says to his father, "It's because I'm bad. That's why she left." I was doing the charts for a couple who were getting divorced, and their little girl came along with the mother. She was about five or six. I was talking to her, and she said, "Daddy left because I'm not pretty enough." You can see how it operates with this little girl – "I'm not pretty enough. I'm bad. I did something wrong. That's why there's this disaster and upset in my life." If you are coming from that place, you have an imagined guilt which motivates you: "I must be good, I must make up for it, I must make reparation."

I think we are getting into the realm of Pluto when you think you have done something bad. You are an evil person, you are a despicable person, and therefore you must redeem it by being helpful. That is one way it may manifest. Someone with Pluto rising has met Pluto very early in life. The 1st house is what you meet early in life. Or if you have Pluto in one of the parental houses, then maybe you have met Pluto in the mother or father, and you sense something dark or bad there, but the badness you feel around them gets introjected. You take it on yourself.

There is something else which exacerbates this thing of self-blame. Children do more than just thinking that everything is connected to them – they also do something which is called magical thinking. Magical thinking is the belief that the thought or the wish for something is actually the same as doing the deed. I first came across this when I was reading Elisabeth Kübler-Ross' book, *On Death and Dying.*[16] She talks about young people whose parents have died. These kids often believe that it was something they did or thought that made it happen, because they are so recently out of the sphere where everything is related to them.

I think there are different kinds of guilt. There is a good sort of guilt – an existential guilt which comes from knowing that you are not living up to all that you could be. That is not such a bad guilt to have. You feel that there is more potential in you than you have realised, and you feel guilty about it. That can drive you into doing things. But

---

[16]Elisabeth Kübler-Ross, *On Death and Dying*, Collier Books, 1997.

there is also a neurotic guilt, an imagined guilt which you feel about something that happens. You have got your wish, your thought made the thing happen, and you feel guilty.

The Yod or "Finger of Fate"

Let me give you an example from a chart I did. I'll just tell you a snippet of the chart. This is a woman with Mercury in Pisces in the 3rd house. Mercury makes a Yod or "Finger of Fate" formation with Pluto in Leo in the 8th and Neptune in Libra in the 10th. This woman came to me as an adult. Let me digress for a minute and talk about the Finger of Fate. I didn't know until very recently that, in the Jewish religion, the holy scroll called the Torah is read with a utensil shaped a bit like a pointer, almost like an arrow. It's used to keep your place while you are reading. This utensil is called a Yod. They love their scrolls, and they unwrap them very carefully, and when you are having your Bar Mitzvah or whatever, you read the traditional lesson from the Torah, and you use a Yod.

Audience: Yod is a letter in the Hebrew alphabet.

Howard: Yes, the letter is that shape. It's interesting that this is something that is used to read the Torah. When a planet gets trapped in a Yod formation, the planet which is the focal point is getting inconjuncts from the other two, which will be in sextile to each other. The planet that is trapped becomes focal in a person's life, in a person's karma, in a person's experience. In some charts you may even have a few Yods. It is as if the planet which is focal is not really free to operate, especially if it is a Neptune-Pluto sextile making the Yod. You get a lot of those, because Neptune and Pluto have been transiting in sextile for a long time. The planet which is focal tries to operate. But there are a lot of unconscious or hidden things influencing that planet, things from the world of Pluto and Neptune, so you have a kind of fate around it.

If we go backward in time, and think about when Neptune was in Virgo and Pluto was in Cancer, what sign would have caught the Yod formation then? Aquarius. So if you happen to have been born when Neptune in Virgo was sextile Pluto in Cancer in the heavens, and you have the Sun or the Moon or Mercury or Venus in a certain degree of Aquarius, then that planet is caught in the fated situation called a Yod. A whole lot comes along with the expression of that planet – some kind of karma which gives weight and significance to it.

Then we had Neptune in Libra and Pluto in Leo. What sign got it then? Pisces. Then we had Neptune in Scorpio and Pluto in Virgo. Who bought it then? Aries. Then we had Neptune in Sagittarius and Pluto in Libra, and Taurus people would have got it. Now who's getting it, with Neptune in Capricorn and Pluto in Scorpio? Geminis. I love it. They deserve it!

Audience: Boo! Hiss!

Howard: Well, you know how clever some Gemini people are at getting out of things, slipping away, avoiding facing certain things – a little bit like Hermes was, a trickster. I think that a lot of people with a strong Gemini influence aren't going to be able to get away with things now. They are getting the transiting Neptune-Pluto sextile making a Yod. They get stuck in things, they get trapped in things that normally they could find ways to get around or slide out of. They really have to be in it now. If you have the Sun around the middle part of Gemini, or if you have Mercury or the Moon or Venus or even Mars, Jupiter, Saturn, or Uranus in Gemini, you will be caught in it. Maybe there is a Yod made to your Ascendant, or to your MC, if it is in Gemini. You may find that you are in what Liz would call an alchemical alembic – a situation where there is a stopper on the flask and everything is getting more and more agitated and intense. Normally you would try to get out of it, but you can't, so you have to grow through being in something you can't escape from. It's pointing at you now. It's you, Gemini!

Audience: It was that Yod that got me into therapy and onto this course.

Howard: Do you want to say more about that?

Audience: Not particularly.

Howard: I have done a lot of charts for people with planets in Gemini, and I've talked about this with regard to the houses involved. It often helps make sense of things for these people. You can't get up and escape and leave a Yod in the middle of the night.

Now let's go back to this woman with Mercury in Pisces in a Yod with Neptune and Pluto. Let's call her Ann. I can't exactly remember how we got into it, but she told me that she had a younger sister whom she felt jealous of. I think her sister is about two or three years younger than her. When she started talking about her younger sister, my eye immediately went to Mercury in Pisces in the 3rd. When you start hearing about sibling issues, go to the 3rd house. See what's on the cusp and what's going on in that house. And look at Mercury. In Ann's case Mercury is there in the 3rd, and on the focal point of a Yod. I wanted to hear more about this. It got my attention because it is a loaded bit of the chart.

Often older siblings have a lot of ambivalence about younger siblings, and I think it is obvious why, especially if you are the first child. You are used to being the centre, used to being the one who is special, and when someone comes along and usurps your centrality, it can leave a fair amount of resentment. But it is a little confusing because we are meant to love this new baby as well. If you observe, you can often see the older child showing a lot of ambivalence towards the new sibling whom they are meant to love. Sometimes they can feel the love as long as the new sibling doesn't get any bigger. Sometimes they can't admit they feel resentment – they can't face the negative feelings. Then the feelings come out in some other way.

I heard a good joke about ambivalence. I hope I get it right. Two Freudian analysts are having tea together, and one analyst says to the other, "Boy, did I make a classic Freudian slip the other day." The second analyst says, "Well, what is it? What happened?" The first analyst says, "Well, I was having scones and tea with my mother, and I meant to say, 'Will you please pass me the butter?' Instead I said, 'Why did you fuck up my life, you stupid bitch?'"

Anyway, when Ann was about six she often had the job of looking after her younger sister. She had negative thoughts about her sister while she was doing this. One day when Ann was looking after her sister, the sister was climbing something and fell off and hurt herself. It was bad enough to have to go the hospital, because she had bone damage. Ann and I talked about this for a long time. I think she has more or less believed, since then, that her negative thoughts, her ambivalence about wanting to get rid of her sister, actually caused that accident to happen. If you are having a very negative thought, like, "Mummy won't let me eat as many cookies as I would like. I hate her! I wish she would die!" and the next day your mother gets ill or has to go away or something bad happens to her, you may believe it was your thought that made it happen.

I think this is quite interesting. You can see how Mercury has to do with both the sister and thinking, and Pluto in the 8th inconjunct Mercury immediately brings out the idea that there is something secret, something hidden in Ann's thinking that has caused bad things to happen around her. The undercurrents around the sister have caused a lot of problems. Ann has spent a lot of her life trying to make up for this imagined badness that she felt attacked her sister. Can you guess what profession she is in? She became a nurse. Neptune is in Libra in the 10th. I am pretty sure that there is a connection between her nursing, her need to make others better in real life, and a making up for the imagined sense of guilt.

Audience: Would the Mercury-Neptune make that worse?

Howard: Can you explain what you mean?

Audience: Well, Ann has this infantile idea that her thoughts can hurt other people, that she can murder or injure people. I was thinking that Mercury-Neptune might make that worse because it fantasises so much. But a good aspect from Saturn could help the problem of magical thinking.

Howard: Mercury-Neptune will tend to have more problems with it. Neptune doesn't have boundaries, so the thinking is more boundless. You can have trouble distinguishing how you are really relating to the people and things you are thinking about. It is also the idea of a wish or a thought being the same as reality. Fantasy is the same as reality. That's a Neptune thing, I would agree.

Both Neptune and Pluto are bearing down on Mercury, and Ann chose to be a nurse. Again, I am not putting down the fact that this might be one of her motivations for nursing. But I do think that it would be good for people in this situation to be aware of it, because as soon as there is a personal motivation, such as trying to assuage guilt or a sense of badness, you have an investment in it. You become too attached to the role of the helper, because that's the only way you can feel better about yourself. And if people don't get better, then you don't get your guilt alleviated.

Audience: Or it could be the other way around – they do get better, and then you don't have a role any more.

Howard: Well, you can find someone else to help pretty quickly. The point I am making is that we are helping others as much for ourselves as for the other person. It is not just coming from that place of a sense of unity with someone. It's not just a response to suffering. There are other, more personal motivations.

Group discussion

I have got a few other things on the list, but I want to hear some feedback. Some of you have already given me some feedback, and I thought it was interesting. I want to hear about whether any of these motivations or reasons make some sort of sense to you, and also if they fit with astrological aspects.

Audience: I have the Moon conjunct Neptune and square Saturn. Those are the two aspects you mentioned before. When I was very young and went shopping with my mother, I used to look at what she was looking at in the shops. I tried to work out what it was she was after so that I could get it for her.

Howard: That's a good example. Alice Miller says that when she was interviewing people who wanted to train as therapists or analysts, she often found that they came from the kind of background where they learned at a very young age to tune into mother. They were really the best people to go into therapeutic work, because they were used to having their antennae out for what other people wanted and needed.

Audience: I have the Moon square Saturn, opposite Chiron, and sesquiquadrate a Mercury-Neptune conjunction.

Howard: So you have got all three of the "helper" aspects. Don't underestimate the sesquiquadrate, by the way.

Audience: I also have Sun trine Neptune and opposite Pluto. I do find myself tending to mother other people and having to be strong for them. The other thing was the story you told about that woman, Ann – the same thing happened to me with my sister. She was in front of me on the slide, and I was right behind her. I saw her fall head first onto the cement, and I kept saying, "I didn't do it, I didn't push her!" Just recently, we were talking about it, and she said, "Oh, I always knew you didn't do it." She remembers it. It was always something I felt guilty about.

Howard: You must do. If you have an experience like that, you tend to have mixed feelings. I don't know what else to say about it. Sometimes I wish people would get up in the morning, look in the mirror, and say, "Not guilty!" – just to be aware that some of these things which cause imagined guilt are really not true at all.

The other chart I'm thinking of is the chart of a man who has Mars in 6° Capricorn exactly square Neptune at 6° Libra. There is an association here, not so much with thinking, but with actions causing something bad to happen. What happened to him was that he opened the door to his grandmother's room and went in, and she was dead in the bed. He told me he really felt that, because he had opened the door, he had caused her to die. He then became very afraid, to the extent that later in life he associated being assertive with causing bad things to happen. He was working in the Civil Service, and everyone else was getting promotion, but not him. He went to his boss and said, "How come I'm not getting promotion?" and his boss said, "Because you're not assertive enough to get promoted." I think that he had guilt about asserting himself. "If I'm assertive, I make bad things happen." He has to go back to what happened when he was a child, in order to free his Mars. In this respect he has to free up the complexes that are hanging around his being an assertive person, because it is a complex that doesn't serve any positive purpose.

Audience: I have a Sun-Pluto conjunction in Virgo in the 4th, and a Chiron-Moon square. I can see that my mother's pain had a big influence on me. I was definitely locked in with my mother. I could see the bad things she was doing. She would sometimes lash out at my brother in a very cruel way. But I couldn't blame her, because she was in such pain.

Howard: Does this connect with now?

Audience: Yes, I think the trauma of all that has made me feel I always have to help people. I feel that, if I don't help them, they will do bad things.

Howard: I think the first step is becoming aware that this is going on, and being a bit more rational about it. I think you do need to know what the rational mind can do to help. You can say to yourself, "I'm an adult now, and my survival doesn't depend on making other people better or making them happy." That frees you up to help them if you want to, and to not to help them if you don't want to. It takes away the compulsiveness.

Audience: I have got the Sun trine Chiron, and Virgo rising. My Chiron is in the 6th house. I also have Saturn on the IC. My father had a weak heart. I work with soldiers with psychological problems.

Howard: That's a very good example of a profession which reflects something to do with wounding in the male lineage.

Audience: There is also the cultural idea that we are all sinners, that we have been thrown out of Paradise and have to atone for our sins. It's a kind of collective guilt.

Howard: I should have mentioned the whole collective thing. Christ is considered to be the Master of the Piscean Age. The idea that he died for our sins leads to the Christian idea that serving is the path to God. It is true that our collective myths absolutely have bearing on why we become helpers.

Audience: I get very angry about the story of Adam and Eve being the cause of evil.

Howard: Especially Eve. Eve did it! By the way, there is something I forgot to say before, not necessarily in terms of what we are talking about now. Yods to any of the angles are very strong, particularly to the MC or the Ascendant, and especially if they are tight. I have one in my chart. I have the Sun in 23° Aries on the cusp of the 3rd house, and Uranus in 22° Gemini in the 5th. I think that is something that led me to astrology. The Sun and Uranus are both exactly inconjunct the MC at 22° Scorpio. In a way, astrology found me – I didn't find it. I was just led by an instinct, a feeling of being pushed along by the Yod formation of the Sun and Uranus to the MC, and it affected my choice of work. It drove me. I didn't have to make a lot of conscious choices.

Magical thinking

Audience: Going back to the subject of guilt and magical thinking, I had an experience in the summer of 1992. I have Mars square Neptune. I was living in a house with a strange lady, and she was driving me bonkers. One afternoon, at around 2.30, I had this feeling of surging hatred. I wasn't in the house at the time. In my mind I said to her, "Fuck you!" She had an accident. She fell over and cut her head. I asked her what time it had happened, and she said, "Half past two."

Howard: Well, you did cause it!

Audience: And a couple of days later it happened again, at 10.00 in the evening. I got home later and she had had a haemorrhage.

Howard: Wow. I'm going to be really nice to you from now on. But this does bring up another issue. You can't make big generalities here, but usually, if someone dies and you have had bad thoughts about them beforehand, it wouldn't have been your bad thoughts which made it happen – there would be a whole lot of other things going on. But there are some people who are very powerful on the mental plane. If you have, let's say, a Sun-Jupiter-Pluto conjunction in the 3rd house in Scorpio, you are powerful on the mental plane. What you think will affect other people, and this will require you to develop a certain sense of responsibility for whatever thoughts you create. What you send out comes back to you. You do have an influence. I have seen people who have power on the mental plane. If they hold someone in a negative light, they may actually influence the person's mood or feelings when they are in that person's presence.

In 1973 I worked for a while as a chef in a vegetarian restaurant. I had to make twelve salads a day, and that was my total responsibility in life. I got paid £22 a week, which I thought was an enormous amount of money. My boss, for some reason, really liked me. She hired me on the spot because she liked me. I could hardly do anything wrong in her eyes. But there was a colleague of mine, a woman, whom my boss really didn't like. It was irrational. It always happened that when I did something wrong, when I dropped a bowl or something, my boss was never around to see it. If this woman colleague dropped a bowl, the boss was always there. Because the boss was holding me in a good light, she never saw when I had messed up. With the person she was holding in a bad light, she was always there when something bad happened. I think the mind can separate us from things, but it can also influence things. Thoughts and events are connected.

This reminds me of something else that happened in the 1970's. I had a flat which I shared with a woman flatmate. When she moved in, she said she wanted to bring her cat with her. Now, I have a kind of mixed relationship with cats. Some I like, and some I don't get along with. Instead of bringing one cat, this woman brought seven. They were all a little bit weird. One used to follow me around – it was called Chicken Legs. The flat started to really stink and smell. I was actually meditating one day, and I thought, "I hate those cats. I wish they would go away." I felt really bad afterward, because they actually developed some kind of terminal illness, and one by one they died. I felt that I had something to do with this. But probably I didn't. I would tend to think that we are usually not guilty. We don't cause death and dying. We may have the mental power to make someone feel bad, if we're around them. But there are a lot of other things involved, too.

Audience: It could be the other way around. Maybe those cats were going to die anyway, and your thoughts were picking up on the fact that they were sick. Maybe their sickness made you feel negative about them.

Howard: Well, that's what I think may be the value of people who suddenly just know that something bad is coming. The value is not in telling other people something bad is coming. The value is in thinking, "All right, I have got this knowledge. What can I do to change things for the better?" It's like being a good witch, a good crone. "What energy can I put in which could help to transmute what I sense is going to happen?" Then you can do magical things. When it gets inflated or out of proportion, then you get power fantasies. The trouble is that there is some truth in it – what we are thinking does create effects, so we have to be responsible.

The family inheritance

Audience: I'm interested in lineage, and what aspects reflect this. You said that Moon-Saturn and Moon-Neptune may mean that you were in tune with your mother, but if your mother wasn't mothered properly either, then you have to be the mother – you have to mother your mother. You can often see the same aspects in both charts.

Howard: Exactly. One of the great things about setting up charts for families is that you will see the same aspects and degrees showing up, and you really see quickly the "family curse" of the parents by looking at that bit of the chart which keeps repeating itself in some way through the different generations. It is a great use of astrology – it can really pinpoint family myths and issues.

Audience: I think the aspects can change through the generations. Something's been transformed and released.

Howard: Yes, maybe there's a trine instead of a square in the next generation. But we can mess up, too, and then sometimes there's a square instead of a trine. I think some people have to redeem the sins of the mothers. Either one works hard on oneself to break out of the pattern, or one passes it down to the next generation.

Audience: I have the Moon square Saturn. Both my daughters have Moon-Saturn aspects. One has an opposition and one has a square. My younger daughter, who just had a baby who has been adopted, has Saturn in the 12th house.

Howard: Who has Saturn in the 12th? The baby or your daughter?

Audience: My daughter. She has the Moon square Saturn in the 12th house, and the baby has a sextile between the Moon and Saturn. It is quite interesting how things have shifted. The baby has got Saturn in the 12th as well, but it's sextile, not square the Moon.

Howard: It is funny, isn't it? Some of you can relate to these very deeply psychological reasons why you become helpers. If you can't, just let the awareness be there, and see what happens over the next weeks or months. See what comes up. You may find that something is going on. Let me talk about a few more of the psychological motives for why we become helpers. Then I'm going to get into other reasons which are less unconscious.

More hidden agendas

Saturn: becoming more lovable

We may want to help save mother or father and therefore we become helpers. We may want to assuage a sense of badness or guilt or imagined wrongdoing, so we become helpers. Related to that is a general feeling of being unlovable or unworthy, and therefore trying to help others in order to make ourselves lovable and worthy. I do think of Moon-Saturn with this. It is so important to understand that the way mother nurtures us really does teach us about self-nurture as well. If she doesn't nurture us, then we not only have the feeling that we are bad or no good, but we also don't have any image of how to look after ourselves in life. But if we get good enough nurturing, then that tends to help our own ability to nurture ourselves, to give ourselves what we need. Some people have a really hard time giving themselves what they need.

I have noticed this with Moon-Saturn – there has been frustration in getting needs fulfilled. When Saturn aspects the Moon, there is a sense of not being good enough. You weren't worthy enough, and that's why you didn't get cared for. Sun-Saturn and Moon-Saturn people, when they grow up, always have to do things to prove themselves. They are still trying to get love by proving that they are worthy, to compensate for their feeling of unworthiness. So they take on a difficult project and they achieve it, and that's supposed to make them feel as if they are worthy. But usually it doesn't, because the deeper complex is still there, so they have to take on something else to feel worthy. You have to somehow break that cycle, by doing some work on the inner child. Probably the inner child needs to experience the kind of parent it didn't get. So you have to do some reparenting. You have to allow your inner child to feel the anger and the guilt and the pain of not getting what you needed. Otherwise you are still going to be looking for good parenting from other people – you are still going to be looking for someone else to be the mother you didn't get. Or you are going to try to be that mother for others.

Moon-Saturn people can sometimes be like gluttons who have to keep feeding themselves with hard jobs. Richard Idemon said that if you want to make someone with Moon-Saturn happy, give them a deadline. Give them pressure. Often they can't relax. The Moon has a lot to do with how we relax, how we let go and let ourselves be. With Moon-Saturn it might actually be hard to relax, because if you are not doing something worthy, then you don't deserve anything. You have to work twelve hours a day to earn one hour of television, and even then you might feel guilty unless you are watching a documentary or a nature programme or the news.

The Moon and self-nurturing

Audience: That's not an exaggeration. I have Sun-Saturn.

Howard: But all is not lost if you didn't get nurturing, or if the bonding went awry. I think the chart is going to show you how to nurture yourself. Look at your Moon-sign and the aspects to the Moon, and that will tell you what you need to nurture yourself, even if you didn't get it back in childhood. What do you think a Moon-Venus contact may need to nurture itself? You need Venus – so that may mean doing something to make yourself look beautiful, or getting massaged every once in a while. You see, any aspects to the Moon will give you a clue about how to nurture yourself.

Audience: What about Moon-Saturn?

Howard: Well, with Moon-Saturn, it may be working hard, or committing yourself to some project. Or it may even be that you need depressions every once in a while to feel good in yourself.

Audience: I have Moon-Saturn, and I have had to struggle with it. I have had Pluto go over it, and I found out that I have had to set boundaries.

Howard: One way of nurturing yourself with Moon-Saturn is to learn how to set boundaries. I find that, when I am getting a transit to Saturn in my chart – a fast transit like Mercury or Venus or the Sun coming to my Saturn – if I do something that I really should have been doing, something that needs to be done but which I haven't been doing, then I feel better. If I sit down and answer letters that should have been answered, or I tidy my desk, then I actually feel really good about the day, even though the day's targets haven't been met. I am doing what Saturn is asking to be done. But if I don't do it, I don't have a good day, because I am avoiding things. You know that Saturn rewards you for the efforts you put into it. It is an exacting kind of justice. If you learn from where Saturn is in your chart, you get rewarded. But if you are cutting corners and not going in, then when something goes over Saturn it is going to make you aware of what you don't know. Saturn makes you tough.

Audience: My problem is that the Moon is in Capricorn as well.

Howard: If you go through biographies of famous people and you look up the Moon, you'll see there is a predominance of Moon-Saturn and Moon in Capricorn people who have become achievers. That is one way they nurture themselves while they are trying to prove their worth. Normally you would think Moon in Capricorn is in its detriment and not such a great place to be, but actually you can compensate in the form of some impressive achievements. The part that bothers me is when they never feel good enough. They can't find the time to pat themselves on the back. I would say to them, "Great, achieve big things. But do take time to let your whole body feel good about the fact that you did it, to balance out this hard critic and judge that you have inside."

Audience: What about Moon-Uranus and Moon-Mercury? How would they nurture themselves?

Howard: I think Moon-Uranus might need to say to people, "Listen, I need time alone!" and go off and do something different. That's how they get nurtured. Or you could study something unusual, like astrology or any of Jung's work – anything to do with Uranus. Do you see what I mean? Or you could work for some sort of humanitarian cause. By doing Uranian things, you are nurturing yourself.

Audience: I have Moon-Chiron in the 12th, in Aquarius. I can do the helping and healing thing only for so long, and then I get bored.

Howard: That's the Aquarian bit, saying, "I need space from this. I need to get out. I want to go someplace cleaner." How would Moon-Mercury nurture itself? Through reading, communicating, writing. Moon-Sun might nurture itself by trying to become special, by performing. You get your nurturing through solar things, through shining. Moon-Pluto needs to go deep into things, or work in a Pluto profession. Sometimes we need to be depressed. Richard Idemon had Moon-Saturn. He said he stopped feeling bad about having times of depression, and just accepted it. He dressed in black and went out at midnight and wrote sad things in his journal, because he was nurtured by times of isolation.

Audience: I have got Moon-Pluto, and I have got a 12th house Sun as well. I am very rarely sad, but when I do get sad, I actually enjoy it, because I can go into it for a few days and know that I am going to come out the other side.

Howard: This is exactly what Richard Idemon talked about. Whatever aspects the Moon is the key to what nurtures you. With Moon-Saturn and Moon-Pluto, it may actually be depression, which is an odd thing. Do you get the point? I don't want to leave those of you who have damaged bonding with the feeling there is nothing you can do about it. Look at it in terms of how the Moon could respond positively to a difficult parental relationship. The chart isn't your doom. You can start nurturing yourself by looking at the aspects, the sign, or even the house that the Moon is in as a way of nurturing yourself.

Audience: How about Moon-Mars?

Howard: I think competition helps – like getting into some kind of competitive sport, or something very physical. Getting nurtured and feeling more connected to life means taking on some sort of legitimate conflict. That's just one way that comes to mind.

Audience: And Moon-Neptune?

Howard: Moon-Neptune needs to do something creative, or something to do with meditation or being a medium. You need time to open up to the infinite. It may be going out into nature and being by the sea a lot, or praying. Or drugs and alcohol may nurture you. Someone with Moon-Neptune once said to me that if you feel like committing suicide, take a bath. Earlier we talked about how we all have a deep memory of being helpless, and therefore we may compensate by trying to be the helper or being for someone else what we didn't get ourselves. Service may also nurture Moon-Neptune.

Let me mention a book to you called *How Can I Help?* by Ram Dass and Paul Gorman.[17] It is actually quite a little gem. I am a great fan of Ram Dass and get a lot from him, and I try to get hold of any tapes of his work, or anything new he has done. He is very contemporary and he has been through a lot of changes. He is an Aries, with the Sun conjunct Uranus conjunct the north Node in Aries in the 10th house. He has a Venus-Neptune square and Cancer rising. Cancer is another sign that tends to help others a lot. Obviously Pisces does, but Cancer does as well. The Moon in Cancer is very sympathetic, but it tends to show its sympathy to those close to you. But if the Moon is in aspect to an outer planet, then your mothering becomes more universal.

---

[17]Ram Dass and Paul Gorman, *How Can I Help*, Knopf, 1985.

The Moon is a nurturing planetary energy, and if is in aspect to an outer planet, then your nurturing is more universal.

Virgo and the 6th house also tend to help others. But I get a different feeling from Virgo and the 6th house. Pisceans and Neptunians often lose themselves through service, rather than having their own identity. They give what other people need. But Virgo and the 6th house have to do with getting a sense of who you are through being of service. You define who you are by being of help. Someone who is serving from a Virgo place gets a sense of identity, so there is a certain pride in doing the thing well and skillfully. A more Neptunian place of service is, "I'll serve because I don't want to think about myself. I want to forget about myself." There is a difference.

Audience: What do you think of the north Node in the 10th, if you take the 10th to be mother?

Howard: Well, I am not sure how it ties in just on its own, but wherever the north Node is, it's an area that is very evolutionary to develop. I always guide a person toward making sure that the area of life associated with the north Node, by sign and house, is something that they are doing a lot of. I can't say how the north Node by itself ties up with mother, other than that something about your relationship with mother needs attention or helps put you in the direction of growth and evolution. In Ram Dass' case, the north Node in the 10th in Aries says, "You are right to be public about your personal experience," and that's what he does. He just gets up there and raps about the way he feels. He has the north Node in a very personal sign, but in a social house. I can't answer your question just in terms of mother. There is too little to go on.

Helping for rewards

I want to tell you what's in this book. The authors make a very good point, a very obvious point. They say that, from very early in childhood, first by parents and then by teachers, we are told, "Be good and help." We get this message. Helpfulness gets encouraged and very often rewarded, and often when parents ask you to help out, it is a kind of euphemism for being obedient and compliant. "Help out and clean your room. Help out and take out the rubbish."

What they say in the book is that, once we come to associate helping with being loved and getting rewards, we start to use helping in the service of a wide range of personal motives, other than the expression of natural compassion – like cleaning your room or taking out the rubbish in order to get the use of the family car. You learn to be good, you learn to help, in order to get a reward. If you feel bad, you help, and then you'll get praise. That's not an unconscious motive. That is inculcated into us. It encourages us to associate helping with gaining rewards, something for personal gain. Again, I am not judging this as bad. I think we should just be aware that this is going on. The more you are aware of it – the more you have a kind of inner witness that can monitor your helping trip – the less you are going to get overly attached to the role.

Audience: You don't really feel your power over the client if these things are unconscious.

Howard: Well, not on the ego level. But it's there underneath. Also, we have a kind of awareness which has a lot of selective perception in it. If I gain my sense of who I am by being a mothering type of person – if I identify myself with being a helper – then, when I look at situations, I am not going to look at them objectively, I'm going to look at them in terms of how can I end up mothering someone, or how can I end up giving help.

Krishnamurti and Abraham Maslow, who is one of the founders of humanistic psychology, both talked about something which is called "choiceless awareness" or "desireless awareness", where you can look at something without having any investment in it being a certain way. Then you can see more clearly. If you need to be a mother, you are going to have an investment in looking at everything in a certain way, to make it motherly. There is a beautiful quote which says, "The truth waits for eyes unclouded by longing." It is a quote really worth thinking about. You can all understand what is meant by it. You look at something without investment.

Power and loneliness

I have often mentioned a book called *Power in the Helping Professions*, by Adolf Guggenbuhl-Craig, who is a Jungian.[18] It has got some good bits in it and is worth reading. I need to say something about what may be a very obvious motivation in the helper – the desire to help others to assuage a kind of loneliness in oneself. It may be that what people are really looking for is intimacy, and they are getting it through a helping relationship. It's something about needing your clients to need you. There is something in doing a chart, when someone is opening up to you and you are guiding and sharing with them – there is a sexual element in it. The person is sharing hidden things with you, and it is almost an 8th house thing. They are sharing their secrets, and you have to be open to them in order to hear and listen to what they are saying. There is a kind of closeness that can happen when you are doing a chart, and when it is going well, that can actually assuage any loneliness that you might have during that time.

When I was doing charts in the early days, I sometimes got people who had very different lifestyles from mine. They were people whom I would never really have come across during the course of my life, but they somehow ended up coming for a reading. While we were doing the reading, provided we clicked, I would feel my oneness with that person. I was very open and receptive, as if we were being very intimate. But as soon as the reading was done and we had to chat while the taxi came or something, suddenly there was separateness again – a kind of awkwardness. It was different. The oneness was gone. I remember once hearing an astrologer in America who was a well known lecturer, a Scorpio. What he said kind of shocked me. He said to the group he was lecturing to, "When I lecture to you, it is as if I am having sex with all of you." There is something that can happen in terms of a strong interaction. There is a certain energy exchange in it. There may be some sort of vicarious sexual gratification or need for closeness or intimacy in being a helper.

Audience: I think you can get that with Moon-Saturn and Venus-Saturn. I have Venus square Saturn.

---

[18] Adolf Guggenbuhl-Craig, *Power in the Helping Professions*, Spring Publications, 1979.

Howard: I would also describe it as a Pluto or 8th house kind of feeling. Maybe if you have Neptune in the 8th, healing or helping comes from something that feels intimate and at one with the other person. We could probably find a lot of different astrological significators to put with it. Again, there is no condemning here – but i t is better to be aware of it, and then maybe you won't get your boundaries blurred or your roles mixed up. There is also the issue of being drawn to helping because of the power it gives you. This leads me into this book by Guggenbuhl-Craig. He talks about the Wounder Healer in the book, and the archetype of Chiron. His main premise is that archetypes come in pairs – they are bipolar, and it is wrong to think of one end of the archetype and not the other end. They both exist. He says there is no healer archetype which is separate from the archetype of someone who is wounded or in need of help, because they go together. He calls this bipolar archetype the Wounded Healer.

He talks a lot about physicians and doctors. I think that certain kinds of professional helper would be more prone to the problem he is talking about than astrologers are. He talks about doctor and patient. Let's call it healer and patient. He says that you need to remember, i f you are a healer, that every healer has a hidden patient inside him or her. Every healer has a wounded bit inside. Guggenbuhl-Craig also says that it's the other way around – every patient has an inner healer. What he is really against is any behaviour or attitude which perpetrates one-sided archetypes. You can get some people in the helping professions, especially given a certain kind of training, who think that it is only their clients who have the problems. They think that people who come to them have a problem, and then they are sorted out by the healer. I don't see this so much among astrologers, but it is possible.

You also get patients who come looking for the doctor to make them better, which means that they are not acknowledging their own inner healer. Guggenbuhl-Craig says that the doctor who hasn't acknowledged their own woundedness is a less effective doctor than one who has acknowledged their own woundedness. If you are a doctor and you haven't acknowledged your woundedness, you will encourage polarisation, and other people will have to carry your woundedness for you. It is a little complicated by the Jungian idea that what you don't own in yourself, you attract from the outside. You live your life vicariously from the outside, through other people. So if you are a healer or a helper or a doctor who is not in touch with your woundedness, then you need other people to be wounded because you need someone to live it for you. And the patient who is not in touch with their inner healer is looking for someone to do it from the outside.

This is one of the reasons why, when we are training people at the CPA, we want them to be in therapy as part of the Diploma course. I believe that, if you work through your own issues, those issues are the things you are going to be best able to help other people with. Also, it is really important not to forget your common humanity. I really don't care how many qualifications you have, or how well you do in your exams. You need the skills, and obviously they are important, but if you start thinking that the skills are the only thing that makes you a good astrologer, you have gone off course. What really counts is your in-touchness with your common humanity – this is at the heart of any healing or change when you are working with someone. The idea at the back of my mind is that, if someone comes for help, the answers are there in the person. Something in them knows what they have to do. There is the guide, the facilitator, the healer – someone who can help enliven that part which already knows what to do, rather than telling them what you think they should do. It is a mental attitude – that the answers are already there in the person who is paying you. There is a kind of *hubris* one should try to avoid, which is the belief that you have to provide all the answers. It is actually easier to fall into than you might realise.

I remember doing a reading for a woman, and it was going really well. I think everyone gets this at some time – it was one of those readings where I was channelling something, and the symbols were really alive for me. I was saying things that really struck home for her, and she was really enjoying it. I started to think, "I am really good at this. I am an oracle." It just went through my mind briefly, because it felt so good. What happened was that I was drinking tea at the time, and just when I was having that thought about what a good astrologer I was, I went to put the cup to my mouth and I missed my mouth and got tea all over me. It was like water putting out my fire.

This client had a lot of Virgo in her chart. I hope you see the point I am trying to make here. We are all helpers, but we are all helpless, too. It is not just the people coming to you who are helpless. As I say, I don't worry about it too much in astrology. I see it more in some aspects of the medical profession, where the doctor has a certain kind of authority. But I must admit that, in my interaction with doctors in the last few years, I have met many who have been very commendable, and who have the gift of seeing and understanding you as a whole person. Chiron had wounds which couldn't be healed, and yet he was the one who could heal other people. The idea is that the person who comes to be helped needs to take responsibility for their own healing. We have to midwife it somehow, and to do that, we have to see our own wounds, our own helplessness. The physician or the healer needs to remember that it is not just other people who have problems.

Saviours and victims

There is another book I can recommend along these lines, by Dr. Bernard Rosenblum. It is called *The Astrologer's Guide to Counselling*.[19] It is worth looking at. I don't know if it is still in print. When I first read it years ago, I wasn't sure about it. Then I reread it when I was getting this seminar together. He makes some very good points in the book. One of the things he says is that, in any relationship, whether it is astrologer-client or friendship or lover or spouse, there is a place in most of us that enjoys being the wise and compassionate one. That's a good feeling. There is a bit of us that gets off on showing somebody the way, on being able to be the one who has the answers. There is some bit of you that feels good about that. You have to be careful that it doesn't lead you into some kind of saviour complex, where you become too eager to lead lost souls into the light.

Now, because of the nature of the subject, astrology does carry this pitfall, and it is not just the astrologer's fault. On the client's side, there is a very human propensity for people to be looking for someone who has all the answers. It is called looking for the Magic Helper, the Ultimate Rescuer, and somewhere in everyone there is a desire to find someone who will give you instant solutions and magic answers. Astrology is a good hook to hang that projection on, because of the fact that it is so amazing. Astrologers can see a person they don't know, and within ten or fifteen minutes, by looking at the chart and talking to the person, they can say some pretty accurate things.

[19]Bernard Rosenblum, M.D., *The Astrologer's Guide to Counseling*, CRCS Publications, 1983.

Astrology has an oracular wizardry. You are cutting through and seeing the truth. Therefore, people who are looking for a person to give them instant solutions and magical answers come to this by getting an astrologer. Then there is the danger that there are some astrologers – and it's in all of us to some degree – who would like to be the kind of person who has the answers. You can see the collusion between the one who wants to provide all the answers and the one who wants to be given all the answers. It is deceptive, because the astrologer is speaking with the authority of the stars. The astrologer can attract very dependent and difficult kinds of people. There are psychic vampires out there, if you know what I mean by that – people who will want to take all your energy. The astrologer, as I say, really enjoys the role of the one who has all the answers. That's really easy prey for a psychic vampire. Do you think there are instant answers and magical solutions? I haven't found any yet. These are inflations and distortions which I think astrologers have to be quite careful about.

Ram Dass uses an expression, "meeting in the space behind your roles." When you are meeting with clients, instead of meeting as the astrologer who is going to help the person who needs help, you somehow meet in a space behind those roles, where you are just two human beings who are talking together and trying to find the best way to find help for a problem. Again, it is the idea of not forgetting your common humanity. It sounds obvious, but if you are doing a lot of charts, and day after day people are coming to you and you are giving advice, it is possible to start thinking that other people have the problems and you are the one who can sort them out. I think you start to lose your effectiveness as a helper when that happens.

Audience: I think one issue that makes it harder is that they are paying us for having the answers. It's the same thing in therapy. Why am I paying this person?

Howard: You still have to try to dispel the illusion as quickly as possible that the astrologer has magic knowledge that will make everything better, and that will tell a person exactly what to do. All my own work comes by recommendation, because I don't advertise – it is all through word of mouth. In general, the illusion of the astrologer having magic knowledge is far worse when you advertise. If you work by recommendation, people will send their friends to you because they know the way you work. But with an advertisement someone might think, "This is Madame Betty of Bayswater here, or Madame Wanda of Wimbledon, who is going to predict the future or tell me what colour to wear on Thursday, and whether I should cut my toenails three days after the full Moon."

Audience: The point is that money changes hands, and there are expectations which money brings with it.

Howard: You have to try to clarify the expectations before the money changes hands. I can tell from a person's voice when they ring, whether they are someone who is looking for a fairground psychic – although some of them may be very good – or someone who is actually looking for an in-depth psychological counselling approach. If I am at all in doubt, I will say to the person, "Who recommended you?" and I might have to say, "Listen, I am not going to sit here and tell you the future. I'll talk about trends, but I am more interested in inner things, in your potentials, in what's blocking you, than in telling you what's going to happen."

Audience: I think that one of the things which is important for the astrologer is to let go of the idea that there is always a solution, that difficulty is not to be tolerated, that we have to get rid of it.

Howard: Yes, that's another thing. Your own attitude to pain and crisis is going to be communicated to the client. That's very important. If you think that pain and crisis are something to be avoided at all costs, then that's going to be your attitude when you're working with people. It is like putting a bandage on things. But if you realise that pain and crisis and suffering are in some ways a gift from the gods, because they make you change or look at certain things that you normally wouldn't look at, then you are a better guide because of your experience and your belief. Of course, you may know from your own experience that suffering can have its rewards and can change you in ways which are constructive, but it's still a little funny to say to someone, "Oh, look, Pluto is conjuncting your Sun and squaring your Moon. Isn't that great! How wonderful this is for you!" It may not be fair, if a person is getting a difficult Pluto transit and is feeling that things are being stripped away. It's a little insensitive to jump in too quickly and say, "Oh, this is a great time!"

Audience: One of the worst things is that somebody with a transit like that may also have a sense of failure. They may be hurting, but they also feel that they are not as good as anyone else.

Howard: Yes, they feel like a victim. Any of you who are doing a fair number of charts will recognise this kind of thing. It was Gurdjieff who said that, if you wish to get out of prison, you first have to acknowledge that you are in prison. I think that, if you are helping people for personal motives, you can become too attached to the role of helping and see the client as the helpless person. Maybe you can't say, "No!" to people because you need to be needed. You need the love and power it gives you, or you need to assuage your guilt. That's when you overbook your diary. That's when you get angry and depressed because people aren't following your advice. The end result of that can be exhaustion and depletion. That's what is so ironic about burn-out – you have actually started out to help people, and to alleviate some of the pain and suffering in the world, but you end up adding more suffering to the universe, which is your own. That's the poignancy of it.

I think you can recognise the signs of burn-out before it gets really bad. You may have been working very hard as an astrologer, and then it starts to get to the point where, when the phone rings and you think it is going to be someone who wants to make an appointment, you cringe. In the beginning, you may be really pleased about getting appointments. "Oh, great, someone gave my name to someone else and they rang me." When you start resenting being asked for help, or the doorbell rings and a client comes in and you immediately feel invaded, you are starting to experience burn-out. Also, you may start to lose faith in what you are doing. You start wondering, "What good is all this anyway? Is it really doing any good?" I think those are the signs that burn-out may be around the corner. What I am saying may be premature if you are a beginner. I am sure that many of you right now would like to get to the point where you did feel burnt out by doing too many charts!

We have time now to do a short guided imagery exercise. It's a very simple one, to give you some time to process and do a little inner work on all this. Just before I give you this exercise, which I will explain to you in a minute, are there any questions or contributions that you want to offer on what we have covered so far? I haven't talked a lot about power and helping, and you might have questions about that.

The astrological Chiron

Audience: You were talking about how archetypes travel in pairs, and that the healer and the patient are part of the same archetype. I was thinking about the healer and the wounder as well. I was thinking about my own family experience. I got to be the person who was the healer, and I feel that my younger sister got to be the wounder, rather than the patient. But maybe the patient and the wounder are linked. Maybe there is another side of the patient that is the wounder, the person who is out to damage other people, rather than the person who says, "Give me help."

Howard: You know the mythological story of Chiron, don't you? He was rejected by his mother because he was half-horse and half-divinity. He was the first centaur, and his mother said, "What's this? Take it away!" The gods turned her into a lemon tree. Chiron was raised by the gods, and he became the first holistic educator and healer. He taught all sorts of things – he taught Aesclepius healing, and he taught Heracles astrology, and he taught Jason how to navigate. He became a kind of foster-parent to the different children of the gods. He also taught warfare. He taught people how to do battle, and then he taught them how to heal the wounds which are incurred in battle. He is both ends of the archetype in that way, too – he is both the wounder and the healer, as well as being the wounded healer.

Psychotherapy is a bit like that because it is about healing, and the process of healing involves bringing the wounds out and clearing them. That can really hurt. I think Chiron is an interesting energy. I do feel that Melanie [Reinhart] is really the authority on it.[20] I call her Melanie of Chironia. She holds that Chiron will give you the answer to everything! In the solar system, Chiron follows Saturn. Anything which is past Saturn takes us beyond the ego. It opens us up

---

[20]See Melanie Reinhart, *Chiron and the Healing Journey*, Arkana, 1989, and *Saturn, Chiron and the Centaurs*, CPA Press, 1996 and 2002.

to seeing life from a broader perspective than our ego or the way the ego would like life to be. The ego wouldn't like to have any suffering at all. The ego is not interested in anything beyond itself. But when you get to the outer planets – and Chiron would be the first of those – then you are getting things which are coming from some other place besides your ego. Something else is making things happen in order to change you, or to tear down your ego and rebuild it in a new way.

Saturn gives you problems. Saturn shows you where you are weak, vulnerable, and inadequate. I firmly believe that Saturn does that. If you look at Saturn by sign and house, you get a sense of where you are weak and vulnerable. But you can actually do quite a bit about Saturn. You can say, "All right, I am vulnerable here, and I am going to do something to get stronger." If you have Saturn in the 3rd, or Saturn in Gemini, and you are insecure about your mind and your ability to communicate, you can work on that. You can get a degree, you can go on courses. You can actually come out quite brilliant as a communicator or a teacher. In the end, you could be someone who could teach other people how to communicate, because of everything you have learned through having to teach yourself.

It is in limitation that the master first shows himself or herself. It is when you find something difficult, something that you really have to struggle with, that you have the potential to be a master. But if it comes easily to you, you are not really masterful at it – you can't really help other people who have difficulty with it, because you don't know what it is like to have a difficulty. You can help others the most with things that you have difficulty with and that you have to master. Saturn is great like that – you can do something about it.

Chiron is a little tougher. There is more surrender in Chiron. There is a wound, where you are damaged or where you have a hole, and you can get very wise and become really evolved as a person in trying to deal with that wound and trying to heal it. But the fact is that the wound won't go away. You still have the wound. You see, with Saturn, you can heal it, and then you don't really have the problem any more – it becomes a strength. With Chiron, you can learn a great deal from the pain, but it doesn't ever quite go away. I think Chiron says that there are certain wounds which never completely heal. There is something healing about having the right attitude towards the wound – learning to live with it and surrendering to it as something which is there to transform you. But it may never go away.

Again, speaking personally, it is funny about Chiron – when it was first discovered, I took to it immediately. I am a traditional kind of person in some ways, with Capricorn rising. When someone comes and tells me that they have discovered a thirteenth planet, or they start talking about invisible trans-Plutonian planets, I tend to say, "Fine for you, but I don't want to know. It is too weird. It is not established enough." That's me. I just get like that. But I was surprised at how readily I accepted Chiron, and how much it seemed to supply a missing energy in the chart. Eventually, when the ephemeris came out, I looked it up and I saw that it is exactly on my MC. There is a reason why I took to it!

I think the asteroids are interesting, but I don't often put them into a chart reading. But I took immediately to Chiron, especially when I discovered where it is in my chart. What has been happening in the last few years is that, amongst other things, Pluto has been bringing out my Chiron, and I am amazed at how Chironian I have become, not only in terms of my walking disability, but also in terms of being a teacher. With Chiron in the 10th house, you are very public with your wounds. There are many, many things that I have gained from the illness. It has changed me in areas where I really needed to change, and I am grateful for it – I can see the wisdom of a higher intelligence which has guided this part of my journey. You are definitely kicked up a grade or two. You have got to go up a few grades to deal with Chiron. It is like speeded-up teaching. It is a challenging part of the curriculum. Even though there are many good things that come from it, it is a wound that is never going to go away. You still have the damage.

Mine is physical to some degree, but it can be psychological, too. For example, you could have a woman who has had real problems with the father. Let's say Chiron is in the 4th, the house of the father, or Chiron conjuncts or squares the Sun. That could mean damage to do with father's pain, or the woman's relationship with him is damaged. It could be the catalyst which leads to an awful lot of growth and change, but even then, although you have got so much through it and you can heal it to some degree, it may be that the wound is still there and never completely goes away. Every once in a while it comes back up again, and you have to deal with it again.

Audience: I was talking to somebody yesterday who has got a Sun-Moon conjunction. They are about 3° apart, and Chiron is right in the middle. She was abused by her father as a child, and has done a lot of work on coming to terms with it. But there we were in the middle of talking, and all of a sudden she just burst into floods of tears. Although she thought she had come to terms with it, she hadn't.

Howard: That is what I am trying to say is the difference between Chiron and Saturn. You can often really do something about Saturn. Chiron, because it is beyond the ego, beyond Saturn, is a slightly different story. In a way it is almost Neptunian or Plutonic, because it is something that you ultimately have to surrender to.

Audience: Isn't that one of the greatest antidotes to *hubris?*

Howard: Yes. Do you all know what *hubris* is? It is when you think you are everything and really great, and you are full of yourself.

Audience: That's where your common humanity is so necessary.

Audience: What orbs do you use for Chiron?

Howard: Most of you know that orbs are a very personal thing, so you should take what you are happy with. I tend to be fairly liberal with them. For a conjunction or square or opposition involving Chiron, I would probably go up to 8°, and maybe even 10°, but probably no more than 10°. For minor aspects like a semisquare or sesquiquadrate, I tighten it up to a 1° or 2° orb. For an inconjunct, I am happy to use 5°. I use those orbs for all the planets. I put Chiron in with the other planets, even though some people would argue about that. What I have observed about Chiron is that, when you get transits to it in the chart, it can awaken people. They may get more into healing, or training as a healer, or working on their wounds, or working on their pain. Even transiting Chiron seems to do that. If you have Chiron in Scorpio, Pluto may be hitting it right now, or if you have Chiron in Capricorn, the traffic jam in Capricorn may be hitting it.

Audience: When I did my therapeutic training, transiting Chiron went over my MC.

Howard: When transiting Chiron hits your Descendant, there will be something in relationships that will bring out Chiron. Either you may be Chiron for the other person, or they may be Chiron for you. The whole situation brings out where you are wounded in a certain way.

A guided imagery exercise

All right, let's do this exercise. This is one of those guided imagings where you will initially be working on your own. Let me just tell you in general what I am going to ask you to do. I am going to ask you to close your eyes and then to do some inner reflecting. Then I will ask you a few questions, when you are in that inward-looking mode. You should keep a pen and a bit of paper near you, so you can write down certain things. Then we will take it from there. The exercise is not too long – maybe five to seven minutes. If, for some reason, you are not comfortable at any point – if you are closing your eyes and going in and it becomes uncomfortable - please, just open your eyes and start writing about what is going on. I will leave that up to you. It probably won't make you uncomfortable. And if the person next to you starts snoring, which is a possibility, just kick them. And do the same if I start snoring.

Now close your eyes and feel how good it is to relax. Take a few deep breaths, and breathe out any tension. You want to get out of your head. Let your shoulders relax. Let your facial muscles drop and relax. Wherever you are holding on, in your hands or neck or shoulders, just let go. Let go of the stomach. You might be tightening your stomach muscles, so let that go. Let your legs be loose. If you are holding on in your feet, just let go. Let go of your tense stuff. Take a few more deep breaths. In your mind's eye, I want you to recall a time you chose to be of service to a person, a thing, or a group. Try to remember a time when you were a helper and were performing a service for someone or something. Take a few minutes to reflect on that experience in your mind and your imagination. See what feelings come up about it. You have a couple of minutes. I will tell you when to finish. Relive that experience – connect to that time when you helped. Now I want you to recall another time when you chose to be of service, or to act as a helper or carer to someone or something. Think of another incident. Take a few minutes to reflect on it. Now, see if you can get an image or

a picture or a symbol of the server in you. It is as if you are watching a
screen – you don't know what is going to come up next. See what flashes
in your mind when you think of yourself as a server. What image do
you see? Now, with your eyes still closed, ask yourself: "Why do I
want to serve?" Just see what comes up when you ask yourself that
question: "Why do I want to serve?" And in your own time, come out of
the exercise gradually. Open your eyes and make some notes about
what you remember and why you want to serve. Come out and do some
writing about it.

What I suggest is that we take our tea break, but while we are
having the break, sometimes it helps to find a partner and talk about
what happened to bring it more to life. I am leaving it up to you.
While you have the break, look around – and if someone wants to sit
and process it with you, go ahead. Find a corner to sit in. You can do a
little bit of that during the break. Meanwhile I will put some charts
up on the board.

Virgo and service

Before we begin with an example chart, I want to say something
in general about Virgo as a sign of service. Our first example has got
quite a bit of Virgo in the chart, so this is going to be an interesting
chart to work on. One of my main interpretations of Virgo and the 6th
house is the idea of trying to get the outer forms of your life to be as
close a representation as possible of what you are inside. I will explain
that. It is a kind of meeting of the inner and the outer. When I say
Virgo tries to get the outer forms of life to be a true representation of
what is inside, I mean things like the job you are doing, and how you
dress. You try to get how you live to be a true reflection of what you are
inside. Obviously this is going to take a lot of adjusting and refinement
all the time, because as you change, your outer forms have to change.
The idea is to get the outer to reflect the inner. Everything that has an
outside has an inside. This is where we get the idea of purity and
efficiency – to get your body functioning as well as possible, to get your
psyche as pure as possible so that you can be a better receptor or
channel for what you are meant to do. Virgo and the 6th house
instinctively know that the purer you are, the better channel you will
be.

The other thing that comes to mind when I think of Virgo and the 6th house is a quote I once heard: "Our true vocation is to be ourselves." You have to think of the Virgo-Pisces polarity, or the differences between Mercury and Neptune. Mercury is the ruler of Virgo. There may be some other planet that has yet to be found which may be a better ruler for Virgo, but for now, think of Mercury. And Neptune is one of the rulers of Pisces. One way we can give meaning to life is to see all the different people in the world, everyone in existence, as part of an orchestra. Each of us has to get the tune we are meant to be playing as right as possible, so that we can contribute to the best functioning of the larger whole. Do you see how I am putting Virgo's specific details and Pisces' bigger picture together? By perfecting who you are, by being a better channel, you are contributing. You are doing your bit to serve the greater whole of which you are part. It is as if each planet in your chart represents an instrument in the orchestra. Somehow we have to get all the instruments to play harmoniously with one another. Don't ask me who writes the score.

Another analogy for Virgo and the 6th house is the idea of the cell within the larger unit of an organ or organism. A cell is a complete thing within itself, and yet it forms a multi-cellular organ or organism, and even though each cell is complete within itself, it contributes to the functioning of something larger. It is like an ideal work force. Each cog in the wheel, each person in the work force, is doing their particular task, their particular specialisation. When you put that all together, you get something larger which is functioning as it is meant to be. Those can be guidelines for the Virgo principle. It gives a great awareness of trying to get the outer to match the inner, and therefore it will also be of service to others in helping them to do the same. Virgo tries to help other people make their outer forms a true reflection of what they are inside, or to help them become more who they are meant to be. Virgos can perform service in that way. They want to see things running efficiently. The idea is to see things going smoothly and efficiently. It is a sign of technical efficiency and health for that reason. It is about fine tuning.

Richard Idemon calls the 6th the house of repair and maintenance, where you have to use whatever energy is around your 6th house just to keep things running well. If you are strongly Virgo, there are lots of times when you have to make readjustments and improve what you are doing. Someone once said that all writers are rewriters. You don't sit down and write something perfectly. It is very unusual to write something perfectly right away, unless you are Mozart. Writing is a process – you are always scratching out a lot and then rewriting bits of it. This is what I think when I think about Virgo. They shouldn't expect to be perfect at something right away. I know many people with the Sun in Virgo or Virgo rising who would make excellent astrologers, but they keep putting off doing charts for people because they are afraid they won't be perfect at it right away. I see some of you nodding. You are afraid you won't know enough. My point is that you will learn through experience.

Someone once told me – I don't know if it is true – that when an aeroplane is going somewhere, it is actually off course 90% of the time. It adjusts its course only 10% of the time, and then it gets where it wants to go. So you don't have to be perfect at something right away. You do it and you learn from doing it. Maybe you make mistakes, or you see what works and what doesn't, or there is something you gain from just doing it, from just being experienced at something. I think of this for Capricorn as well. It has always bothered me when Virgos who have abilities at things like doing charts are afraid to, because they are so afraid of saying the wrong thing or taking the responsibility involved. It isn't a bad thing to have that kind of worry, but it can mean that they never get around to really perfecting themselves at something – they are not actually doing it enough. They aren't doing it enough because they are afraid they won't be good at it right away.

Leo has a similar problem. Sometimes Leo is afraid to try, just in case they might fail. It is easier to imagine what a great astrologer you could be, and how much better you could be than other people. It's harder to actually try it and risk not being so hot. Leos need to get over cowardliness and fear of failure. But Virgos are more afraid of not doing it as well as it could be done.

There is a kind of Pisces shadow with Virgo. My experience is that they are usually very good at sensing when something is out of place or when something isn't quite right and needs to be adjusted for someone else. Someone with a Virgo Sun or Virgo rising will be one of those people who goes around factories and checks the safety procedures, or goes around restaurants and checks the health and safety requirements. I know that when people with strong Virgo come for readings, it is actually quite funny – when they are around, I tend to notice everything that is wrong around me, like the dust on the cassette recorder. If someone else had come in, I wouldn't even notice, but somehow the very presence of strong Virgo brings out what is weak or what is flawed. If you hang around a Virgo person for long enough, i t will make you aware of everything that is not quite right in your life. It just happens. They don't have to say anything. That is a funny way of serving, but I also see it as quite a practical service. I think that Virgo, as an earth sign, would say, "Great, you have all this inspiration, and you have all these ideas, but what good are they? How can you put them to practical use in an everyday way?" I have found Virgos personally helpful in very practical ways.

When I was in Australia, there was a Virgoan chap looking after me. He was perfect. He was actually a Scorpio with the Sun in the 6th house and the Moon in Virgo, and he knew exactly what my needs were. He wasn't invasive – he could see when I could handle something – but he also knew what would really help me. Virgo is about the ability to provide help, and to help something run more effectively. The idea is that your true vocation is to be yourself. If we can really be ourselves – if all of us could be who we are and be a true reflection of ourselves, and cut through everything and say the truth of what we really are – everything would fit together. Someone, I think it was the Queen Mother, said, "Work is the rent we pay for life." Then there is another story, which I have told many times. When they were building St. Paul's, a man went up to one of the workmen and said, "What are you doing?" and the workman replied, "Laying bricks." He said to a second workman, "What are you doing?" and that workman replied, "I'm earning money." He said to a third workman, "What are you doing?" and that workman replied, "I'm helping to contribute to the building of a great cathedral." It is all in your attitude. Work means different things to different people. It is the attitude behind the work which is important.

They say that technique is the liberation of the imagination, which, again, is a Virgo-Pisces thing. It is the idea that you can have a great Piscean imagination or great Neptunian inspiration, but you need the technique, you need the skills in order to put it to use, whether we are talking about healing ability or some other ability. You can have great healing ability, but if you are a Virgo, you need to train at something. You need to find some medium which gives you the chance for your healing ability to come through, whether it is reading the Tarot cards or doing charts or doing something like massage or body work. It is training, learning the system, learning the method, which allows the creativity or the healing to come through. I remember when I did some charts for people from the Royal Academy of Music. There were two types. There was the Piscean type, who had great feeling but didn't have the skills, and there was the Virgo type, who were very technical but didn't necessarily have the inspiration. That is the polarity of Virgo-Pisces. Mercury is a planet of detail, and Neptune is a planet of oneness.

Audience: A lot of Virgos can be mistaken for Pisceans. I find that it is sometimes just the opposite of what you say.

Howard: Any sign can look like its opposite. An awful lot of Librans seem like Aries, and an awful lot of Aries seem like Librans. Ultimately, your Sun-sign is extremely important for you to feel fulfilled. You have to develop the qualities of your Sun-sign in the most constructive way. But you also have to develop the qualities of the whole cross that your Sun is on. If you are a Virgo, you really need to develop the whole mutable cross to come into your own.

Audience: Sometimes a person doesn't want to face the Sun, doesn't want to live that energy.

Howard: That's sometimes the case. I think the solar energy is what we are really here to develop and build in this lifetime, in order to define our uniqueness. Some people are afraid of defining their individuality too much, but it is through the Sun-sign that you do it. The other thing about Virgo is that, because its ruler, Mercury, is so adaptable and flexible, you have to look at how Mercury is placed in the chart to really get an idea of what kind of Virgo the person is.

An example chart

Mercury and the Moon

Miriam has the Sun in Virgo, and Mercury is also in Virgo, trine Saturn, trine Jupiter, and square the Moon. If you have a Virgo who has Mercury conjunct Neptune, they are going to be a very different kind of Virgo from a Virgo with Mercury conjunct Saturn. So if you start saying, "Virgo likes to be precise and neat and have everything in place," and the Virgo has Mercury conjunct Neptune, saying that is not going to mean that much to them. But if they are a Virgo with Mercury in good aspect to Saturn, then it will probably be true.

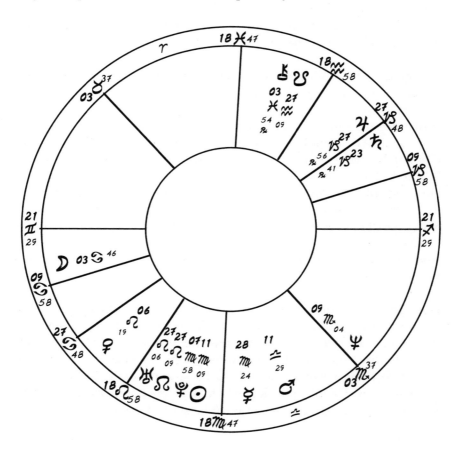

Miriam
3 September 1961, 11.25 pm, Paris
Placidus cusps

What's nice about Miriam's chart is that Mercury has got those trines to Saturn and Jupiter. The square to the Moon is a slightly different thing. It is an out-of-sign square, but I would want to talk about that. To have Mercury in Virgo trine Saturn in Capricorn, in terms of the ability to be orderly or pay attention to details, what would you think? It would encourage that. The trine to Jupiter is a real blessing, if it can be used well, because it gives the the Jupiterian ability to see the bigger picture at the same time that you are seeing the details.

Miriam: I am working on that. I know that I can do that. When you were talking about Virgos doing charts, I was thinking about a time when I came out of someone else's lecture and thought, "I'll never do astrology, I'll never be any good. I'll never be able to do it like that."

Howard: Was this after one of Liz' lectures? Yes? How did I know?

Miriam: A friend of mine said, "You can't always be so negative about yourself."

Howard: Be you. Be yourself. Don't try to be Liz or me or anyone else.

Miriam: This friend said, "I know why you think you can't do astrology. It's because you can't be perfect." I said, "Well, yes." She said, "Well, don't try to be perfect, because when you do a chart, you will be fine."

Howard: Good advice. That's also what I meant earlier. It is important to have the technical proficiency, but ultimately you have to meet in that place which is behind the roles with another person. Then you use your knowledge in the best way you can. This is the thing people say when they are putting down Mercury or Gemini or Virgo – they can't see the wood for the trees. Their noses are in the details. When Mercury is trine Jupiter on the cusp of the 9th, it helps to offset that tendency. You can see the bigger meaning and also the details. It is like having broadened awareness and focused awareness at the same time. That ability is there in you. If you believe in past lives, you must have worked at it before, because you have the talent. It is just a matter of bringing it out.

The Moon square Mercury adds a little bit more chaos, though, especially with the Moon in Cancer. I don't see Cancer as a very organised sign, to tell you the truth, in spite of what you might read in books. It is a sign of moods and changing feelings, and your thinking will be influenced by your moods. If you have a Moon-Mercury square, then Mercury, which is the planet of the mind, conflicts with the Moon, which is the planet of emotion, especially in Cancer. Then you will get fluctuations. Also, the Moon-Mercury square does contribute to some self-doubt, because the mind says one thing but the heart says another. Or your feelings say one thing but your reason says another. It is a head-heart dilemma. Mercury square the Moon can also worry about being misunderstood or misunderstanding other people. If you think in terms of childhood, Miriam has some nice aspects to the Moon, which are great, but the Moon square Mercury may mean that there were some communication problems with the mother.

Miriam: The most common problem arising around communication with my mother was that, if I didn't want to talk, she would try to force me to talk. But if I was answering back, I was told to stop answering back. If I wasn't answering, then she would say, "Why don't you ever talk to me?"

Howard: It is a double message.

Miriam: I didn't know what to say, and I was always trying to adapt.

Howard: I think your mother's stuff gets in the way of your Mercury functioning as well as it could. What I have noticed about the Moon in Cancer, or the strongly Cancerian person, is that they have to respect their rhythms. If they are in one of their pulling-inside-their-shell rhythms, woe befall the person who tries to poke them out. They'll just drive the Cancerian type in more, and they won't come out until they are ready to come out. Your mother tried to poke you out of your state of mind to get you to talk. That is an insult to Cancer – they need to be true to their own rhythms. If she had just left you alone, eventually you would have come out. When you did, it wasn't the right time for her. That's the Moon-Mercury square.

Ideally, one would have Moon trine Mercury or Moon sextile Mercury. Then there is a better mental understanding and better communication between you and mother than when you have the square or the opposition. The square or opposition can give a problem later in life, because mother is the first prototype for relationship. Later on, you might feel, "My partner doesn't understand me," or "I can't communicate my needs." In the earlier scenario, you are trying to communicate with your mother – "I need food," or "I need space," or "I need closeness" – but she isn't able to read you right, and that's what sets up the expectation of misunderstandings later on.

Even though one wouldn't think a Moon-Mercury square would be that difficult an aspect, it is tricky. Moon-Mercury interaspects in synastry are also very tricky. It is a beautiful aspect if you have a Moon-Mercury conjunction with someone. If Miriam meets someone whose Mercury is 3° Cancer, or someone meets her who has the Moon at 28° Virgo, then they have a Moon-Mercury connection. Usually, provided it is not impinged upon by other aspects, they immediately understand what you feel, or you are receptive to what they say, or they understand your emotions. Sometimes it is amazing – you don't even have to speak to know what is going on. But even if you have some beautiful synastry contacts with someone, if your Moon is square the person's Mercury or the other way around, it can be very frustrating. When you try to talk or communicate your feelings, you run into some sort of difficulty.

Audience: Uranus is in the 4th and opposing the MC, and what Miriam seems to be describing about this mother is quite perverse and contradictory. Is that anything to do with Uranus?

Howard: Yes, I would agree, that's part of it, if you take the 4th house to be the mother. Even if you take the 10th to be the mother, the opposition to the MC brings in the Uranian side. But I think the Moon-Mercury square and Moon-Mars square are the keys to most of the problems with mother. I have tried playing around with the 4th house as mother. What I find, in all honesty, is that if I look at my chart and I read the 10th house as mother, I can get a very interesting reading, but if I read the 10th house as father I get a very interesting reading as well, and I learn something from both. It may be because the 4th and 10th houses are a polarity, and polarities often swap in living out things. So I am not really rigid about it. Or I'll talk to the person and see which house seems to work best with the description they give me.

Audience: What happens when you get the ruler of one parental house in the other one?

Howard: When you get the ruler of one parental house in the other parental house, sometimes you get one parent playing both roles.

Miriam: My father was working all day, and I only saw him in the evening. There were a lot of things he didn't know about.

Howard: What was going on? I'm sorry, maybe I shouldn't ask. You don't have to tell.

Miriam: It's all right. My mother was very unbalanced, and could behave in very wild ways. She could get violent. But then she would say, "If you tell your father, I will beat you." So I couldn't tell my father.

Howard: That must have been pretty horrible. There you are again with that difficult Moon-Mercury communication, and the Moon-Mars, which is the violence.

Miriam: When my parents split up – my brother is eight years younger than me – he suffered a lot more than I did, in a way. Now we both say to my father, "Did you know that she was unbalanced?" "No," he says to us, "I never knew." Surely he must have known! But we were trapped by not being able to tell him yet expecting him to know.

Howard: I was going to say something about that. The Moon is sextile Pluto, trine Neptune, and trine Chiron – it's part of a grand trine. And you can be deceived into thinking that when your Moon is trine something, that has to be good. But when you get the Moon trine or sextile an outer planet, it is not necessarily an easy ride. Don't be fooled into thinking that the person had an easy time with mother just because it is a trine or sextile. If you have the Moon in aspect to Chiron, Neptune, or Pluto, you met those energies via your mother. The trine or sextile says that maybe you can process it or come out of it better than someone who has them in square. The aspect shows how the ego deals with the problem. With squares or oppositions, the ego has more resistance to dealing with the energy. With the trines and the sextiles, the ego is sometimes more creative in bringing those energies together. You may know how to deal with a Plutonic or

Neptunian childhood and not get as damaged as someone who has the square or the opposition.

Audience: One thing to remember about a grand trine, Howard – if it is a very close grand trine, you have actually got a dynamic where each planet is on the midpoint of the other two. Chiron is on the Moon-Neptune midpoint here.

Howard: We should also say something about the kite formation. A kite is when you have got an opposition to one point of a grand trine, and sextile the other two points. In this case you have got Chiron opposing Pluto, the Sun, and Uranus. If we also include midpoints, then we have Chiron = Moon/Neptune = Sun/Uranus = Uranus/Pluto. You can see how this really looks like a kite.

Audience: It looks like a volcano to me, with Chiron at the top.

Howard: When you have a kite, the idea is that the focal opposition motivates you into action. But the Sun-Pluto has a sextile to Neptune. There seems to have been difficulty with the father as well.

Miriam: Not often.

Howard: Maybe it was difficult because he didn't realise what your mother was doing.

Miriam: As I grew up, my brother and I were the only ones there for him. I feel guilty a lot of the time. He makes me do things I don't want to do. He says things like, "Will you do a chart for a friend of mine?" I say, "But I haven't got the time," and he phones up and says, "You promised you would do it." I say, "I didn't promise."

Howard: What advice would the rest of you give her about that? Should she do what he wants or not?

Audience: No!

Audience: She should get paid for it.

Howard: I think that, with this stuff down here in the 4th – if you take the 4th to be your father – there is a need to stand up to him. It is a Plutonic need. I think you have to risk confrontation with him to get your own power back. Am I being too pushy?

Miriam: You are saying it is a power issue.

Howard: Yes, it is a power issue between you and your father, and I would like to see you take your power back.

Miriam: We argue, and then I put the phone down and say, "It doesn't matter that I put the phone down." But it does matter. Then I ring back, and he's at the other end of the phone straight away, saying, "Oh, I knew you would call back." That really infuriates me. Then we start arguing again, and I end up saying, "I'm sorry."

Howard: There is something here about learning how to say, "No!" without feeling guilty.

Audience: I was thinking about what Miriam said, about her and her brother being the only ones there for her father. They are apparently the only people in the world who can help him. But he makes them feel that way. It may not be true.

Miriam: When he says it, I feel he is saying it for a reason.

Howard: Yes, there is a reason: manipulation. I would think it is important to keep working on standing up to him, and to risk it. I think you have to do it from a very clean place in yourself, where you say, "Listen, Dad, I would like to be able to help you, but I can't right now," and bear the brunt of his anger. If you take the 4th house to be the father, with your north Node and Uranus there in Leo, there is something about being true to who you are rather than selling out to keep the peace or win his love. It seems like a risk. It is a solar battle. Some people have to fight the mother to become an individual, but you have to fight the father.

Miriam: I left my mother. I have nothing to do with her. I don't see her. I can't see her, and I know I can't see her, and I don't want to. She wants to see me, and I just don't want to. I don't mind not seeing her. Now maybe my father thinks I am going to do the same to him, so I can't do it to him.

Howard: How has it been with Jupiter around your Sun recently? Did you notice anything opening up between you and him?

Miriam: No, that's when we had a big argument.

Howard: It's true that Jupiter can bring out difficulties. That's what you always have to watch with transits of Jupiter. You think it's going to be great, but if the planet it is transiting has an opposition or a square natally, then it brings out the whole thing. It reveals everything to you. Now, I would watch this transit, because Jupiter is going to come back over the Sun again. This could actually be a good time to bring things out more, and experiment with other ways of handling your father than you have done in the past. You need to look at where you really want to come from. I would sense that there is a lot of fear around standing up to him, or even losing him.

Miriam: Yes. I am afraid that if I stand up to him, he might die. What if I have an argument with him and he dies and I won't be able to bring him back?

Howard: This is what I mean about coming out cleanly. Do you know how we can react from a complex? It's like someone hitting a button. A complex is like that. Before you can help it, your ego is pushed around.

Miriam: If anyone can wind me up, he can.

Howard: Yes, some people know just where to go, and suddenly all your buttons are pushed. I think you could work on that therapeutically with someone, so that you can get to the point where, when he does it, you say, "Oh, yes, there is my complex getting pushed." Then you could come from a place which says, "I am sorry, I really would like to help you, but it is not convenient for me now. It's not something I can do now." You are really clean then, and if he should die the next day for some reason, I know it would be hard and you might blame yourself at first, but in actual fact you are clean. But if you are just reacting from the complex, then you are still caught. It is sometimes easier said than done, but I think that the Jupiter transit might help.

Miriam: It has been over my Sun twice.

Howard: I am looking at Jupiter bringing out the whole Pluto-Chiron-Sun opposition.

Miriam: When he wanted me to do the chart for his friend, he said, "Do it quickly. Write anything, it doesn't matter." I couldn't do a chart properly with that kind of pressure.

Howard: He is being a little too generous with your time. The other way to depersonalise this to some degree is to look at your chart as if it was someone who came to see you with this problem. What would you say to them? You may have to do a little more inner work on it before you are really ready, but it would be an appropriate time to work on it now, since we are talking about it.

Signatures of the helper

Let's stay with the theme of the helper, because you do have a lot of the significators I would give to helping – Virgo, the Moon in Cancer, Chiron in Pisces in the 10th, and also Neptune in the 6th. The 6th house has a lot to do with what kind of service we do for others, or what kind of skills we have, and Neptune can be healing skills. Whatever planets are in the 6th can show resources or abilities. I do think the 4th house has a lot to do with what comes out in us as we get older. You are just thirty now, so you are moving out of your Saturn return. As we get older, the 4th house tends to be revealed more, and we get more of a grip on it, because we go deeper into ourselves and we look at ourselves more. With the Sun in Virgo conjunct Pluto in the 4th, and with the Sun ruling the 4th house, and with Chiron in Pisces in opposition, I think that, in many ways, this is the chart of someone who is a server, who is meant to be a helper. You probably need to develop techniques or skills in some field, or even some speciality of a field, to really come into your own as a server. This is my own way of looking at it, when I think of Virgos coming into who they really are. If they are a nurse, I tend to think they should find some branch within nursing to specialise in. Virgo needs to go for the particular, and the more of an authority you can become in something particular, the more the Virgo side of you feels good, because you have got a speciality.

Miriam: Yes. It is why I do astrology, and I wanted to go into psychological astrology combined with counselling. Defining that goal has really helped me.

Howard: You will come into it more and more. I think there is a lot in the chart about your finding fulfilment through your work, and through becoming skilled. I get the idea, with Virgo in the 4th, that even when you are old, you will still be working. You will still want to be productive. The 4th house is what comes out as we get older, and with Virgo there, as you get older, it will be important to have something that you are really being productive and useful with. However, Leo on the IC says that, even if you do have work that you find important and special, the Leo energy and the Uranian energy will make you need to take time away from it. It is awfully good advice in general – if you are an astrologer – to be able to take time away from people's psyches every once in a while.

Miriam: That's what my friend said last week. She said, "You're a Virgo?" I said, "Yes." She said, "All they do is read astrology books." I do read a lot of astrology books. But I find that I have got to read other things.

Howard: I understand perfectly what you mean. When I read novels, I feel guilty because I am not working.

Miriam: Yes!

Howard: But you learn so much from a good novelist. I sometimes sit and watch the news with a book of charts. I think they should put on the news when and where the person they are talking about was born. There are some incredible stories that happen to people, and you wonder what their chart is like to have that happen.

Audience: They often say, "So-and-so, age twenty-nine, was arrested for whatever." You often hear that age of twenty-nine mentioned.

Howard: Of course you know immediately that the person is going through the Saturn return. When I was in Australia there was a horrible programme called *Hard Copy* or *Hard News*. I think it is an adaptation of an American show. They do tabloid exposées of rather horrific things. There was one story of a woman who had been kidnapped and kept in a cupboard under the bed and used as a sex slave for seven years. She had survived the experience and was relatively okay. You think to yourself, "What was in her chart? What was going on?"

Audience: That sounds like Pluto.

Howard: It definitely sounds like Pluto, and Saturn too, and maybe also the 12th house. You do start wondering. Anyway, to have Virgo in the 4th house suggests the need to be productive as you get older. To have Uranus in the 4th but ruling the 10th also suggests that, as you get older, work will be important and you will find something to do. But work needs to be balanced with the need to do things just for yourself.

Miriam: That is very hard for me.

Howard: Otherwise you will get resentful in the end. Also, this is about the ability to say, "No!" To have the north Node conjunct Uranus means being able to tell people, "No!" You have to become a bit Uranian. To be a bit Uranian means you have a right to challenge people.

Audience: Howard, would you also counsel her to find a balance and give enough attention to her own wounds? I think the chart is really clear about her vocation – to be of service and a helper – but there are also very, very painful parental wounds, with Pluto and Uranus in the 4th and Chiron opposite the Sun. And with Saturn in Capricorn in the 8th, she may be helping other people as a way of looking for closeness.

Miriam: When I get help from other people, I don't think I deserve it, with Saturn in the 8th. If someone really wants to help me, I make it hard for them, because I find it hard to talk openly. If they ask me about my childhood, I say I had a good family. Someone once said to me, "You are very private. I tried to ask you things, and you didn't take any notice of my questions."

Howard: Sun-Pluto will hide a lot. Maybe you need to find someone you could work with, a therapist with whom you feel safe enough to let stuff out.

Miriam: I did some therapy, and it really helped. At first I wanted her to talk to me. I tried everything, and she just sat there. After a few months I thought, "No!" and started listening to myself, and it really helped. It came back to the fact that I could only be helped if I helped myself as well.

Howard: I think there is some inner action that still needs to be taken.

Audience: I was looking at the chart ruler in the 5th house, and thinking that perhaps Miriam should do something creative.

Howard: Yes, something that she does just for herself. I'm getting that from the chart too. It is both Leo at the IC and, as you say, the ruler of the Ascendant and Sun-sign in the 5th. It needs to be some sort of hobby or creative outlet which you do just because it gives expression to something in you, or because you get pleasure out of it.

Miriam: I do enjoy astrology.

Howard: That's in the other direction, the direction of the helper. I'm looking for some sort of creative expression.

Miriam: I write.

Audience: There's a Mars-Mercury conjunction in the 5th. I was thinking of craftsmanship.

Miriam: I knit and do tapestry work.

Howard: I think the whole idea with any chart is to try to make room in your life for as much of the chart as possible. You do have things in the chart which have to do with your own expression, which is just as important as your career.

Audience: Chiron is in the 10th. Could you say something about that?

Audience: Mother Theresa has Chiron in the 10th.

Howard: Do you have her chart details? I was searching like mad to find her data for this seminar, and I didn't find it. I would love to know it.

Audience: It's in the *AA Journal*.[21]

Howard: There were a few charts I wanted to look at, in terms of the theme of the helper, and I have to apologise because I didn't have time to get all the data. I was interested in Mother Theresa and Florence Nightingale. Elisabeth Kübler-Ross is very interesting in terms of life experience leading to service, but I used her at the Vocation seminar and I didn't want to use the chart again.[22] It's interesting to see what happened in these people's lives that led them in a certain way, or what chart aspects fit with what they are doing.

Bob Geldof is an interesting example which I was going to bring up, in terms of how he was maternally deprived. He has the Moon in Sagittarius in the 12th house, and his mother died when he was young. He then got into feeding the world. It is as if he became a mother to the world. Sometimes we use 12th house energies for the sake of the greater whole, and not just for ourselves. He has one of those Sun conjunct Neptune in Libra square Uranus in Cancer charts. In the 1950's there was a Uranus-Neptune square from Cancer to Libra, and the Sun played into it every time it went through a cardinal sign.

The Sun-Uranus square is interesting in terms of Bob Geldof's rebelliousness against authority, but it got mixed up with Neptune in terms of the service he performed. He also wrote an autobiography. It

---

[21]For the reader's interest, the chart data for Mother Theresa as given in the *Internationales Horoskope Lexikon* is 27 August, 1910, 2.25 pm, Skopje, Yugoslavia.
[22]See Part One, p. 33.

is often a good thing to find some famous person that you are interested in, and to read their biography or autobiography and look at their chart – whether it is Isadora Duncan, or Zelda Fitzgerald, or whomever you are into. It is a good way to learn. Also, if you want to use them as examples, it is great, because a lot of them are dead and they can't talk back!

Let's go back to the Moon trine Neptune in Miriam's chart. Remember, I was talking earlier about Moon-Neptune squares indicating trouble, but even the trine can be a problem in terms of boundaries between you and mother.

Audience: What about the misrepresentation between the Moon in Cancer and Gemini rising? Gemini tends to say a lot of things, but the Moon is saying something else. If you look at the elements, the airy element is very strong, so the Moon in Cancer might not be able to communicate its feelings.

Miriam: I know I am sometimes very blocked in my emotional expression. I can stay locked in my emotions because I don't know how to express them. I can't have emotions and talk about them.

Howard: There seem to be two ways to work with that. One would be to find some other form besides the literary, verbal form – whether it is picking up paints, or sculpting, or dancing, or playing music. The other way might be harder. If you can let go enough and risk the indignity of it, you could let out a lot of feelings through some kind of primal work.

Audience: If Mercury is ahead of the Sun, we tend to speak out personally. I think that is very encouraging, because it means Miriam could learn to do that.

Howard: You know, I read that too, when I first started studying astrology.

Audience: You told me that when you did my chart!

Audience: Get your money back!

Howard: I probably said that there is this theory about Mercury ahead of the Sun, but I haven't found it to be of any use myself.

Audience: But there is a grand trine in water. That would give ease in showing feelings.

Howard: Yes, but because Neptune and Chiron are challenging planets, I think it is still hard to express feelings.

Miriam: I cry very easily. I cry when I watch ice skating. A friend said, "What's the matter?" I said, "Nothing, I'm just watching television." He looked at the television and there was an ice skating championship being broadcast, and he said, "What are you crying for?" I said, "It's so beautiful, the music is so beautiful."

Howard: Maybe it has something to do with your sensitivity to beauty, to anything exquisite.

Miriam: I find that if somebody forces me to express my emotions, I will cry instead of speaking.

Audience: I don't believe that you don't feel, or that your feeling function isn't working, I think it is more that you don't trust other people with it. Saturn in the 8th and Sun-Pluto have left you feeling damaged, so it is frightening to express feelings and lose your sense of control over them.

Howard: I agree with all of that.

Miriam: What I do is I cry. I don't talk about what I feel.

Audience: Somebody, I forget her name, had a theory about the kite formation. She said it is not the easy or creative aspect people say it is. I have it in my chart. The focal point where the kite discharges is the point which really has to carry the brunt of all the difficult stuff. You said that before, Howard. Pluto in Miriam's chart is the central issue in her life – finding out where her power lies.

Miriam: My power is with my father.

Howard: Yes. And you'll have to take it back.

Audience: Your father was an illusion in your family. You idealised your father as the good father, but he let you down by not being there.

Miriam: I was really close to him.

Howard: I think you are on to something. I think the parental relationships are really at the core of a lot of things here. It is very understandable that you might have trouble exposing your real feelings, because when you tried to as a child, you were probably trampled on in some way. There may have been a thing in the family about certain things never being said, and you have a whole issue about that. But the chart looks better and better as you get older. I feel very good about you coming more and more into your own.

Miriam: Thank you very much.

Howard: Well, I think we should end now. Listen, have a Merry Christmas and – what do they say? – an Awesome New Year. We'll see a lot of you in January. That's it.

About the author

Howard Sasportas was born in Hartford, Connecticut, USA, at 1.46 am EST on 12 April, 1948. His parents, Max and Edith Sasportas, came from a long line of devout Sephardic Jews, and although he was later to become open to all dimensions of the spiritual life, these roots remained of great significance to him. He received his B.A. from Tufts University and took a Masters degree in Humanistic Psychology from Antioch University. He moved to London in 1973, and in 1979 he was awarded the Gold Medal for the Faculty's Diploma Exam. In the same year he became a tutor for the Faculty, and also began to establish himself as an immensely popular speaker at the Astrological Association of Great Britain.

Howard continued his exploration of psychology and spiritual studies as well as astrology over the following years. He was a graduate of the London-based Psychosynthesis and Education Trust and also of the Centre for Transpersonal Psychology founded by Ian Gordon-Brown and Barbara Somers. In 1983 he and Liz Greene founded the Centre for Psychological Astrology, for which he remained co-director until his death. From 1987 to 1991 he was series editor of Penguin's Arkana Contemporary Astrology Series. He authored two books on his own, *The Twelve Houses* and *The Gods of Change*, co-authored *The Sun-Sign Career Guide* with Robert G. Walker, and produced four volumes of seminars with Liz Greene under the Seminars in Psychological Astrology Series published by Samuel Weiser, Inc: *The Development of the Personality, Dynamics of the Unconscious, The Luminaries,* and *The Inner Planets.* He was constantly in demand, in Great Britain and internationally, as a teacher and lecturer, and also maintained a full astrological and counselling practice.

In his later years Howard battled constantly with chronic ill-health. He bravely endured two major back operations in an attempt to correct a congenital spinal disorder known as ankylosing spondylosis. These operations virtually crippled him. At the same time he had to face the remorseless progress of AIDS, to which he finally succumbed. Toward the end he gave much of his time to the Oasis Centre in North London for AIDS sufferers, and although wheelchair-bound in his last year, he continued to travel and lecture worldwide. His final triumphant lectures were given from his wheelchair, between blood transfusions and nights in hospital, at the Easter 1992 UAC Conference in Washington, DC. Howard died at 5.11 pm BST, on 12 May, 1992.

About the CPA

Director: Liz Greene, Ph. D., D. F. Astrol. S., Dip. Analyt. Psych.

The Centre for Psychological Astrology provides a unique workshop and professional training programme, designed to foster the cross fertilisation of the fields of astrology and depth, humanistic, and transpersonal psychology. The main aims and objectives of the CPA professional training course are:

•   To provide students with a solid and broad base of knowledge within the realms of both traditional astrological symbolism and psychological theory and technique, so that the astrological chart can be sensitively understood and interpreted in the light of modern psychological thought.

•   To make available to students psychologically qualified case supervision, along with background seminars in counselling skills and techniques which would raise the standard and effectiveness of astrological consultation. It should be noted that no formal training as a counsellor or therapist is provided by the course.

•   To encourage investigation and research into the links between astrology, psychological models, and therapeutic techniques, thereby contributing to and advancing the existing body of astrological and psychological knowledge.

History

The CPA began unofficially in 1980 as a sporadic series of courses and seminars offered by Liz Greene and Howard Sasportas, covering all aspects of astrology from beginners' courses to more advanced one-day seminars. In 1981 additional courses and seminars by other tutors were interspersed with those of Liz and Howard to increase the variety of material offered to students, and Juliet Sharman-Burke and Warren Kenton began contributing their expertise in Tarot and Kabbalah. It then seemed appropriate to take what was previously a random collection of astrology courses and put them under a single umbrella, so in 1982 the "prototype" of the CPA – the Centre for Transpersonal Astrology – was born, with the adminstrative work handled by Richard Aisbitt, himself a practising astrologer.

In 1983 the name was changed to the Centre for Psychological Astrology, because a wide variety of psychological approaches was incorporated into the seminars, ranging from transpersonal psychology to the work of Jung, Freud and Klein. In response to repeated requests from students, the Diploma Course was eventually created, with additional tutors joining the staff. The CPA continued to develop and consolidate its programme despite the unfortunate death of Howard in 1992, when Charles Harvey became co-director with Liz Greene. Richard Aisbitt continued to manage the administration with great ability and commitment until 1994, when the burden of increasing ill-health forced him to restrict his contribution to beginners' and intermediate classes. At this time Juliet Sharman-Burke took over the administration. Richard himself sadly died in 1996. Finally, in February 2000, Charles Harvey tragically died of cancer, leaving Liz Greene as sole director. In the new Millennium, the CPA continues to develop along both familiar and innovative lines, always maintaining the high standards reflected in the fine work of its former co-directors.

Qualifications

Fulfilment of the seminar and supervision requirements of the In-Depth Professional Training Course entitles the student to a Certificate in Psychological Astrology. Upon successfully presenting a reading-in paper, the student is entitled to the CPA's Diploma in Psychological Astrology, with permission to use the letters, D. Psych. Astrol. The successful graduate will be able to apply the principles and techniques learned during the course to his or her professional activities, either as a consultant astrologer or as a useful adjunct to other forms of counselling or healing. Career prospects are good, as there is an ever-increasing demand for the services of capable psychologically orientated astrologers. The CPA's Diploma is not offered as a replacement for the Diploma of the Faculty of Astrological Studies or any other basic astrological training course. Students are encouraged to learn their basic astrology as thoroughly as possible, through the Faculty or some other reputable source, before undertaking the In-Depth Professional Training Course. The CPA offers introductory and intermediate courses in psychological astrology, which run on weekday evenings.

THE CPA DIPLOMA DOES NOT CONSTITUTE A FORMAL COUNSELLING OR PSYCHOTHERAPEUTIC TRAINING. Students wishing to work as counsellors or therapists should complete a further training course focusing on these skills. There are many excellent courses and schools of various persuasions available in the United Kingdom and abroad.

Seminars in Zürich

Certain seminars from the CPA programme are available in Zürich. Please write to Astrodienst AG, Dammstrasse 23, CH-8702 Zürich-Zollikon, Switzerland, www.astro.com for details. However, those wishing to enter the In-Depth Training Course will need to attend seminars and supervision groups in London in order to obtain the Diploma, and should apply through the London address.

Individual Therapy

In order to complete the In-Depth Professional Training, the CPA asks that all students, for a minimum of one year of study, be involved in a recognised form of depth psychotherapy with a qualified therapist, analyst or counsellor of his or her choice. The fee for the CPA training does not include the cost of this therapy, which must be borne by the student himself or herself. The basis for this requirement is that we believe no responsible counsellor of any persuasion can hope to deal sensitively and wisely with another person's psyche, without some experience of his or her own. Although it is the student's responsibility to arrange for this therapy, the CPA can refer students to various psychotherapeutic organisations if required.

Criteria for Admission

The following guidelines for admission to the In-Depth Professional Training Programme are applied:

• A sound basic knowledge of the meaning of the signs, planets, houses, aspects, transits and progressions, equal to Certificate Level of the Faculty of Astrological Studies Course. The CPA's own introductory and intermediate courses will also take the student to the required level of knowledge.

• Being able and willing to work on one's own individual development, as reflected by the requirement of individual therapy during the programme. Although a minimum of one year is required, it is hoped that the student will fully recognise the purpose and value of such inner work, and choose to continue for a longer period.

- Adequate educational background and communication skills will be looked for in applicants, as well as empathy, integrity, and a sense of responsibility.

Enrolment Procedure

Please write to the Centre for Psychological Astrology, BCM Box 1815, London WC1N 3XX, for fees, further information, and an application form. Please include an SAE and International Postage Coupon if writing from abroad. The CPA may also be contacted on Tel/Fax +44 20 8749 2330, or at www.cpalondon.com.

PLEASE NOTE:

- The CPA does not offer a correspondence course.
- The course does not qualify overseas students for a student visa.
- The course is for EU and Swiss residents only, although exceptions may sometimes be made.

About the CPA Press

The seminars in this volume are two of a series of seminars transcribed and edited for publication by the CPA Press. Although some material has been altered, for purposes of clarity or the protection of the privacy of students who offered personal information during the seminars, the transcriptions are meant to faithfully reproduce not only the astrological and psychological material discussed at the seminars, but also the atmosphere of the group setting.

Since the CPA's inception, many people, including astrology students living abroad, have repeatedly requested transcriptions of the seminars. In the autumn of 1995, Liz Greene, Charles Harvey and Juliet Sharma-Burke decided to launch the CPA Press, in order to make available to the astrological community material which would otherwise be limited solely to seminar participants, and might never be included by the individual tutors in their own future written works. Because of the structure of the CPA programme, most seminars are "one-off" presentations which are not likely to be repeated, and much careful research and important astrological investigation would otherwise be lost. The volumes in the CPA Seminar Series are meant for serious astrological students who wish to develop a greater knowledge of the links between astrology and psychology, in order to understand both the horoscope and the human being at a deeper and more insightful level. The hardback volumes in the series are not available in most bookshops, but can be ordered directly from the CPA at www.cpalondon.com, or from Midheaven Bookshop, 396 Caledonian Road, London N1, Tel. +44 20 7607 4133, Fax +44 20 7700 6717, www.midheavenbooks.com. Paperback volumes are available from Midheaven Bookshop and from the Wessex Astrologer at www.wessexastrloger.com. They are also available in many specialist bookshops in both the UK and the USA.

Hardback volumes available in the CPA Seminar Series:

The Astrologer, the Counsellor and the Priest by Liz Greene and Juliet Sharman-Burke

The Family Inheritance by Juliet Sharman-Burke

Venus and Jupiter: Bridging the Ideal and the Real by Erin Sullivan

The Astrological Moon by Darby Costello

The Art of Stealing Fire: Uranus in the Horoscope by Liz Greene

Incarnation: The Four Angles and the Moon's Nodes by Melanie Reinhart

Water and Fire by Darby Costello

Where In the World? Astro*Carto*Graphy and Relocation Charts by Erin Sullivan

Planetary Threads: Patterns of Relating Among Family and Friends by Lynn Bell

Relationships and How to Survive Them by Liz Greene

Earth and Air by Darby Costello

Astrology, History and Apocalypse by Nicholas Campion

Paperback volumes available in the CPA Seminar Series:

The Horoscope in Manifestation: Psychology and Prediction by Liz Greene

Apollo's Chariot: The Meaning of the Astrological Sun by Liz Greene

The Mars Quartet: Four Seminars on the Astrology of the Red Planet by Lynn Bell, Darby Costello, Liz Greene and Melanie Reinhart

Saturn, Chiron and the Centaurs: To the Edge and Beyond by Melanie Reinhart

Anima Mundi: The Astrology of the Individual and the Collective by Charles Harvey

Direction and Destiny in the Birth Chart by Howard Sasportas

Barriers and Boundaries: The Horoscope and the Defences of the Personality by Liz Greene